HIGH DESERT, HIGHER COSTS

HIGH DESERT, HIGHER COSTS

BEND AND THE HOUSING CRISIS IN THE AMERICAN WEST

JONATHAN BACH

Oregon State University Press

Corvallis

Oregon State University Press in Corvallis, Oregon, is located within the traditional homelands of the Marys River or Ampinefu Band of Kalapuya. Following the Willamette Valley Treaty of 1855, Kalapuya people were forcibly removed to reservations in Western Oregon. Today, living descendants of these people are a part of the Confederated Tribes of Grand Ronde Community of Oregon (grandronde.org) and the Confederated Tribes of the Siletz Indians (ctsi.nsn.us).

"High Desert, Higher Costs" originally appeared in the May 14, 2021, edition of the *Portland Business Journal*. Portions are reused with permission and the author's gratitude.

Cover photograph © Nate Wyeth (https://commons.wikimedia.org/wiki/File:Old_Mill_District_2019.jpg). CC-BY-SA-4.0

Cataloging-in-Publication Data is available from the Library of Congress.

ISBN 978-1-962645-28-7 paper; ISBN 978-1-962645-29-4 ebook

∞ This paper meets the requirements of ANSI/NISO Z39.48-1992 (Permanence of Paper).

Oregon State University
OSU Press

Oregon State University Press
121 The Valley Library
Corvallis OR 97331-4501
541-737-3166 • fax 541-737-3170
www.osupress.oregonstate.edu

For Makenna

As this wave from memories flows in, the city soaks it up like a sponge and expands. A description of Zaira as it is today should contain all Zaira's past. The city, however, does not tell its past, but contains it like the lines of a hand, written in the corners of the streets, the gratings of the windows, the banisters of the steps, the antennae of the lightning rods, the poles of the flags, every segment marked in turn with scratches, indentations, scrolls.

—Italo Calvino, *Invisible Cities*, 1972

CONTENTS

ACKNOWLEDGMENTS

High Desert, Higher Costs began as a cover story in the *Portland Business Journal* (*PBJ*). First and foremost, a big thank you to all my *PBJ* colleagues. Managing Editor Andy Giegerich closely guided the execution of my article, "High Desert, Higher Costs: The Dark Side of Bend's Runaway Housing Market," as its main editor, keeping in focus the business angle for our readers. Despite its positioning as financial news, we attempted to keep humanity front and center. This is not an impossible feat in business journalism, nor is it all that uncommon, but it was especially important in this instance, as I was writing about my adopted hometown. When I proposed turning the article into a book, our executive editor, Suzanne Stevens, backed the idea enthusiastically. In fact, I can't count how many meetings I had with Suzanne where she asked me how the book was going and gave her trademark "go get 'em" encouragement, just like she did for any big story. Publisher Candace Beeke also became an ardent supporter of *High Desert, Higher Costs*. My *PBJ* coworkers spent years listening to me talk about this project as I wrestled with its complexities, and I am grateful their feedback. Matthew Kish, thank you for helping me through the early stages of crafting a proposal. I am equally grateful to everyone at the *PBJ*'s parent company, American City Business Journals. I started covering housing for the Portland *Oregonian*/OregonLive in 2024, and I thank my newsroom colleagues for their support.

For years, I talked with my friend and professional mentor, Peter Laufer, about writing a book. He always encouraged it. After the *PBJ* published the article, Peter pushed me to make something more substantial out of it. A longtime author, Peter showed me how to pitch my work to publishers, and he edited my efforts along the way. We traded emails while I wrote the manuscript. It was an immense reassurance to have someone who'd seen these streets before helping me to maneuver its potholes. Likewise, peer reviewers consulted by Oregon State University Press provided crucial feedback to both the proposal and the manuscript. Jonathan Thompson, Lori Tobias, Edwin Battistella, and two anonymous reviewers offered indispensable advice. I want to offer special thanks to Jeff Mapes, the reviewer who dissected both the proposal and manuscript. After reading the book's first official draft, he went above and beyond by suggesting a new structure that, frankly, made the whole thing click. A cohort of others lent their perspectives to early copy. My thanks to Claire Withycombe, Bill Poehler, Scott Greenstone, Andrew Berzanskis, Kristin DeNovellis, and Bruce Hammond.

Oregon State University Press was fantastic to work with. Acquisitions Editor Kim Hogeland, who understood precisely how to shape this narrative into a story of policies affecting people, deserves special mention for making my experience with the press such a good one. Over many conversations, Kim pushed me to connect the dots for readers. The story is far richer for the hard questions she posed. To her, Tom Booth, Micki Reaman, Katherine White, and the entire staff at OSU Press: thank you so much for seeing the importance of this housing story. Thank you, Ryan Schumacher, for your diligent copyediting. I want to express gratitude to OSU Press for the elegant book design.

The book is nothing without the participation of several sources. To everyone in Bend and beyond who spoke to me for this book, thank you so much. Those who work behind the scenes to pull together interviews don't often get the spotlight. Delia Hernández with Oregon Housing and Community Services was immensely helpful, as was Vanessa Krueger with the US Department of Housing and Urban Development. Thank you for coordinating conversations that were crucial to helping readers understand how state and federal officials are trying to ease this crisis.

Friends motivated me to see the project through. I send much appreciation to Troy Brynelson, George Plaven, Steven and Liann Garcia, Soren Odom, Jacob Motl, and Sheldon Cabrera-Miller. Family members supported this project, too. To my sister and brother-in-law, Katherine and Nicholas Paige Bach, and my dad, John Bach—thank you. I think my mother, Kelli, would have enjoyed reading this book, and afterward, she'd tell me exactly where she agreed and disagreed with me. To my in-laws, Tom and Julie Carrico, who let me have a writer's retreat at their house in Corvallis that jumpstarted my writing when I was in a lull, thank you. Savannah Carrico and David Majeski boosted my morale, as did my grandmother, Diane Rush.

My wife, Makenna Bach, believes in journalism, believes in me, and believes this project can help people. She has had my back since we were college kids at the University of Oregon. I could not have done it without her.

PREFACE

This was her last house before the end. The single-level residence sat on the rimrocks of Terrebonne, overlooking the Central Oregon high desert. It had three bedrooms and hardwood floors. A spacious shop would hold the many boxes and totes accumulated over my mother and father's cross-country moves.

"We sign tomorrow, 7:30 a.m.!" Mom texted me early in November 2016.

"Congratulations!" I replied that night. "Love you so much."

Two days passed before she told me, "It is done, the house is ours!" She and Dad, both in their fifties, were renters no more. I fired off a couple digital stickers of the cute gray cartoon cat Pusheen, one with a heart above its head.

On November 5, I asked, "How's the new house?"

"Just got here," she said. "I love it! But I will say it's smaller than anything I remember except the first house when we got married."

Perhaps the rural Central Oregon house was smaller than the others in which they'd lived. By now she and my dad had lived all over the United States since their 1990s breakup with Southern California, where they'd gotten married and had two kids. My parents moved us from California to Oregon, first renting in the Portland metro area and then in Bend, where Mom got a management job at Bend Cable. My sister, Kati, and I sometimes went to Bend Cable after school let out from Elk Meadow Elementary. Once when Mom was coming back into her office, I mischievously spun around in her desk chair and yelled, for everyone to hear, "I'm an angry Bend Cable customer, and I wanna know what you're gonna do about it!" She loved it. When we weren't at work with her after school or with Dad at home before his shifts at the grocery store Fred Meyer, we frequently went to our babysitter's. The sitter, Cindy, waited tables at Jake's Diner along Highway 97 on the south end of town, where semi drivers pulled in and a cacophony of forks and knives on eggs and pork chops rang clear. Kati and I spent hours either at Jake's or farther south at the babysitter's house in Deschutes River Woods. Her single-detached home rested on an expansive lot; looking back, I'd guess it had to be more than an acre. Her sons and I all raced BMX bikes on dirt tracks around Oregon. My parents bought me a premium Redline bike and all the protective gear, from the gray full-face helmet on down to yellow Fox racewear. My dad spent hours out on the BMX tracks with me during practice, getting out there with his own bike and gear. At races my parents yelled from the sidelines, "Pedal, pedal, pedal!"

During round one of living in and around Bend, my family rented in Deschutes River Woods, on Tall Pine Avenue, and in a development called Conestoga Hills, giving us a view of different parts of the community. The houses all looked different, but the place remained the same. Our homes and the sitter's house reflected Bend in the early 2000s: a densely forested truck-stop town with plenty of single-detached homes for families like ours.

The author's mother, Kelli, in the family's two-story home on the outskirts of Bend. (Photo by Jonathan Bach)

Relocating often for work and medical care following Mom's diagnosis with kidney failure, we hammered down stakes across the county, sometimes more than once in the same state but always in rentals. In 2004, near Poplarville, Mississippi, the rental had a pool that saved us from the heat and humidity of the Deep South. Mom worked temporarily across the border at a Bogalusa, Louisiana, call center. After that, we moved on again. Mom's diagnosis came in 2005 while we lived in Billings, Montana. It came as a shock to the whole family and upended our lives. She worked remotely for a company called Liveops, and her dialysis pole stood by her desk with a hanging bag of fluids while she sat there. We spent time in a few houses in Billings, but my favorite, the one where I recall the IV pole, was in the hills outside the city, south past the Yellowstone River. Wild turkeys gobbled on the rocky, underdeveloped portion of Briarwood Boulevard that led out to our place. In the slippery winter, the hill up to our house was treacherous, even for our burly gray Land Rover. That house was my favorite because of the view: looking south was scraggly country with few homes as far as you could see.

Later, outside frozen-in-time Kingman, Arizona, we stayed in a small, squat house on a dirt lot along a dirt road with panoramic views of dirt. When we changed houses, we scrubbed the walls and steam cleaned the carpets, ensuring we'd get the precious security deposit back. Life for a family of four could be a mess. Laundry and dishes piled up, and often we didn't unpack all the boxes from prior moves. Why bother? But hopefully a stranger wouldn't know we were ever there by the time we finished cleaning. Naturally, in high school, I took a job as a housekeeper at Sunriver Resort in the Central Oregon community of Sunriver, for fun money, scrubbing toilets for the guests who could afford wooded views and sun-soaked golf courses. My sister also started in housekeeping in Sunriver as a teen, and she stayed in hospitality for years, moving through the ranks at the nicest hotel in downtown Bend, the Oxford.

Kati and I had begun making friends in Arizona when my parents told us we were relocating to Bend once again—for medical care, if I remember correctly. Mom could still drive in the desert but had started using a walker to get around. Kati and I made our parents swear this would be our last move for a while. It was around 2007, and my parents held to their word. Our move back to Central Oregon included cycling through a few rentals, but in time, we landed in a yellow, two-story home on a road called Barlow Trail on the city's eastern outskirts. It was outside Bend city limits, technically, but the mailing address still said "Bend." Rent cost $1,200, by my dad's recollection. This was 2009, so that would be roughly $1,700 in 2023 dollars. We had no idea how many friendships we'd get to forge in the relatively affordable rental.

Mom had to be wheeled around the house with a sling held up with a hydraulic lift, akin to a crane with a sturdy metal frame and four small wheels, when she wasn't in a wheelchair or in bed. Her mobility deteriorated with her health; the newly installed hemodialysis machine whirred in the corner of Barlow Trail's bottom floor. After years of rolling around America, mostly in the West, the house let the rest of us tread and retread the same steps on the same carpets and wooden floors thousands of times, up and down the same stairs. We took night walks with a flashlight in the freezing cold, stars dangling in the black sky. Kati and I brought a parade of Bend Senior High friends to hang at our place. I walked dogs and talked philosophy with my friend from the school bus, Nicholas, who would one day marry my sister. I'd amble from Bend High, past the Safeway and under the railroad bridge, into the city's compact downtown. My friends and I clambered up the most climbable tree in Drake Park. I drank Irish breakfast tea at Townshend's on Northwest Bond Street. There was Everywhere Else, and there was Bend, where, for me, memories for once had time to settle in. I graduated from high school in 2012 and went off to the University of Oregon (UO).

The author spent hours and hours in downtown Bend after school with friends as a teenager.
(Photo by Jonathan Bach)

Four years later, Mom and Dad bought a place of their own in Terrebonne, a rural town north of Bend but still well within Central Oregon. A US Air Force veteran, Dad used a Veterans Affairs home loan for the purchase.

I asked Mom about their new house, "How do you like the view?"

"Pretty, pretty, pretty, pretty, pretty," she said.

This new home, some forty miles north of Barlow Trail, stood along the aptly titled Southwest Rim Road. Just off the back deck was a precipice and then, farther out, Crooked River Ranch's golf course. The view reminded me of the rimrocks in Billings. Mom described the drop to friends as "next stop, Splatsville."[1] Distant from city-light pollution, the Terrebonne nights glittered. Daytime was no slacker either: the sun illuminated the surrounding desert. Dad loved Arizona so much that we hauled what seemed like a million-pound tote of *Arizona Highways* magazines that dated back decades. It made sense that when they bought a home, it sat in a part of Oregon that approximated, to the highest degree possible in the drenched Pacific Northwest, the look and feel of the bone-dry desert. Mom showed off the view through a window toward open country, triangle-tip hills or mountains pushing up to the east, set against white clouds. One friend asked why they moved. "After almost eight years in the same house, it was time. These vagabonds had never stayed in one place that long," she responded. "We are just 30 minutes from before, 20 away from Kati and the kids, and well, the same three hours over the Cascades for Jonathan . . . It was a great move for us."[2] We all loved the Barlow Trail rental. But Mom and Dad managed the climb up Mount Homeownership. The property was in my father's name, but it was a summiting achievement for them both. They had no landlord demanding rent. Yet Mom would only live in the house until the following March. She got the experience of owning a home for a fraction of her fifty-two-year life, more than a decade of which she spent sick and frequently hospitalized.

On New Year's Eve 2016, she seemed in high spirits. They had firmly settled into the Terrebonne home. Mom sent everyone an email about a big trip, the kind of thing we used to do all the time when she could walk. Often we would go on day trips to places like Montezuma Castle in central Arizona. "As a final family gift this year, we are renting a beach house in Waldport," on the Oregon Coast, she informed the family. I was in the Willamette Valley, where I'd taken a job as a reporter out of college, and my sister remained in Central Oregon. Mom was looking at May: "We will be there the entire time, and you can work around whatever schedule you need." She promised room enough for everybody. No one knew the May trip would never come.

In March 2017, her illness put her back in the hospital again. I came back from the Valley. She lived to see her daughter's children and meet the woman who'd become my wife. But she should have seen so much more. Done more. She lay on life support in a bed at a St. Charles intensive care unit room in Bend, the community around which she invested so much of her life, surrounded by family. When it was time for her to pass on, I sat beside her and lay my head down as the monitor beeps became more distant from each other. Her heart relaxed to a stop. I slept in an overwhelmingly dark spare bedroom at the Terrebonne house that night.

▲   ▲   ▲

I thought about my mom a lot while I wrote this book. For a blessed stretch of time, Barlow Trail and Terrebonne gave my parents what many dream of in the West: panoramas from single-detached homes. The Barlow Trail rental sat on an eye-watering four-and-a-half acres. My parents lived squarely in the camp of those who'd prefer to have land to call their own instead of being cooped up in an attached unit. An overwhelming majority—89 percent—of American homebuyers said loud and clear in a 2019 Redfin survey they'd take a single-detached home and a backyard over living in a triplex, even if the commute from the triplex was shorter.[3] The real estate company's chief economist, Daryl Fairweather, summed it up, "As long as Americans are willing to pay a premium for detached homes, developers are likely to continue building them."[4] This makes sense to anyone who's ever shared a wall with a noisy neighbor who blasts music or argues with their roommate. Still, there was hope for attached-home advocates. As Fairweather noted, "Homebuyers are more willing to settle for a condo or another unit with shared walls if the home itself isn't the defining feature of why they're choosing a city."[5] People move to Bend for the natural beauty, not just the homes, so attached housing surely had a place in the supply mix where residents are spending a lot of time outdoors.

I don't recall thinking about a housing crisis when I was a kid. Sure, the Great Recession was in the news—but what does that mean to a high schooler? My parents, perpetual renters into midlife, were lucky to lock in their slice of high-desert heaven, particularly with reasonable rent. My outlook on housing changed when I graduated from the UO in 2016 and went to work as a news reporter for the Salem *Statesman Journal*, which hired me to cover city hall and business in the state capital. There I learned developers sit right in the sweet spot between private business and public policy, because they often obtain taxpayer-funded grants and loans. If residents didn't like a proposal for new housing, I would write about it. If police swept a homeless camp, I would cover it. If a developer opposed the construction of a homeless shelter, it was my story. Through work, I met fellow journalists writing about homelessness, advocates for the houseless, lawmakers, developers, and everyday residents. I gained a clearer picture of what was at stake in Oregon's housing circles. I found myself thinking about home more and more.

Of course, people far smarter than me made clear what was going on nationally. Sam Khater, Len Kiefer, and Venkataramana Yanamandra of Freddie Mac's Economic and Housing Research Group noted some reasons for a national shortage included a worn-out and thinned-out construction workforce, onerous land-use rules, zoning restrictions that hindered development where the greatest demand exists, neighbors who vocally opposed new development—known widely as the NIMBY, or "not in my backyard," crowd—and a shortage of developable land. The rising cost of critical building materials such as lumber further frustrates builders. Researchers pointed to an even more pernicious and long-standing problem in our present woes: since the mid-1970s, America has underbuilt starter homes, meaning entry-level houses measuring smaller than 1,400 square feet. As the Freddie Mac researchers observed in 2021, "The combination of low supply (especially entry-level) and high demand (especially entry-level) is causing entry-level prices to rapidly escalate well above overall prices, triggering affordability issues for buyers to come up with even larger down payments." A broad-based decline in homebuilding, not just for starter homes, has taken hold nationwide over the decades, and its effects continue to show. Khater, Kiefer, and Yanamandra estimate that the overall US deficit of homes went from 2.5 million units in 2018 to 3.8 million in 2020.[6] The problem is not getting any better.

Like most of the United States, Bend suffered greatly in the wake of the 2008 financial crisis. My parents, it turned out, were luckier than I thought, paying a bargain basement price on such a nice bit of land for so long: they lived at Barlow Trail until 2016. As the Economic Policy Institute reported, "A growing housing supply shortage is a key contributor to the housing affordability crisis. Following the Great Recession, the share of homes being built fell significantly, causing buyer demand to exceed housing production. In fact, fewer new homes were built in the decade following the Great Recession than in any decade since the 1960s."[7] Lorelei Juntunen of Oregon economics firm ECOnorthwest, in a 2017 deep-dive into Bend housing, brought the crisis home. Juntunen wrote, "Housing units are not available at the price points that are demanded in the current market" and "while the number of overall housing units in Bend may be in line with the population, there is a mismatch in need and affordability."[8] The big-picture US housing shortage, worsened by the Great Recession, made it more difficult for everyone who made Bend run to live there.

I left the *Statesman Journal* in January 2020 to take a job covering real estate with the *Portland Business Journal*. My wife Makenna, a cellist, and I heaved our belongings and our aging orange tabby, Sunny, from our six-hundred-square-foot, one-bedroom Salem apartment into a U-Haul and, as I'd done automatically my whole life, I left for someplace new. This time I was behind the wheel of the truck instead of staring at the dashboard and the highway beyond from the passenger seat. We drove up Interstate 5 to southwest Portland, and one of Makenna's longtime friends from Corvallis, where she grew up, unpacked our things from the truck and brought them into our new, two-bedroom apartment with us that night. The ground-level unit was less than a thousand square feet, but Makenna and I would use the second bedroom as a music room and office. I had been excited to start life in the big city, similar to the life my parents left when they departed Los Angeles: the newsroom was in the heart of downtown Portland, right near the brick-laden Pioneer Courthouse Square. But in March, as the COVID-19 pandemic struck, the publisher pulled us all into the newsroom and said we'd be going remote, so I got very used to hanging out with Sunny in the rental all day. Makenna and I went on long neighborhood walks during the shutdown, admiring all the cozy, low-slung homes. Covering real estate full-time, I became more and more interested in homeownership as a topic. By 2021, I still watched Bend from afar, trying to understand what was happening with the housing market as prices exploded. I pitched a story on Bend housing, and my editors approved. I talked to a bunch of residents and experts, leveraging my rusty local knowledge. The article that came through cried out with residents' frustration and anxiety. My *PBJ* editors ran it large on the front page. Yet there was so much more to tell than the few thousand words conveyed. There was so much more research to do on the forces that were roiling the city.

That's how *High Desert, Higher Costs* came to be. While I look at the historical roots of Bend and the West's housing problems, I spend many of the following pages in the period from 2010 onward, the influential post-Great Recession years, when Oregon lawmakers, recognizing a need, worked hard to encourage new construction. They implemented public subsidies meant to get developers off the sidelines and zoning reforms to inform what, exactly, they should build, with a special emphasis on increasing townhomes and other dense kinds of homes. Legislators make laws, but state officials have a strong hand in implementing the policies that determine whether things get done. As such, I focus at great length on Oregon Housing and Community Services, the housing-finance agency that spearheaded an innovative way to spur housing production by combining federal tax credits and state money. The agency hit significant roadblocks. Similarly, US senator Ron Wyden, an Oregon Democrat, attempted the near-Sisyphean task of trying to pass legislation to create a tax credit to stimulate middle-income housing construction. In December 2023, Wyden told me of jammed-up Washington politics, "It's hard to get sixty votes for a tuna fish sandwich around here these days."[9] The results of those efforts and more are laid out in the following chapters.

Bend's troubles are not unique. Through interviews with housing officials across the West, I learned about different ways cities are reacting to explosive demand. Especially important to cities situated near natural beauty is the question of how much vacation rentals reduce the stock of available homes for long-term residents. I take the approach of using vacation rentals to tackle part of the broader question of how housing investors affect supply.

Reporting on the western housing crunch, I met a political hopeful forced to move from rental to rental around Central Oregon after suffering a massive setback; a remote worker who arrived mid-pandemic from Seattle, starting over in a new town; a density proponent who made his voice heard from Bend to the capital city; a local reporter who settled in Bend only to have to make a sacrifice; and an nonprofit worker who tried to build more housing for the homeless but might have to leave herself because of rising housing costs. I followed many of their journeys for more than a year to try to find answers in a story that explores gentrification, urban planning, amenity migration, and why homes do or don't get built.

Along the way, I hoped to answer the most pressing questions for residents: How do you endure in a housing market, both for renters and owners, that has become so hostile to the West's working class? Whether you were born in a city like Bend or came to it later in life, how do you keep your place as costs become unreasonable and untenable? What concessions do you make? How can we make our cities fairer for everyone? Like my family, everyone in this book is trying to do right for themselves and their kin, with the money they have at their disposal. It's a matter of available resources and the speed and type of construction. I find the West adapting under immense strain. So many people want to live here, and builders haven't kept up. The kinds of homes we need are changing, and it's hard to shift supply so abruptly away from single-detached homes—the kinds I mostly grew up in. Yet plenty of ideas are gaining traction, such as a push for workforce housing, subsidized by the government or employers themselves. Land trusts are taking hold here and there as an affordability measure. Townhomes are rising within eyeshot of apartments and detached homes. Residents of cities like Bend are vocal about the need for reasonably priced places to live. Is all this enough?

CHAPTER 1

Crossing into Bend

The exceptionally adequate, yellow, two-thousand-square-foot house in downtown Bend was listed for a breathtaking price. We were in the car, on the way to a friend's place in Tacoma, Washington, when my wife, Makenna, riding shotgun, came across an Instagram post from an account that showed off old homes for sale. Built in the 1920s, the residence had three bedrooms and two bathrooms. Downtown and within walking distance of the Deschutes River, it was a Craftsman house.[1] It was a popular style for those living near the center of Bend at that time, as it was both cheap and easy for local builders to construct with local materials.[2] Today this Craftsman, with pillars at the entryway, was anything but cheap, its list price nearly $1.3 million. Makenna read out some of the Instagram comments as I drove down the highway. Many were justifiably aghast. One person dubbed Bend "a little Los Angeles now except with Patagonia jackets and Stanley cups."[3]

Neither the price nor the comment shocked me. By the time this house was on the market in 2023, I had already spent more than two years investigating Bend's housing shortage, the catalyst behind this home's outrageous valuation. I wanted to understand what happened to the place where I spent much of my childhood. The crisis worsened, ironically, as Bend recovered from the Great Recession: population rebounded but homebuilding failed to keep up with demand, sending prices soaring.[4] Examples like the downtown Craftsman—which last sold for $292,000 in 2004 and went for $1.15 million after the Instagram post, a nearly four-fold increase within twenty years—underscored how out-of-hand things had gotten.[5]

▲ ▲ ▲

Bend has long been a destination for its natural wonder. The only skyscrapers in Central Oregon are mountains. In the evenings, whiskey sunsets fade behind the treasured peaks of Bachelor and the Three Sisters. These are just a few of a chain of mountains, formed atop a subduction zone, one summit after the other, along a rough-and-tumble six hundred miles from British Columbia to Northern California, terrain marked by glaciated volcanoes, spilling waterfalls, and wooded valleys.[6] "Towering volcanoes, part of the Cascade Range, rise like islands above an undulating sea of blue-green forests," wrote Raymond Hatton, a Central Oregonian geographer and historian. Cold snow rests on high mountain slopes into the summer. Lakes glimmer behind the cover of trees.[7] Hatton wasn't alone in his appreciation for the region: at least one guidebook claims the views offered by the Cascades are among the best you can find in the lower forty-eight.[8]

The Cascades define more than Bend. They serve as the major geographical and cultural divide in Oregon. To the west, the green and damp Willamette Valley lies between the high peaks and the lower Coast Range. Strung through the 150-mile valley are Eugene, Salem, and Portland, our largest metropolitan areas. Since the Second World War, around two-thirds of Oregonians have made the mossy valley their home.[9] But the mountains catch the clouds and create a rain shadow; east of the Cascades is the high desert of Central Oregon, where Bend has long been the population center. Sagebrush and juniper sprout low on Bend's north flank, leading to the outlying communities of Redmond and Terrebonne. To the south, mile after mile of deep green, crowding conifers tower overhead, away to Sunriver and La Pine.[10]

The area between what we now call Bend and the Columbia River, the waterway along the border between Oregon and Washington, is the Confederated Tribes of Warm Springs' original homelands. The Northern Paiute, Wana Łama (Warm Springs), and Wasq'ú (Wasco) people stayed on a seasonal basis, and the Klamath Trail trade route stretched northward to trading grounds at Celilo Falls, nurturing commerce among tribal nations.[11] In 1855, with orders to clear out Indigenous peoples, Oregon Territory superintendent Joel Palmer negotiated a treaty to establish the Warm Springs Reservation. The Wasco and Warm Springs tribes ceded some ten million acres "but reserved the Warm Springs Reservation for their exclusive use," as the Confederated Tribes of Warm Springs noted in a regional history. They kept rights to harvest food and fish away from the reservation in the places they had before. The forced relocation dramatically altered how they lived: the salmon didn't swim in such multitudes as they did in the Columbia, and farming became more difficult in the poor soils and unfavorable climate. Their former economy no longer functioned in the same way. "In addition," notes the Warm Springs history, "federal policies to assimilate the Indian people forced them to abandon many of their customary ways in favor of modern schools, sawmills, and other infrastructure foreign to the tribes."[12]

White settlers didn't situate Bend near the Deschutes River by accident. Native people had found ways to cross the raucous river, and the newcomers did, too.[13] Wagon trains aimed for safe river crossings and looked for the landmark Pilot Butte, the lifeless cinder cone protruding like an earthen boil some five hundred feet high.[14] During the mid-nineteenth century, United States survey teams and scouts explored what is now Central Oregon. Oregon became a state in 1859, and in 1877 a claim was put in for a ranch called Farewell Bend near a crook in the Deschutes, south of present-day downtown.[15]

In 1903, a new local paper, the *Bend Bulletin*, started printing from a hand press inside a log building.[16] In one of its first issues, the *Bulletin* forecast "unprecedented" prosperity to come as the railroad opened the desert to more people. The young paper vowed, "We shall at all times work for the development of Bend and the upper Deschutes country. . . . It shall be our constant aim to foster and further the efforts of settlers who may intend to make their homes and fortunes in our midst."[17] The name Bend became the shorthand for Farewell Bend, where passing travelers glimpsed the Deschutes River one last time.[18] In 1905, Bend's five hundred or so people transformed their rough community into a proper city.[19] Kelly Cannon-Miller, the Deschutes County Historical Society's executive director, told me in 2021, "The people who were coming here in 1905 really wanted the same things as the folks who are coming here now: a place where they felt comfortable and could enjoy life while making a living."[20]

The wealthy caught notice of the high desert's splendor. Alexander Drake, a moneyed Minnesotan, rolled into Farewell Bend by covered wagon in 1900, before residents voted to incorporate.[21] Drake went on to earn the moniker "the father of Bend."[22] The *Bulletin* described him as "a Midwestern capitalist who was reportedly lured West by irrigation possibilities and the availability of good fishing. . . . Drake worked at surveying and platting the town in 1901 and 1902, and in the spring of 1903, he had the streets laid out with a horse-drawn plow. His Pilot Butte Development Company began the first delivery of water to lands adjacent to Bend in early 1904."[23] Drake's wife, Florence, had a hand in guiding the town's layout. "Mrs. Drake loved every one of the cow trails on which these streets are located today," Elmer Ward, who helped with the work, recounted in a 1953 interview with broadcaster KBND. "She insisted that we locate the streets of Bend along those contours that formed the cow trails of those days. And we followed instructions. And that's why we have the winding streets."[24]

Drake, a well-groomed gentleman with a narrow jaw and trimmed mustache, wasn't all business.[25] He had gotten word from a traveling companion of a gleaming river that brimmed with trout, and he soon constructed a pine-log home within eyeshot of Mirror Pond.[26] His and Florence's home "became a center of Bend social and civic life," the historical society recorded.[27]

Like many in the West, Drake wanted acreage. In April 1904, the newspaper reported of his fastidious care, "A. M. Drake has devoted a great deal of attention to the improvement of the 3-½ acre lot in which his residence is located. It has been plowed, harrowed, rolled and scraped to perfect smoothness, and given sufficient slope for convenient irrigation. It will be converted into a model lawn."[28] Drake's preference for a log cabin and lawn fit into a historical timeline. From 1825 to 1875, many Americans no longer viewed outside residential space as just a place to plant vegetables or herbs, and the mowing machine's advent meant smooth lawns replaced meadows previously snipped by sheep or scythe. The best home rested within a garden or manicured lawn. "The revolutionary change in attitude that this represented can best be appreciated by recalling that for the first four thousand years of urban history, congestion had meant security, with the very walls of the city representing safety from invading hordes or rampaging bandits," historian Kenneth T. Jackson observed.[29] The Romantic movement of the late 1700s to mid-1800s, which begat many of the world's most expressive literary and musical works, was also paired with a growing sense that wilderness should be seen as national cultural asset, inuring many to wild country. And pride still flowed from settlers' earlier "conquest" over nature.[30]

The Drakes were among the first of many well-heeled residents to embrace Bend, something that would become a persistent theme through its history.[31] But they left for Southern California the same year the railroad arrived in 1911. The train's arrival triggered a population boom as new sawmills that benefited from the rail line turned the community into a mill town.[32] "When the railroad comes in 1911, you immediately get entrepreneurs kicking into gear," said Cannon-Miller, from the historical society.[33] Big on superlatives, the state's official *1911 Blue Book* deemed a lack of means by which to transport goods "the most serious obstacle" to progress in Oregon. Steam and electric railways were being constructed across the state. "In anticipation of this railroad activity, there has begun a rush of people into the heretofore unsettled interior portions of the State which bids fair to populate those sections very rapidly," the *Blue Book* reported.[34] With excitement running high in 1912, railroad builder James J. Hill projected "within five years the population of Central Oregon will be 300,000. Within ten years, it should be more than a million."[35] Timber added fuel to the fervor. The *Blue Book* dubbed Oregon the "Switzerland of America," noting its "greatest natural endowment" came in the form of vast wealth stored inside marketable timber, much of it Douglas fir cut for shipbuilders. Oregon trees were thought to account for around a fifth of the nation's total merchantable timber supply. The trees held an estimated worth at the time of $5 billion. The *Blue Book* forecast, "Fifty years will see every stick of this vast forest cut and sawed if the present demand keeps up."[36]

Newcomers crowded into Bend, where emerging businesses were poised to cash in on the timber. Two competitors, Shevlin-Hixon Company and Brooks-Scanlon, opened mills in 1916, and scores of houses rose thereafter.[37] In January 1916, a newspaper advertisement marketed "Built it Yourself Houses" with sawed and numbered materials to assemble: "Knock-down homes from Portland for as low as $205—economically built homes, permanent, substantial and attractive."[38] Adjusted to January 2023 prices, that's just under $5,900 a dwelling. With employment opportunities came disparities. "So great was the influx of people into Bend that in January 1916, despite temperatures down to -19° F, some families were forced to live in tents because of a housing shortage," Hatton wrote. A group called the Bend Benevolent Association assisted families in finding temporary quarters.[39] Neighbors' attempts to help others struggling with housing would remain a fixture into the modern day.

The dueling mills got to processing wood. Lumberjacks wielding axes and crosscut saws felled ponderosa pines from nearby forests.[40] Bend established itself as a town for loggers, becoming Central Oregon's largest community and, in 1916, the seat of Deschutes County. Mill managers and workers spilled in from Great Lakes states. Railroad workers got laid off but found mill work, as did high-desert homesteaders. And the economy seemed to sustain new home production. "By the 1920s the famous and near-famous were coming to the area to enjoy its scenery and world-class trout fishing," wrote historian Thomas Cox, who was raised in Central Oregon. "Along Mirror Pond, a park-rimmed impoundment of the Deschutes that ran through town, fine homes soon lined the waterway." Homes not clustered on the pond looked modest. There were brothels and bars, and violence occasionally visited the community. Loggers tended to spend lots of time in camp in the woods, moving by rail when the cutting changed from here to there, often miles from town.[41] Many of the homes built in Bend from 1910 into the 1950s were Craftsman bungalows, but for the workers out in lumber camps, the mills built fourteen-by-twenty-foot timber houses, designed to sit on flatbed railway cars so they could roll from one encampment to the next. Loggers saw their shelters uprooted as the work demanded. In the 1940s, the mills began selling off the timber homes. They, too, now dot the downtown.[42]

Through the decades, the mills rumbled across the Deschutes from one another, processing hundreds of millions of board feet a year at peak production. But their sturdiness softened when timber supplies weakened. Brooks-Scanlon bought Shevlin-Hixon in 1950. In 1994, Brooks-Scanlon's new owner, Crown Pacific Limited, closed the legacy mill for good because timber supplies had further diminished. Crown Pacific claimed logging restrictions to safeguard the northern spotted owl on federal lands were to blame for the shutdown. Others ruled the mill's cause of death unsustainable logging. "Shevlin-Hixon, Brooks-Scanlon, and Crown Pacific all had aggressively clearcut their landholdings with little attention to replanting," historian Joshua Binus wrote for the Oregon Historical Society. "Over time, when the available harvest on the company's remaining private lands dwindled, the company became increasingly dependent upon the federal government for subsidized timber sales off public lands. When those sales could no longer be sustained, the mill found itself without a reliable source of timber."[43]

▲   ▲   ▲

Bend could no longer rely on all that money stocked within the bark. But the city's profile with outsiders rose. Raymond Hatton described how the trend of urbanites wanting to live there was nothing new. He wrote, "Curiously enough, one of the attractions of Bend and of Central Oregon in 1910—as it still is today—was the attempt to flee the 'big city' and return to the country."[44] Hatton quoted a tradesman from Chicago, who pined after Oregon thusly in a 1910 copy of the *Bulletin*:

> I, along with many more, am getting tired of this humdrum life, and long for the quiet of the country. . . . Living expenses in Chicago are getting to be so high that even the most common of food is getting to be a luxury and rents are going up all the time, so that a man making a small salary has to be a genius to make both ends meet. Hence the tendency toward the farm, and the desire to "Go West."[45]

Chicagoan or otherwise, people have been acting on feelings like the tradesman's long since 1910. Hatton's sentiment about fleeing the city proved evergreen. The first and second editions of his Bend history came out in 1978 and 1986. Hatton himself first cast his eyes over Central Oregon in the 1950s and 1960s, traveling on a summertime Highway 97.[46] English by birth, he ran track for the University of Idaho and picked up a few master's degrees as a new American, including from the University of Oregon, landing at Bend's Central Oregon Community College as a geography professor in 1969. Hatton climbed mountains, hiked trails, and wandered lakes and lava flows.[47] He spent most of his life in Bend and became an expert on Central Oregon, publishing ten books before his death in 2015 at age 83.[48] And he was right about Bend's appeal, which only increased over the decades he lived there.

The rush of outsiders pushed Deschutes County to become Oregon's fastest growing county: from 1960 to 1970, the population more than doubled. Though growth slowed during the tough economy of the 1970s, the population explosion didn't stop.[49] By the mid-1980s, Bend's status as a happening place achieved new heights. Shoppers drove to retailers like those found in larger communities, and Bend's recreational facilities were enough to turn other cities green with envy.[50] Data across a forty-year period underscored the point. In 1960, Deschutes County's population was 23,100. In 2000, it was 115,367. It was around this time Bend ranked sixth among America's fastest growing cities. But with the timber economy diminishing, a deeper transformation took hold, one that went beyond adding headcount. From Bend's beginning, shipments of lumber, agricultural products, and cattle had supported the regional economy. But Central Oregon farms and ranches were now being sold off. Riding horses and llamas replaced cattle on what turned into hobby farms.[51]

How much and when Bend came to rely on tourism is murky. There is evidence to suggest the downward spiral of the mills thrust Bend and similarly positioned lumber towns toward economies fueled by the commodification of their surrounding natural beauty—think selling tickets to ski slopes.[52] But another strong argument is that tourism was with Bend from the start. Americans were having a change of heart about the nation's wild country by the late nineteenth century. Frontier days were coming to a close. "By the 1890s sufficient change had occurred in American life and thought to make possible a widespread reaction against the previous condemnation of wilderness," environmental historian Roderick Frazier Nash wrote in *Wilderness and the American Mind*, first published in 1967. "The average citizen could approach wilderness with the viewpoint of the vacationer rather than the conqueror,"

Nash continued. "Specifically, the qualities of solitude and hardship that had intimidated many pioneers were likely to be magnetically attractive to their city-dwelling grandchildren."[53]

Recreation was burgeoning around the region. As far back as 1900, people camped close to the Staats post office and store, snoozing on the hay inside a barn owned by the Staats family.[54] William Staats was a pioneer who arrived in the region in 1879 and watched it develop. He died in 1931.[55] In addition to camping, recreators could go mountain-climbing and canoeing. Portlanders in 1912 rode by rail to Bend round-trip for $7.45. The city advertised its recreational and scenic goodies during the San Francisco Exposition of 1915, including having maps that showed Bend as a stopover between Portland, the Columbia River, and Klamath Falls. Motorists visiting Oregon's Crater Lake overnighted in Bend.[56] Today the highway route is roughly one hundred miles, southbound, from city to lake. President Theodore Roosevelt, the conservationist, worked with Congress to set aside national parks for the American public, including Crater Lake in 1902.[57] The *Bulletin* in August 1919 reported, "Central Oregon is coming into its own as a country of tremendous attraction to tourists and sportsmen. As tourists are welcomed this leads to more business and more developments and a brush with the outside world."[58] Economic Development 101: More people—doesn't matter where they're from—equals more commerce equals more growth. In Bend's case, its well-established relationships with tourism and timber appeared to nurture population growth over a sustained period.

Amenities developed throughout the twentieth century. The Mount Bachelor ski area west of Bend was founded by businessman Bill Healy in 1958, starting "with a rope tow and a single lift," which has since grown into "one of the largest ski resorts in the U.S." Out-of-state money took an interest when Utah-based Powdr Corporation bought the Mount Bachelor ski area in 2001.[59] Beer went well with tourism. After Governor Vic Atiyeh approved legislation in 1985 permitting brewers to produce and sell their beers on one premises, Deschutes Brewery opened in Bend in 1988, and Central Oregon's brewpub culture expanded from there.[60] In the 1990s, developer Bill Smith joined six investors to buy for $6 million the 270 acres where the mill workers once toiled, transforming the storied land into a sprawling riverfront shopping center called the Old Mill District, whose first tenants, including Ben & Jerry's and Regal Cinemas, opened in 2000.[61] I saw the Dwayne Johnson classic *The Scorpion King* to celebrate my birthday at Regal with my mom and a few friends in 2002 and watched *The Dark Knight Rises* in the cushy theater seats there a decade later, and indulged in plenty of Ben & Jerry's ice cream. As a young man, I engaged in

The three distinct smokestacks are a signature feature of the Old Mill District, a riverfront shopping center established where Bend mill workers once toiled. The brick building is today home to outdoor gear co-op REI, an obvious reminder of where locals' passions lie. (Photo by Jonathan Bach)

outdoor recreation and tourism, camping with friends in the woods and float-ing the river, even when it left my back swollen with insect bites, like when I spent hours out on the Deschutes, lolling past the sun-drenched countryside, my back a chew toy for the waterway's habitués.

In-migration, outdoor recreation, and tourism became fundamental parts of Bend's identity. Yet conflicting ideas emerged over what Bend should *be*; whom it was *for*. Some longtime Central Oregonians felt the place they cherished was fading as newcomers brought values that clashed with their own. Cox described a widening community schism, "They came seeking the natural rather than the social environment; indeed, they tended to look down on, when they did not ig-nore, what was already in place." Bumper stickers pleaded, "Don't Californicate Oregon." And housing troubles didn't help. Redmond, the next (and less popu-lous) city north of Bend up Highway 97, slowly became a place from which locals commuted thanks to its less-expensive homes. Cox, who grew up in Redmond during the 1940s and '50s, took it hard when the landscape shifted: "When those of us who have left return for class reunions or familial visits, we share the disquiet that has developed. What happened to the place we once knew? We grieve over the unfamiliar place Central Oregon has become."[62] Elements of Cox's lamentation hold true, namely the sense of unfamiliarity for many, myself included, as time rolls on. Yet he paints with too broad a brush: I found out-of-state newcomers reinforcing a sense of community in Bend, whether by working at the local newspaper, in local eateries, or for local nonprofits.

Come the 2000s, Pilot Butte loomed on the east side of a growing city, over a changing populace and fresh construction. Bend drew people from around Oregon and beyond. They arrived from California, yes, but also states like Colorado and Washington. Locals still wanted chunks of property to call their own. Single-detached homes were the signature dwellings, not stacked apartments.[63] For many, Bend was a place to which to escape and stretch their legs. But two major calamities would shape local housing markets in the coming years: the 2008 financial crisis and the global coronavirus pandemic.

▲ ▲ ▲

It was a bruising and rambunctious place to go through adolescence. Once a friend I made on the school bus, John, who was, like me, equal parts into biking and video games, drove us in his pickup to Phil's Trail, the signature single-track system on Bend's west side. Perfectly pale brown dirt tracks wove through trees as light wove through overhead branches. John had the idea to take our bikes to the top of a steep downhill. We got to the top, got on our bikes, then careened down, John first. I caught air on one of the first big jumps but screwed up the approach and flew off course. I seemed to come at a trailside log in slow motion. My right leg absorbed most of the impact. The log violently cleaved the skin along my knee, the bloody injury immediately screaming under my pantleg. I pushed myself up, with most of the track left to ride. I'd eaten it untold times during BMX, like when an older kid tried to teach me how to get air when I was a baby cyclist, so I inspected the damage, limped back onto my bike, sped down, and quickly rallied back to John. The decline didn't allow for a sluggish descent. We rolled on, going onto other parts of Phil's Trail. My crash didn't suck any fun from the outing: this was a war story I doubtless brought to my other school buds.

From 2002 to 2006, homebuilders were getting, on average, more than 3,100 new houses permitted every year in the Bend-Redmond area, which were linked in government reports by their proximity. That was a peak, according to federal housing officials. But the economy tanked, and new home construction in Bend and Redmond plummeted with it. "From 2008 through 2012, an average of 520 homes were permitted annually because construction financing was difficult to obtain," the US Department of Housing and Urban

Development (HUD) stated.[64] The housing bubble popped.[65] The effect on Bend was calamitous.[66]

I was in high school during the recession. One day our PE teacher sat our class down on the gym bleachers and asked if anyone wanted to talk about what was happening. One kid said their dad's retirement savings got wiped out. Deschutes County in spring 2009 ranked fourth in the United States for "some of the most serious recession pain in the land" measured by "unemployment, foreclosures and bankruptcies," according to the Associated Press Economic Stress Index. Rankings were for counties with at least twenty-five thousand residents. "This city in Oregon's scenic high desert once had one of the nation's hottest economies," the Associated Press stated as it set the scene. "Resort developers, bankers, construction workers and luxury car dealers rushed for a piece of the action. Now some locals call Bend 'poverty with a view.'" The phrase "poverty with a view" stuck around for years as a way to describe how, for many Bendites, wages were too low and housing costs too high.[67] I certainly heard "poverty with a view" years later while reporting on the very different COVID-19 housing market, with Bend now divided among "the haves and the have-nots."[68]

One-and-a-half million construction workers across the United States lost their jobs in the Great Recession, resetting industry employment to a low not seen since 1998.[69] As with the rest of the country, Central Oregon contractors fell on some of the hardest times. In Bend-Redmond, the logging, mining, and construction industries accounted for nearly half the local jobs lost in the recession.[70] In a 2009 dispatch that said, "Bend, Oregon was a 21st century American boomtown," Adam Brookes of BBC News focused on some good things, "The sunshine is warm, the air crisp and filled with the scent of bitterbrush and pine. Its people are gracious, their gorgeous surroundings imbuing them with a certain American languidness." He also noted some of the bad, such as the unemployment rate nearly quadrupling from two years prior to 15 percent that summer. In spite of the tough economic indicators, Brookes expressed a certain optimism that Bend would recover. But one point was almost prescient. He said, "No-one expects the housing market ever to revert to its previous, ferocious levels of activity. And many will tell you they have no desire for it to do so, that Bend has learned a lesson about bubbles."[71] Ironically, insufficient construction coming out of the recession got Bend-Redmond into trouble as the economy recovered and expanded from 2012 to 2019. More people were coming into the region than leaving, motivated by the outstanding quality of life and improving economy. That migration strained the housing market, which demanded fresh construction. "This dynamic contributed to an average annual increase of 600 jobs, or 11.2 percent, in the mining, logging, and construction sector, which has been the fastest growing sector in the (area) since economic recovery began in 2012," HUD wrote in 2021. In the coming years, the agency forecast, "the mining, logging, and construction sector is expected to add jobs at a strong pace to support the housing needs of the growing population."[72]

The need for more builders in Bend became apparent in a state-mandated report called a housing needs analysis. In August 2016, Bend had a fresh analysis showing the city's estimated needs all the way to the year 2028. Building permit data—this time down to the Bend level, excluding Redmond—showed residential development for all housing types rising year-to-year from 2000 (with 969 new units permitted) to 2005 (2,608 permitted), then falling to a trough in 2009 (132 permitted). Homebuilders regained some momentum by 2013 (907 permitted), but it still looked nothing like the construction frenzy of 2005.[73] And a frenzy would've helped—just without the subprime mortgages. According to the city's own analysis, Bend needed close to 17,000 additional homes to accommodate a probable increase in population from 76,551 people in 2008 to 115,063 people in 2028, representing a 50 percent increase in residents over two decades.[74] In other words, Bend needed to churn out homes thanks to a straightforward problem of supply and demand. As state economist Josh Lehner pointed out just a year prior in 2015 as he evaluated the region, "Population growth has returned . . . but new home construction remains subdued. Vacancy rates for both rental and owner-occupied housing are very low. The result is rising prices." If construction didn't accelerate over the next few years, Lehner warned, housing affordability would become a big problem.[75] That homebuilding? It didn't keep up.

The housing analysis called out the need to find ways to house three burgeoning demographics, which were not all mutually exclusive: baby boomers looking to downsize, Hispanic and Latino residents, and millennials. Report authors stressed that Bend needed *attached* housing, even though single-detached homes long predominated most new construction. What did attached housing mean, precisely? The authors wrote, "These demographic changes, combined with the existing and growing need for affordable housing, shows a growing need for *single-family attached housing (such as townhomes) and multifamily housing*" (emphasis added). "Multifamily housing" is another way of saying apartments. The authors quickly added that this didn't mean the extinction of single-detached homebuilding: "While the majority of new housing will continue to be single-family detached housing," they conceded, "the type of single-family detached dwellings may change, with more emphasis on smaller and more affordable new single-family detached housing and a decrease in demand for large-lot single-family detached housing."[76] Essentially, Bend should definitely ramp up apartment and townhome construction, and at the very least, it needed to shrink the size of new single-detached homes to make them more affordable to average residents. It's worth dwelling on this assertion from the 2010s, because it came to define what Bend needed in the 2020s: more apartments, more townhomes, more—and, notably, *smaller*—single-detached homes.

Oregon economics firm ECOnorthwest was more aggressive in 2017 when it followed up on the housing needs analysis with its own report. Lorelei Juntunen was a housing whiz; in her career, government and industry officials alike would regularly call on her to explain and, in Oregon's case, even shape policy. She was raised in rural Idaho, honed her craft in Seattle and at the University of Oregon, joining ECOnorthwest in 2004.[77] She ran point on the Bend report and was unsparing as she called out "The Mid-Market Housing Challenge." Juntunen wrote, "The Bend housing market has seen rapid price increases that affect renters and homeowners at all but the highest income brackets." She delivered the stunning fact that, "Median for-sale home prices . . . now rival prices in the much larger market in Portland." If you were a homebuyer, you didn't want to see the kinds of numbers her report had inside—but they probably wouldn't surprise you, either. You needed to make $81,400 a year to afford a median home. The city's median household income was not $81,400. It was $59,400. A typical Bendite couldn't afford to buy a typical home. Renters, naturally, didn't get it any easier. They got a 1.1 percent apartment vacancy rate (a measure of the share of empty rentals in need of tenants) in 2016, falling from 2.6 percent the prior year, according to Central Oregon Rental Owners Association data. All but a few of Bend's rentals were spoken for, so people had little in the way of choice and high rents for their trouble. Supply goes low, rent goes high. Average rent for a two-bedroom apartment—like for a young family or just a bedroom and an office—was $975 in 2016.[78] Juntunen summarized the challenges faced by middle-income residents: "Median income homebuyers earn enough to afford a home in Bend priced at $250,000. However, supply at this level is very constrained." Of the Bend homes that sold in 2016, only around 15 percent closed at $250,000 or less, reflecting the very constraint she was describing. "Median renters earn substantially less," she said, "and can afford only $850 per month in housing costs. Until just recently, the median renter could afford the average unit available in the Bend market, but as of 2016, this is no longer the case."[79]

By all appearances, 2016 marked a turning point, a year in which lack of appropriate supply caught up with residents. What's more, because there was a deficit of lower-cost housing, low-income residents were increasingly doubling-up in homes or paying more than they could reasonably afford, since they had to strain into the sets of homes more commonly "affordable" to middle-income Bendites. That had the effect of affecting, and even limiting, the housing supply available to middle-earners. The poor and middle-class jostled and jockeyed for limited supplies in their price ranges and, all the while, the wealthy had their pick of the listings, the ECOnorthwest report evidenced. Juntunen wrote that "while the number of overall housing units in Bend may be in line with the population, there is a mismatch in need and affordability. The price distribution makes much of the market impossible for middle-income families to reach. The vast majority of surplus housing is on the market at a price point affordable only to households earning more than $150,000 per year, above 250% of AMI for a family of four." "AMI" means area median income, a standard local economic measure. Even if the total number of homes was commensurate to population, the level of affordability wasn't, because so many homes were selling so far above what a low- or middle-income family could pay.[80]

Builders weren't cranking out new construction quickly enough as the Great Recession faded into the past. Even though far more permits were being approved since 2012, those permits weren't keeping pace with demand, the 2017 ECOnorthwest report confirmed. "Bend's housing market will continue to fall behind because at this moment the number of permits being approved for new housing units are not keeping up with the rate of population growth," Juntunen said, echoing state economist Josh Lehner's 2015 warning. "Since in-migration of higher income households is likely to continue in the near future, this shortage of housing production is likely to heavily impact and cost-burden middle income households."[81] And, it went without saying, impoverished locals would feel the brunt, too. The ECOnorthwest report's policy takeaways resembled those from the 2016 housing needs analysis, particularly in advocating attached homes, but with a fresh emphasis on how building all kinds of different homes could smooth out price spikes. Yes, the report recommended building "at all price levels," but it highlighted the need for additional for-sale homes marketed to middle earners who made 80 to 125 percent of the area median income. ECOnorthwest concluded with a familiar call for density, stating unequivocally, "It will not be possible or practical to support growth in Bend only through expanding the urban growth boundary. New higher density housing types such as duplexes, triplexes, and quads will also be necessary. These housing types are often referred to as 'middle housing' types."[82]

There will be more on middle housing and urban growth boundaries later. The thing to know was that, even in 2016 and 2017, before anyone heard of so-called Zooms towns—a COVID-era catchphrase—and only a few years following the global financial crisis, Bend needed to build more. As the years crept along, signs emerged that construction wasn't keeping up, leading to uneven experiences in the housing market depending on how much money you made. In 2019, the *Bulletin* reported Central Oregon was in a "housing crisis."[83] Brenna Visser, who wrote that story, told me that housing "was bad when I moved to Bend in 2019, and it only got exponentially worse." Like so many before her, Visser was an outsider before she became an insider. She grew up in the small central Washington city of Wenatchee and vacationed to Bend as a kid. She went into newspapering as a young woman and moved to Oregon, working at the *Daily Astorian* in Astoria, situated on the Columbia River close to the coast. She was ready for her next step when a colleague flagged an open spot at the *Bulletin*. She emailed an editor there and said she wanted to work for her. Visser got the position and moved inland. She picked what could have been the exact wrong time to take a job at the Bend paper. In May 2019, Western Communications, the Bend-based owner of the *Bulletin*, was spiraling through a bankruptcy, mired in some $30 million of debt, with plans to sell its Pacific Northwest papers and dissolve. Buyers crouched in anticipation.[84] "It was a crazy time to come to Bend," Visser recalled. "I had a lot of people be like, 'Why are you doing this? You have a stable job here at the *Astorian*. Why would you leave this to go to a newspaper that may not even exist in three months?'"

Visser started off at $17 an hour at the *Bulletin* and couldn't nail down a single-bedroom apartment that wouldn't eat up most of her paycheck. She said, "I ended up being resourceful and having connections through my publisher at the *Astorian*, (who) knew someone in advertising at the *Bulletin*, who then connected me with someone who had a room that she was able to rent." There was no "resistance-less path" when she tried to find a home "through a normal application process, trying to move here." At the one-story house in north Bend, about $800 a month got her a room, bathroom, utilities, Internet, and streaming services. "That was a rude awakening, because I was renting a two-bedroom apartment in Gearhart," on the coast, fifteen miles from Astoria, "for $900 for myself."

Still, she sensed things would work out. Maybe it was hindsight bias, but the bankruptcy saga had something of a happy ending after all: keeping owner-ship local, Oregon-based EO Media Group won ownership of the *Bulletin* and its companion newspaper to the north, the *Redmond Spokesman*, following a fifteen-minute auction in late July. To beat two other bidders from out-of-state, EO Media Group bid $3.65 million.[85] I had fond memories of EO Media from a college summer interning at its *East Oregonian* in rural Pendleton. EO Media already owned the *Daily Astorian*, Visser's prior haunt, meaning she went back to working for the same parent company. "We joked about that," she told me. "They're like, 'We just followed you to Bend.'" Another happy twist: on a dating app, Visser quickly met a woman who'd become her fiancée. In fact, they both met within their first week of getting to Bend. Visser was making a life. Yet her work covering housing was sobering. "There are tons of people who work in this city, who do not get paid enough to live in this city, but they need to be in the city," she said. "We need journalists in this city. We need the people who are servers in the city. We need social service providers in the city. We need janitors and park attendants, and we need all of these people to run a society. The whole city can't just be remote tech workers. . . . There's so many of us in the city that are holding on to stay here, but barely can."

Bend for decades relied on a broad mix of laborers across industries to thrive. But only those at the uppermost income levels seemed to be rewarded with the choicest homes in town—or the choice to stay in town. Housing supply had constricted before, like when the mills first opened and too many workers crowded in.[86] Same went for the post-Great Recession and COVID-19 years: in a cruel twist, working-class people who made Bend a magnetic place to live were rejected by its reinvigorated economy. COVID-19 didn't produce the local housing troubles; they predated the pandemic. But during COVID, the schism dividing "haves" and "have-nots"[87] widened because of inadequate supply. Could a movement to build more point the way to a fairer future?

CHAPTER 2

"Big City Problems"

Colleen Sinsky and Greg Delgado were the kinds of people who really got into making their community a better place. Sinsky, who like many northwesterners nurtured a sense of awe about the natural amenities that separated the region from other parts of the country, worked at a Bend nonprofit. Delgado was by turns a community organizer, political hopeful, and service-industry worker. But their experiences underscored how, despite its smaller size and remote setting, the city was encountering some of the same urban challenges as West Coast metros like Portland. Vacation destination Bend was by no means immune to homelessness and eviction.

A doctor's daughter, Sinsky was the blonde eldest sibling of four. She grew up in cul-de-sac house in the suburb of Escondido in Southern California, close to Interstate 15. Her family's four-bedroom home had a yard with a swimming pool for parties, all on just under a half-acre, said Colleen's father, Jerry Sinsky, a semi-retired gynecologist. Jerry described it as "classic middle-class, upper middle-class, somewhere in there, nothing fancy." The neighborhood was quiet. For her part, Colleen was both easygoing and studious as a kid. "She was always philosophical, even when she was young," Jerry said. He observed once that Colleen might just be happy as "a head in a box. She loved thinking about things." The family wasn't intensely outdoorsy, but they hiked. As Colleen got older, however, she camped, rappelled, rock climbed. She got to know Oregon by coming here to see her paternal aunt, whom she visited as a kid. Traveling to the Beaver State added nuance to her worldview. As Jerry told me, "I'm sure that first trip—and I forget how old she was—to visit it was the one that really made her realize that the world isn't all like San Diego and L.A."

Unsure what to do as she prepared to graduate from Santa Clara University, Colleen learned about a group called Jesuit Volunteer Corps Northwest, for which she could volunteer in Oregon. She packed lightly for the trip north, a suitcase and backpack in the trunk of her car, as she remembered later. She traveled with friends to spend a weekend in San Francisco before crossing state lines. California had an expensive goodbye present in store. She parked her car in Haight-Ashbury and went to get her nose pierced, but she finished and came back to see her car was gone, along with the few belongings inside. She panicked, called the cops. But she couldn't remember any details, like the car's VIN or license plate number. As it turned out, no one stole it. She'd blocked someone's driveway. It'd been hauled off. Getting the car back cleared out her meager, fresh-out-of-college savings. "That was like a $1,200 day," she told me. Her parting sentiment was (censorship hers), "Eff you, California." Sinsky cut her weekend short, made for Oregon, drove to an Ashland hostel just past the state line, and she fell in love.

For her Jesuit Volunteer Corps Northwest time, she entered the complicated world of homeless services in our biggest, most populous city. Sinsky volunteered with the Portland nonprofit JOIN. "I went from never having talked to somebody who is homeless to doing the nighttime street outreach," she said. She maintained the group's blog. In October 2010, at the conclusion of her third week with JOIN, she wrote in a post titled "the Rookie" that her day-to-day work was building relationships, doing street outreach, moving furniture when people got into homes, and compliance paperwork. She felt lucky that JOIN had brought her on, and she expressed a youthful eagerness to see how the year would pan out.[1]

Her written excitement belied some discomfort. Sinsky was in unfamiliar surroundings, helping some of Portland's worst off, and she felt guilty about having her own place to sleep at night and took it upon herself to sleep on the floor by her bed the first few weeks. She finally fessed up to a coworker. "They thought that I was the biggest idiot, and that was a really dumb thing to do," she recalled. "I was like, 'Yeah, yeah, you're right.'" Still, it was part of her self-admitted journey of reconciling her guilt and privilege and working in homeless services. She explained, "It came initially from just this realization like, 'Holy shit, the world doesn't work for everyone the way that it works for me.'" She understood her advantages in life, but she did a job that helped people in worse straits.

For Sinsky, a year at JOIN became years. She took up retention work for the organization and kept on writing, too. One of her final missives came in August 2014, when she wrote more than six hundred words, published in the local newspaper *Street Roots*, on the dehumanization and isolation that come with homelessness. JOIN workers like her were often the only emergency contacts listed on apartment applications for people they helped. "When our folks are in the hospital or hospice, it's not uncommon for us to be their only visitors. And when they pass away, we grieve and honor each of them by carrying their memory forward with us," she wrote in *Street Roots*. "This real and compassionate level of authentic human connection is as necessary as housing."[2]

She'd detour before arriving in Bend. In her twenties, she felt as though she saw her future roll out before her and understood that if she didn't pause and take a step back, she'd be married with kids in a fulfilling Portland job. She wasn't ready for all that yet. Still single, she did what many young people do and set off and saw the world: Greece, China, Alaska. She cobbled together work along the way and basked in her own sense of fearlessness. By October 2016, six years after her initial "Rookie" post for JOIN in Portland, Sinsky had returned to Oregon once more. "Oregon pulled me back across the border by my heartstrings, and I actually had a silly moment alone in my car of literally screaming with happiness at being back inside of Oregon," Sinsky recounted on a personal blog. "Every time I come back I get this same flooding warm feeling of a happy welcome that I haven't found anywhere else. . . . After living there for about five years, even while working in the 'ugly underbelly' of urban homelessness, that feeling of *home* hasn't changed."[3] She relocated to Bend in November 2016. "It snows a lot in Bend," she wrote on the blog in January 2017. "No one told me this before I moved here. I haven't seen the ground for a month."[4]

A local social services group, J Bar J Youth Services, soon hired Sinsky to manage a drop-in center where teenagers went twice a week for a meal and a safe place to hang out. J Bar J helped connect young people with shelter and housing if they needed it. She worked with teens to get in touch with mental health services or obtain food stamps. Diving back into homelessness services proved smart: She knew the ropes and helped resilient eighteen- and nineteen-year-olds who survived despite living outside or couch-surfing. She felt confident in the work. But within a few years, even with steady nonprofit employment, Sinsky was forced to confront the possibility of leaving the city as housing for workers like her became more tenuous.

▲   ▲   ▲

Sinsky's Bend fantasy turned into a stress dream. By late 2020, there was talk of in-migration and soaring home prices against a backdrop of so-called Zoom towns, as remote-working urbanites arrived in small cities with big paychecks.

Sinsky, now thirty-two years old, had moved on from J Bar J and landed at a small homelessness and affordable housing nonprofit called Central Oregon FUSE, working as its program manager. She submitted a column to the *Bulletin* that published in November, leading with the depressing prediction that she wouldn't live in Bend in three years' time. "That should matter to you," she told fellow locals reading the paper, "because Bend needs people like me to build a life here." The ravenous hunger for Bend housing was eroding her own hope of becoming a homeowner and raising a family within the city. She acknowledged she wasn't special; rather, she represented a class of residents making essential contributions to the community: restaurant workers, teachers, childcare providers, healthcare workers, police officers, all of whom understood the severity of Bend's housing crunch. The crux was a personal question that carried implications for weavers of the social safety net like her. "How can I continue to pour myself into my work when I feel so financially insecure and alienated from the future of this community?"[5]

In early 2021, I was trying to find sources for a story about Bend's housing crunch I'd pitched to my editors at the *Portland Business Journal*. I came across Sinsky's op-ed and read through it. It stuck out to me. As luck would have it, one of my sources, a tenant advocate, knew her and put us in touch by email. I told Sinsky what I was up to, that I'd read her column, and that I wanted to know more about her story for my piece. Sinsky replied and was happy to talk. "I've been amazed at the response I've gotten from that article," she wrote by email of her *Bulletin* op-ed. "It's been a flood of friends and even strangers thanking me for naming what's been going on for them."

Sinsky told me her story when we talked for the first time soon afterward. She rented an approximately 1,100-square-foot house with her boyfriend. She worried over whether her lease would be renewed, as she'd heard about landlords selling their properties from under their tenants. She figured if she were smart, she'd leave Bend because there wasn't enough housing for someone making what she did. She didn't want to leave Oregon again, but her conversations with others frequently circled back to the unstable nature of Bend housing. "I feel cut off from the future of my community," she said. She was making $2,450 per month working part-time at Central Oregon FUSE, though she expected to earn more after she graduated with her master's degree in social work.[6] But this was the net result of housing insecurity for Sinsky: she was trying to improve Bend, but it was unclear whether she'd share in that future prosperity.

I interviewed several other locals to get at the story: State Senator Tim Knopp, a Bend Republican, said, "It's almost impossible for people to find

Colleen Sinsky was among the local workers trying to make Bend a more affordable place for the least affluent to live. But the hyper-competitive housing market left her wondering whether she herself could stay. (Photo by Jonathan Bach)

something that they can afford." Damon Runberg, a regional economist with the Oregon Employment Department, said, "We're all guilty of being tourists here at one point." Louie Hoffman, president of the Central Oregon Association of Realtors, said of new arrivals, "They've got the dough." Katy Brooks, CEO of the Bend Chamber of Commerce, said it "costs you, as a human being, more to live in Bend." The resulting article ran in the *Business Journal* in May, bringing my hometown's story to Portland readers.[7] Sinsky's life, along with everyone else's, carried on. So did the housing dilemma.

▲   ▲   ▲

Sinsky kept busy with work and school. She completed her master's degree, and in August 2021, Central Oregon FUSE brought her on as its executive director. The year represented FUSE's transition from, in effect, a small start-up toward becoming more of a stable organization with programs and goals. In a 2021 report, Sinsky described a motivating and exhausting year. "It's still hard for me to believe that we're actually creating permanent-supportive housing opportunities that hadn't existed before," she wrote in the report. "Sometimes, at the end of a long day in front of my laptop, I'm struck by the fact that tonight, there are already seven people who will be sleeping safe in their own apartments that night, after having experienced the trauma of homelessness for years."[8]

The most ambitious initiative of which FUSE was a part, from a construction standpoint, was a project called Cleveland Commons. This was billed as "Central Oregon's first Permanent Supportive Housing development."[9] Common in larger cities like Portland, permanent support housing is defined by the state as "affordable housing designed to serve households experiencing chronic homelessness."[10] The plan was for Cleveland Commons to open in 2024, bringing thirty-three apartments to southeast Bend. Along with FUSE, other local groups on the project included Housing Works, Epic Property Management, NeighborImpact, and Deschutes County Behavioral Health.[11] If Cleveland Commons could succeed, so might others like it. Deschutes County commissioners had so much faith in Cleveland Commons that they set aside $2 million toward it from the American Rescue Plan Act, the pandemic cash infusion from the federal government. According to the county, Cleveland Commons would have "on-site healthcare, behavioral health supports and trauma-informed resident services." Colleen Thomas, chair of the local Homeless Leadership Coalition, said in a written statement, "Right now in Central Oregon, we have very limited options for permanent supportive housing and the proposed project at Cleveland Commons will serve those meeting the chronic homeless definition."[12]

What does it mean to be chronically homeless? The definition was important, as the feds were anything but casual with their rules. Documentation outlining a 2015 clarification to define "chronically homeless" ran to fifteen pages in the *Federal Register*.[13] It is perplexingly complicated. According to the US Department of Housing and Urban Development, someone is chronically homeless if they have a disability under what's known as the McKinney-Vento Homeless Assistance Act and the person "lives in a place not meant for human habitation, a safe haven, or in an emergency shelter, and . . . has been homeless and living as described for at least 12 months* or on at least 4 separate occasions in the last 3 years, as long as the combined occasions equal at least 12 months and each break in homelessness separating the occasions included at least 7 consecutive nights of not living as described." The asterisk denoted that "a 'break' in homeless is considered to be 7 or more nights."[14]

The chronically homeless definition could further apply to someone who "has been residing in an institutional care facility for less [sic], including jail, substance abuse or mental health treatment facility, hospital, or other similar facility, for fewer than 90 days and met all of the criteria of this definition before entering that facility**; or . . . a family with an adult head of household (or, if there is no adult in the family, a minor head of household) who meets all of the criteria of this definition, including a family whose composition has fluctuated while the head of household has been homeless." The double asterisks stated that "an individual residing in an institutional care facility does not constitute a break in homelessness."[15] Point being, it's stunningly complex whom the federal government does and doesn't consider chronically homeless, and who in turn gets the housing resources under that definition. Still, this was a segment of housing Bend needed. "It's possible that we'll target folks who are timing out of shelters, or timing out of rapid rehousing," Sinsky told me. Deschutes County commissioners and all the project leaders were banking on Cleveland Commons. Groundbreaking was scheduled for 2023, and tenants were expected to start signing leases the following year.

Housing Works, the regional housing authority, was the developer of Cleveland Commons, and Sinsky described herself as a "sidekick" on the project. She was coordinating long-term funding for the social services to be offered on-site and figuring out a plan to implement them. One hurdle was that the property needed a service provider to be there around the clock. Any number of groups in Portland could fill that kind of role because there were so many permanent supportive housing buildings there. Portland was accustomed to dealing with a sizable homeless population, as Sinsky experienced firsthand. But Bend didn't have much in the way of options. No local agency seemed well positioned to assume the responsibility. "They've asked my organization to do it, but it just doesn't make sense for us to try to scale up from essentially one person to having a 24-7 team," she said. Outsiders might be able to come in and help, but for her, the dilemma exemplified how Bend's rapid growth meant it was outpacing its resources. Sinsky identified it as an urban-rural conundrum. "It's an embodiment of the fact that Bend is growing so quickly," she said. "All of a sudden, we have these big-city problems of urban, visible homelessness. But we don't have those well-established organizations yet that can implement the best practices."

Though growth had been part of Bend's identity from the get-go, the city was buckling under the weight of newer, big-city challenges, and people like Sinsky were trying to rapidly construct the low-barrier, low-cost housing that the most vulnerable had to have. At the same time, Sinsky, working for a homeless services nonprofit, had herself grappled with whether she could afford to lend a hand. Her dilemma pointed to the compounding nature of Bend's housing crunch: the market was hostile to the people whose job it was to provide the low-income housing that research had proved Bend needed. If relatively stable workers like Sinsky struggled to find places to live, the poor didn't seem to stand a chance. What's more, if forced out, the Sinskys of Bend wouldn't be around to build lower-income, affordable housing for those who needed it. The ecosystem of reliance between workers of different incomes was apparent. That's why, for instance, the community needed more middle-income homes: to sustain the people who'd construct the Cleveland Commons-type developments of the future. Brenna Visser, the writer, had argued much the same point: Bend couldn't be all techies. It also required people like her and Sinsky to make the civic gears turn. There needed to be enough homes at reasonable prices for local workers to have local addresses.

By the time I was trying to turn the cover story into a book, I knew I needed to talk to more people. Through local connections, Sinsky learned about a man named Greg Delgado, though she didn't know him personally. She passed my contact info to him. It was July 2021 when I got an email from Delgado with his phone number: "Feel free to contact me at your convenience."

▲   ▲   ▲

Competing ideas have taken shape around identifying the largest contributor to America's housing troubles. These ideas apply to Bend. One increasingly mainstream argument, laid out by journalist Conor Dougherty in his authoritative book *Golden Gates: The Housing Crisis and a Reckoning for the American Dream* and by Brookings senior fellow Jenny Schuetz in her writing for that think tank is that we must fill a Mariana Trench-deep deficit of homes where Americans want to live and businesses want to operate.[16] Others, namely sociologist David Madden and urban planner Peter Marcuse in their *In Defense of Housing*, contend the real problem is the transformation of homes into commodities, whose free-market economic value becomes more important than their use as dwellings. Once a home is a commodity, they write, its highest purpose is to make an investor money, not to shelter residents.[17]

It's worth meditating for a moment on why we treat homes as assets. Commodification is contentious enough that a United Nations official specializing in housing warned in 2017, "Many States have been too deferential to the dynamics of unregulated markets and have failed to take appropriate action to bring private investment into line with the right to adequate housing. By providing tax subsidies for homeownership, tax breaks for investors, and bailouts for banks and financial institutions, States have subsidized the excessive financialization of housing at the expense of programmes for those in desperate need of housing."[18] The Economic Policy Institute describes the financial pressures that push owners to keep their home values as high as possible, at a time when retirement-savings accounts and entrepreneurship can't always be counted on to build familial wealth:

> The United States also has one of the weakest social safety net arrangements among Organization for Economic Co-operation and Development (OECD) countries, making the acquisition and maintenance of individual family wealth necessary for economic security. Our economic system is full of pitfalls that are avoidable for families who have secured individual wealth but can be devastating for those who have not. The rising costs of health care, higher education, and other living expenses are all defrayed by having a valuable asset like a home to borrow against or sell when times are particularly hard. The value of a home even matters intergenerationally, as homes are an asset that can be easily transferred to one's children or used to otherwise support their economic goals.[19]

Whether you agree with the economic, supply-and-demand argument (we have too few homes to fulfill demand, so we need to build more) or decry commodification (and believe that viewing homes first and foremost as moneymakers undermines the goal of providing "the residential good life" for all[20]), both schools of thought arc toward the same practical conclusion: our way of doing things leaves the poorest among us either homeless or barely in home.[21]

Difficulties associated with that struggle compound when eviction enters the equation. First and foremost, it can make finding another place to rent more difficult if the landlord sees your past eviction.[22] What's more, if "residential stability begets a kind of psychological stability, which allows people to invest in their home and social relationships," then eviction begets the opposite. When landlords and courts evict tenants, the evicted lose not only their home but their neighborhood, too. Their place in the local tapestry is rended. The evicted must frequently settle into substandard living arrangements. "Eviction does not simply drop poor families into a dark valley, a trying yet relatively brief detour on life's journey," sociologist Matthew Desmond wrote in his Pulitzer Prize-winning book *Evicted: Poverty and Profit in the American City*. "It fundamentally redirects their way, casting them onto a different, and much more difficult, path. Eviction is a cause, not just a condition, of poverty."[23] Such was the case for Greg

Delgado, who was kicked out of his longtime rental on a violation of his lease terms as home prices were ballooning in 2021, while state and federal COVID-related eviction bans were still in place. Delgado was caught in the crosshairs of two systemic issues: a justice system that allows evictions over relatively minor infractions and the state legislature's focus on non-payment as a cause for eviction while still permitting evictions for other, non-criminal reasons.[24]

▲   ▲   ▲

I got in contact with Delgado in the summer of 2021, the first of several conversations we'd have over the next two years. He grew up in Sahuarita, Arizona, a community outside Tucson.[25] His family grew produce and raised animals on a small farm. As he got older, he traveled quite a lot: through Mexico and Texas, back to Arizona, then Estes Park, Colorado, which was "beautiful but cold as heck." In the early aughts, a few friends planned to move to Bend, so he made the more than thousand-mile trip with them. Once in town, Delgado wandered into a watering hole, where someone at the bar sized him up and said, "You look like you could use a drink."

"Yes, I could," Delgado said.

"This one's on me," came the reply.

Locals welcomed Delgado. "It's hard for me to feel welcome places because [being] a person of color in an all-white community is very scary," he said. Still, he and others certainly wouldn't ignore Oregon's many issues when it comes to race. He enmeshed himself in the community and pushed for Latino advancement. He became an organizer for Causa, a prominent immigrant rights organization. Congressman Greg Walden was an Oregon Republican whose congressional district blanketed Eastern and Central Oregon, including Bend.[26] Walden was also a favorite demonstration target. In 2014, when Walden was at the Bend Deschutes Brewery meeting with the local commerce leaders, Delgado joined other protesters outside the bar and voiced support for migrant workers. "We need him to be a leader in our communities and hear our voice," Delgado said of Walden.[27] Delgado's activism landed him in handcuffs later in 2014, when he and another activist went to Walden's fourth-floor office in a building on Bend's Northwest Bond Street, then sat there and refused to leave while perhaps a dozen sign-carrying protesters demonstrated outside. A responding police officer, Scot Eliott, recounted in his report that Delgado and the other person in the Republican's office were "part of a group protesting for immigration reform. They and their group feel like they have exhausted all legal means to have their voices heard. They believe only by being arrested for trespass will they be able to have their voices be heard. . . . Congressman Walden would not see them so they would not leave without being arrested." The police placed the two activists in handcuffs until they reached the first floor, where police uncuffed them and cited them for trespass. As police completed the citations on the ground floor, the crowd chanted outside. Eliott saw that "Delgado offered them fist pumps, although I'm not sure they could see them through the tinted glass." The two emerged outside to cheers, proudly holding their citations high.[28] The charge, second-degree criminal trespass, was later dismissed.[29] Delgado was a community activist, a gatherer of people. He was agitating for change in the city that had welcomed him years ago.

Pivoting from public action to chasing public office, Delgado in 2016 ran an insurgent campaign as a Democrat against State Senator Tim Knopp, the Republican incumbent of Senate District 27. The cover photo of the Delgado campaign's Facebook page was him next to Democratic governor Kate Brown, and his platform skewed unsurprisingly left: tax corporations, incentivize green construction, fight urban sprawl by developing city centers, build less-expensive homes. The campaign social-media page stated, "We can't allow the working-class members of our community to be uprooted by gentrification."[30] When he described his campaign to me later, Delgado emphasized how few opportunities Latino residents, in particular, have to own homes and how challenging it is to put down roots. Even as Bend blossomed into a larger city over decades, its population remained overwhelmingly non-Hispanic white.[31] Latinos had come to Oregon as far back as the sixteenth century, when explorer Juan Rodríguez Cabrillo sailed from Mexico's port of Navidad to what's now the California–Oregon border. During the 1600s, a Spanish commander named Martín de Aguilar described Oregon's coast in a logbook. He became one of the first people to put observations of the haunting shore in writing, describing a "white cape" that's now believed to be near modern-day Port Orford. In the early twentieth century, Union Pacific Railroad, the Oregon Short Line, and the Oregon Railroad and Navigation Company hired Mexicans as laborers.[32] Fast forward to the twenty-first century, and the Latino community in Central Oregon was, as one report from the Latino Community Association put it, "vital and stable." It grew even through the Great Recession. Central Oregon's Latino population would log a more than sixfold increase, from about 3,300 in 1990 to 20,500 in 2018, with many living in Bend. Still, housing costs tended to burden Latinos more than white residents.[33]

Bend's two main newspapers were split on Knopp and Delgado when they published endorsements for Senate District 27 in October 2016. The *Source Weekly* kicked off its editorial by noting that readers frequently reported their concerns about living wages and affordable housing to the alt-weekly, problems that could, in the worst extremes, force people to double up, live in cars, or camp outside. Affordability, then, stood among the top issues for Bend's most vulnerable. Delgado wasn't someone who thought about living-wage employment and housing affordability in the abstract: he worked two jobs to live in Bend. "Delgado will be entering the legislature as an untested politician," the *Source* wrote, "but when it comes to being a voice of the working person, it's a worthwhile test."[34]

Taking the other side, the *Bulletin*'s editorial board praised how Knopp's professional background, including with the Central Oregon Builders Association, meant he knew affordable housing and construction. Much of the *Bulletin*'s appreciation for the incumbent came down to its view that the troubled state pension system needed an overhaul, and Knopp was the reformist for the job. The editorial board appraised community organizer Delgado next, noting how he wanted to give rent control a close look. It also noted his two DUI arrests in 1995 and 2008, but in that regard, the paper called Delgado "admirably honest that he has made mistakes in the past." The editorial board ultimately supported Knopp.[35] In November 2016, so did local voters, sending the Republican back to Salem. Delgado, who secured 39 percent of the vote to Knopp's 61 percent, didn't plan to rip out his carefully cultivated roots. In an interview with a local podcaster, Delgado, then fifty-one years old, said, "What I wish for my future is someday to actually own my own home or business or both here in town. That's personally. As a community, I think I wish that we could work harder at making opportunity and this life in this community equal for everybody."[36]

▲   ▲   ▲

As much as Delgado yearned to own, he did cherish his rental apartment's placement on Northwest Greeley Avenue, just outside the city's innermost neighborhood, Old Bend. It was where he lived while he campaigned for office. Friends got ready for big events there: political marches, community meals, Día de Muertos (Day of the Dead). One friend, Cait Boyce, recalled how there'd be papier-mâché crafts for Day of the Dead. She remembered the overgrown flowers and herbs, and the barbecues Delgado put on at the apartment building. He paid $900 a month in rent and testified in support of statewide rent control in 2019, telling Oregon lawmakers, "I love my apartment, and the community I have been able to create around it."[37]

Greg Delgado made a name for himself as a community organizer and political hopeful in Bend, but an eviction during the pandemic threatened to tear up his carefully cultivated Central Oregon roots. (Photo by Jonathan Bach)

While this was Delgado's home, the reality was he didn't own it. An entity called Second Half Enterprises LLC owned the building. The company was owned by a man named David McDonald, who bought the building with his wife, originally thinking they'd put some kind of small business on the first floor. The ground floor was too small, they realized, and they kept the building a rental.[38] The property manager, meanwhile, was a Bend company called Partners Property Management and Sales. As Partners would outline in an eviction case against Delgado, "The rental property is comprised of a building that is split into an upper and lower unit, the rental property includes outdoor space as common areas for both tenants."[39] Partners filed to evict Delgado in 2021 for leaving debris and personal belongings in common areas, and the case went to court on June 3 of that year.[40]

Delgado's eviction trial took place in the courtroom of pro tem circuit court judge Andrew Balyeat. The lawyer for the landlord, a local attorney named Frances Zars (whose last name has since changed to Mann), started by telling the court, "This case is simply about which party is legally entitled to possession of the rental." She straightforwardly asked the court to grant possession of the unit to her client. Zars called as a witness Brandi Snow, who worked as Partners general manager. Snow appeared via video and began by describing Delgado as "a respectable person."

"We usually remedy any issues that usually have come up during the time that he's rented," Snow told the court.

As Zars got a little deeper into her direct examination, she homed in on the personal property argument: Were tenants allowed to leave personal property in common areas, according to the lease? Snow said they weren't, and she sent a notice of termination in December 2020 because there had been "an abundance of personal belongings all around the building in all of the common areas." Snow testified that she got in touch with Delgado about fixing the problem and went as far as to describe a shed that Delgado purportedly rented. To press her case, Zars had Snow read notes from an inspection aloud. The notes said, "During the site visit with Greg, he stated the items being stored in the common area belonged to a friend of his who was having medical issues. He said he was securing a trailer or truck to move the (items) as soon as possible."

Snow went on to testify that by early 2021, Delgado continued to claim some items were not his, so she offered to help haul them off. As of March 2021, the property management team continued to drive by the rental at the request of the owner. It looked clean, though it appeared at that point Delgado was working on some sort of project outside. One Partners employee thought they might be piñatas, Snow said. "He was actively working on it, not just storing items." That made a difference: Partners didn't issue another termination notice then because nothing appeared to be stored. However, a month later, boxes, a mattress, the purported piñatas, and other items came into view outside, including items that had been in the yard back when Partners issued the first termination notice in December, she told the court.

Zars got to her point, asking her witness, "Why are you evicting Mr. Delgado?"

Snow said, "Simply for the lease violations of the belongings in the common area."

Soon enough, it was Delgado's turn to take the stand. Delgado's lawyer was Rebecca Straus of the nonprofit Oregon Law Center, which provides legal aid to low-income renters.[41] Balyeat swore Delgado in, and Straus asked how long he had lived in the unit.

"I think since 2013," Delgado said.

"During that time, have you placed items, furnishings, belongings in the common areas?" his lawyer asked him.

"Generally speaking, it's usually potted plants, a barbecue grill, and patio furniture."

"Have you received a violation notice or a notice of termination other than the ones that have been submitted into the record in this case?"

"No."

Straus oriented Delgado back in time a few years. "In the summer of 2019, did you have personal belongings in the common area?"

"Yes."

"Can you describe what was out there?"

"I set it up with couches, chairs, patio furniture, a barbecue grill," Delgado recounted.

"How long was that out there?" Straus asked.

"Probably from like April 'til October."

"Did you have tents up?"

"No tents."

"Have you ever been behind on your rent? Have you ever missed a rent payment?"

Delgado responded, "As of recently, because of COVID, but not before that. There were a couple times that I forgot to pay the rent, but I had it the next day. I just forgot to drop it off." He said he paid a late fee but took care of it right away.

Delgado's attorney came back to the termination notices, asking if, when he got the first notice in December 2020, he believed all the belongings in the common area to be his.

"No," Delgado told Straus. "There was a lot of debris in the back." A homeless person appeared to have left stuff there, he claimed. Some of the items belonged to his upstairs neighbors, according to Delgado, as they had "a rotation of people up there."

Soon enough, it was Zars's turn to cross-examine him.

"Hello, Mr. Delgado," the landlord lawyer said. "You signed a month-to-month lease, which is Plaintiff's Exhibit 1, is that correct?"

Delgado said he assumed so, as he didn't have it in front of him.

"I apologize that you don't have the exhibits," Zars told Delgado. "I can share my screen with you if that is possible. What you are looking at here is—can you see my screen?"

"Yeah."

"Great."

Zars showed Delgado the lease and asked if he was familiar with it. He was. She stopped screen-sharing. "You were keeping some personal property in the common area, is that correct?"

"Yeah, patio furniture," he said.

"And you received the December 22 notice from my client?"

"Yes."

"Did you object to the notice or contact the landlord that the property in the common area was not yours?"

"Yes," Delgado replied.

"Okay," Zars said. "Did you inform the landlord that you believed the property was the other tenants' property?"

"Yes," he testified.

"Okay, we don't have any record of that. I am sorry," Zars told him.

She moved on: Following the first notice, Delgado did remove the stuff, but what about for the April termination notice? Delgado said he had told Partners he "was trying to get a truck." He then made the claim that he was told "to remove (the items) within like forty-eight hours," and when he called to say he needed at least another twelve hours because he had work, someone (it was not clear who from his testimony) allegedly responded Partners was going to cancel his lease.

"That's what they told me," Delgado said.

The April notice stated he had ten days, Zars countered. Delgado stuck with his statement that he was given forty-eight hours to get the debris out of the yard. This was a new development, but it quickly fizzled and went unproven. Zars again apologized, telling him she didn't have any record of such a conversation. She finished her cross-examination. The rest of Straus's and Zars's questioning of Delgado dealt with the forty-eight hours he claimed he had been given. Delgado clarified his testimony during Straus's redirect, telling the court that on April 21, "They posted on the door that I had forty-eight hours to remove the mattress and the desk that was in the yard." When he followed up to say he needed a little more time, that's when someone allegedly told him they were just going to discontinue the lease anyway, and they issued the ten-day eviction notice, according to his testimony. He claimed someone else at the Partners office, not Snow, made him aware of this. But aside from his sworn testimony, neither Delgado nor his lawyer produced evidence in the trial, namely a copy of this purported forty-eight-hour notice he said was posted to his door, to back up the claim.

Snow and Delgado were the only witnesses called during the eviction trial. The court proceedings to decide whether he'd be kicked out were exceedingly brief. Because this was not a jury trial, the case soon went to Judge Balyeat for a decision. The judge reiterated that the issue at hand was whether Delgado violated the lease by leaving personal items within the common area. He acknowledged Delgado's testimony that a homeless person may have left items, and that other people were coming and going from the second rental on the property and might have also left items. "But what I also heard was him acknowledge that the mattress and the desk," the judge continued, "that he had promised to remove those, and I also heard testimony that was not refuted, that when confronted with the need to remove this personal property, his response was that he didn't have any place to put it. He had a shed rented, but it sounds like it must have been full, and then it was pointed out to him that he had a two-bedroom apartment, and he just simply could not store things in the common area."

The judge returned to Delgado's claim about a forty-eight-hour notice: there was no evidence presented aside from the renter's testimony. In the end, that line of defense came to nothing. Balyeat said, "When the defendant says in response to complaints about the personal property that there's nowhere else to put them, I deem that to be an admission, and when he says he's going to remove the mattress and the desk, but that he needed forty-eight hours, and I have seen these photographs,"—there were photos presented in evidence—"and I am just persuaded by the evidence that he did violate the terms of his lease agreement by leaving personal property in the common area."

Balyeat concluded: "I'm going to grant the eviction."[42]

The ruling cast Delgado into uncertainty. On June 8, Delgado and his lawyer made a last-ditch effort to keep him indoors for as long as possible. The defense suggested there would be an appeal of the Deschutes ruling and asked the court for Delgado to be allowed to stay in his rental and pay his $900 rent while their appeal played out.[43] Delgado promised he would pay rent on time and follow the rules of the rental agreement. "I still live in the unit and have nowhere to move," he told the court. "I would lose my home and suffer irreparable harm if forced to move prior to resolution of this case on appeal."[44]

Within a few days, Delgado and the landlord arrived at a settlement, one that made Delgado abandon an appeal. Partners Property Management and Sales agreed to pay Delgado $1,500 and he would be allowed to stay at Greeley Avenue until July 11, a little more than a month after the court granted the eviction. In exchange, he agreed to hand over the rental keys in July and drop the appeal threat.[45] For his part, property owner David McDonald was tired of the rental headaches. He felt Delgado had been given ample notice of issues at the unit before it came to an eviction. By selling, the property owners would get their money's worth out of the place. In September 2021, McDonald's Second Half Enterprises LLC sold the Greeley Avenue property for $818,500. McDonald reflected later, "The market was red hot."[46]

Delgado clung to his low-rent downtown apartment for years, paying the rent dutifully. The evidence presented in court indicated he had, in point of fact,

left personal belongings in the common areas of the building, and the judge followed the evidence to reach his ruling. No COVID eviction protections helped
Delgado guard against the case. Just like that, he carried an eviction on his record that could make it more difficult to sign another lease elsewhere in Bend.[47]
Why would another landlord lease to someone who had been through an
eviction when there were clearly other tenants with untarnished records who'd
pay market rents? Stacking the odds against Delgado further was the housing
shortage. It's difficult to find an open door when there are only so many in town.

▲   ▲   ▲

With nowhere to go, Delgado leaned on the social ties he'd forged since arriving
in the early 2000s. His friend, Cait Boyce, called him up. She didn't know if he
wanted to come to Terrebonne, but if he needed a place to live, she was offering
hers.

"For how long, though?" Delgado asked over the phone, as Boyce recalled
the conversation.

"For as long as you need to be here," Boyce told him, by her memory.
Delgado's recollection of the terms was that he could stay for six months.

Boyce came to Central Oregon in 2004, straight from San Francisco. A
surfer, she had lived on 32nd Avenue and Vicente Street, down the street from
the beach. There's no ocean in the high desert. And the mountains? "I like it
on a postcard," she said. But she had married a falconer—rather, the Falcon,
Christopher Boyce, the subject of the spy flick *The Falcon and the Snowman*
who served time for espionage before his release from prison in the early
2000s—and he wanted to be somewhere quiet.[48] She didn't blame him, and
rural Central Oregon seemed suitable. First, they moved to just outside Sisters,
a low-miles-per-hour town near the Three Sisters mountains. There was culture
shock. Boyce was accustomed to the vibrant diversity of Northern California.
She once commented to a friend about Central Oregon, "There's white guys
with teeth and white guys without teeth, and that's the level of diversity here."
By the time of our conversation, she noted, "Things have changed a little bit."
Boyce bought her three-bedroom, two-bath Terrebonne house in 2006. Around
2014, both she and Delgado got to know each other through a group called the
Human Dignity Coalition, with which they were both involved. She was the
community organizer.

After the eviction in 2021, Delgado moved in with her for free. Boyce had
never had roommates. She didn't have any kids. Her new roomie stayed in a

back bedroom and had the hallway bathroom, by her account. Delgado told me he lived out of a suitcase and a few trash bags with his stuff inside them, stored on the floor at the end of his bed. Pants, shirts, undergarments—all were divided among the sacks. His other belongings were bagged in the garage, he said. Delgado was there during what Boyce called "Reign of Frank," so-called for Boyce's beloved royal standard poodle. (Sadly, Frank has since passed away. Lymphoma. "He was just the love of my life," said Boyce.) Thrust together, housemates Delgado and Boyce cooked more often than not. Others came over for dinner. Most importantly, the exiled Bendite had a roof overhead.

Smith Rock State Park, within a short drive of Terrebonne, is among the most popular recreation areas north of Bend. (Photo by Jonathan Bach)

Coming off the trial and tribulations of the past few months, Delgado was now more or less stable. He certainly appreciated it. But this was no perfect setup. To make money, he worked the cash register at a restaurant, Está Bien, in Bend. Terrebonne to Bend is twenty-two miles down Highway 97, generally a half hour by car but, as Delgado experienced, longer with traffic. That's a long slog when you're not used to it, and it stressed him out. He couldn't maintain much of a social life because of the after-work commute. Delgado was joining the many Central Oregonians who rolled into the biggest regional city for work. In 2019, half of Bend's nearly 56,000 local jobs were filled by inbound commuters. The rest of those holding down Bend jobs resided in the city, much like Delgado had.[49]

For people like my parents, Terrebonne is somewhere to love. The entire community lies low on the horizon, a checkpoint on the highway from Redmond to Madras. In the fall, people gather within a short drive of Smith Rock, its crags jutting from the desert, to celebrate Halloween with face-painting, pumpkins, and a petting zoo with pigs and sheep. My family enjoyed one such fall celebration to the fullest. Situated close to Terrebonne, Smith Rock itself is a trademark destination for high-desert climbers and hikers, cars piling into parking spaces outside the state park on a typical afternoon.

Yet this wasn't where Delgado spent years creating his community. Now in Terrebonne, he tried to work through the anger that he felt at being thrust out of Bend. He tried to push down the negativity, but he blamed Bend's housing boom for displacing him. He knew he'd have to save enough money to even think about renting in the city again. Sure, he paid $900 a month in rent for his old two-bedroom apartment. But he figured he would have to pay $1,100 to $1,800 for a comparable one-bedroom these days. On top of it all, he limited his activity because of a recent toe amputation, which didn't let him work many hours. He told me, "I will be working less hours and having to pay almost twice as much in rent if I was to stay in Bend, so the prospect of staying in Bend is quite a challenge, because I don't think that as a working-class person that I'll have enough income to be able to do that." He continued, "I have all my friends and all my relationships—my life is here in Bend, so moving to Terrebonne basically just severed all of that."

CHAPTER 3

Zoom Towns and Amenity Migrants

In June 2020, barely a few months into the COVID-19 pandemic, the Pew Research Center found that one in five American adults had already moved or knew someone who relocated because of the outbreak.[1] As a feeling of apocalypse drifted over the country, millions clambered for somewhere else to shelter in place from the terrifying and often fatal coronavirus. Desk jockeys like yours truly went home to become "remote workers," and many piled into so-called Zoom towns like Bend: out-of-the-way destinations with stunning views. The person who got the phrase pinging around the Internet was Conor Sen, a Bloomberg opinion columnist who, in August 2020, called Zoom towns "the places where corporate executives, Wall Street barons, Hollywood stars and more than a few journalists have fled to escape the perceived dangers of crowded cities filled with people who might be carrying the coronavirus." Sen noticed a trend: "As well-paid knowledge workers who can do their jobs anywhere now flock to these 'Zoom towns,' home prices are surging and housing inventory is dwindling."[2] Indeed, whatever effect on in-migration Zoom towns may have, the focus remained on housing inventory, a problem that predated and would outlast the pandemic.

Sure enough, the catchphrase caught on and similar stories started popping up online. "'Zoom towns' are exploding in the West," reported *Fast Company*, "and many cities aren't ready for the onslaught."[3] NPR's *Planet Money* preferred a Dickensian angle, publishing a piece titled, "Zoom Towns And the New Housing Market for the 2 Americas."[4] Because there's always a tech angle, a *Forbes* contributor pontificated on whether Zoom towns would welcome self-driving cars. The verdict: "The odds are that Zoom Towns are going to welcome self-driving cars with great eagerness and support."[5]

Urbanites had plenty of reasons to uproot themselves and scooch. Rebecca Lewis, a University of Oregon land-use expert, told me in 2021, "Particularly for a place like Bend, there's this access to the outdoors and this recreation playground where people are making lifestyle choices about where they want to live, because they don't have to work in an office in a big city, or they don't have to work in the corporate headquarters in the Midwest." The West offered a bounty of mid-sized cities with high qualities of life, where residents didn't have to deal with crushing traffic. Lewis said, "You still get a larger house for your money than you would in downtown San Francisco or downtown Seattle." Newcomers sought relief during the public health crisis, going where they could relax and enjoy natural amenities. Their fresh-aired surroundings contrasted with concrete jungles.

But when higher earners move into rural communities for their amenities, economic and social distinctions are laid bare. Sociologist Ryanne Pilgeram posited, "Amenity migration reorganizes rural space for consumption, transforming relatively open and unregulated spaces into more controlled spaces where nature has been packaged for consumption and monetized. . . . These spatial transformations create very real barriers across social classes, as the spaces of the New West are organized to suit the leisure and recreation needs of the affluent."[6] You don't need a sociology degree to surmise that class barriers harden when housing is scarce, as the wealthy not only steep themselves in recreation, but also maintain the privilege of comfortable, in-town living.

One big advantage some amenity migrants have over locals: They don't have to settle for the smaller wages typical of the cities to which they moved. To explain, Bend economist Damon Runberg drew on the idea of the second paycheck, a concept describing the noneconomic value a person gets out of living in one place versus another.[7] Runberg told me, "Normally, when we're talking about the second paycheck, it's some sort of equation that you're trying to make up in your own mind." He used himself as a hypothetical: He could either be an economist in Bend or work for Amazon as an economist in Seattle, and he'd have to calculate in the second paycheck. "The math is really easy for people who are not changing jobs but are able to literally pick up their wages—their first paycheck—and move that first paycheck wherever the heck they want."

Newcomers bringing out-of-city paychecks into town didn't have to depend on Bend wages. This gave them more power as they went out to buy homes. Runberg said, "The people who are moving from parts of California or moving from Seattle are actually moving a wage that's above the market rate for that occupation here locally, and they're bringing oftentimes cash-in-hand from the sale of a home that was of a higher-value market, and so they're not just getting second-paycheck benefits. They're also getting tangible financial benefits on top of that, where their dollar goes further. Their actual first paycheck dollar goes further because of lower cost of living" compared to whence they moved.

Without seeing bank statements, it would be difficult to track individual movers' incomes and expenses. But the point about amenity migration stuck out to me. Consider Portlander Patty Brun and her husband, John, both around fifty years old. They got married in 2019, the first marriage for both, and relocated to Bend in the pandemic. They had property in a few different places: she rented out a home she owned in southeast Portland. He had a place in Underwood, Washington. They lived together in north Portland. "He has worked as a contractor for Boeing on-and-off most of his professional life, and I am a middle school teacher," Patty told me. (John later went to work for the Jeff Bezos spaceflight company Blue Origin.)

Patty went on sabbatical for the 2019–20 academic year, working as a substitute teacher in Everett, Washington, while John was on a Boeing contract. But like millions of others, John was told in March 2020 to go remote. There were also a few coronavirus cases in Patty's school district. The newlyweds packed their car and tried to find somewhere with mountain biking and fishing for what they assumed would be a working vacation of two, maybe three weeks. On March 10, they pulled into Bend. Within days, the world shut down.

Patty and John didn't have any trouble finding a vacation rental company that would rent to them for two months. In fact, their five-year plan as a couple had been to try to find somewhere like Bend to live. They'd thought about another city, Hood River in the Columbia River Gorge east of Portland, but landing work there as a teacher would have been difficult for Patty. Bend-LaPine Schools is a larger district with, in all probability, more job opportunities. "We decided to try to move here (to Bend) full-time. We had wanted to move to the Gorge or someplace like it with biking and fishing close by. Bend hadn't seemed possible before then," Patty said, "but living there for that brief time was lovely, and we began to try to make it happen."

Because they weren't at retirement age yet, they needed steady income. "I needed somewhere local, but John, it was looking like he was going to be able to continue to do remote work. So then Bend became a viable place to think about." Patty tried and failed. In July, the two gave up on Bend and left. But their luck turned when Patty got an interview call and, in mid-August, a job at Bend's Pilot Butte Middle School. "I got a job, but we had no house," she said.

Now they had a problem to solve. Their hunt began in earnest around Christmas. As soon as one home went for sale, though, someone snapped it up. In January, word of mouth led them to a home near Pilot Butte. Patience sealed the deal. They waited to move in so the sellers could stay while they decided what to do next. Set on a dead-end street, the new-to-Patty-and-John house held wide windows and luscious plant life, with vine maple out front and cherries for the birds to eat. Poppies and strawberries adorned the back, which had a deck. "We feel really happy our five-year plan got pushed up," Patty told me. We first connected in July 2021. When I checked in with Patty in April 2023, after she'd spent a good few years settling into her new life, she explained, "We are still here. We are happy about our decision. My only struggle is with allergies. We love our house and the outdoor activities we can enjoy so close."

Patty and John wanted to live somewhere like Bend, where they could enjoy outdoor activities, a straightforward example of amenity migrants making their move during the pandemic. On their first pass through the city, they utilized the infrastructure of the vacation rental market that has built up in Bend. Though John could work remotely for Blue Origin, Patty did have to find work in Bend as a middle school teacher, connecting herself to the local public school employment market and its wages. This leavens the Zoom town conversation with nuance: if a household moves into a Zoom town, there's no guarantee all income-earning family members are going to be checking into their employer's Slack via their home-office laptop. They may very well be in a situation similar to Patty and John, where one partner needs to bind themselves to the local employment market. This would be a theme when I spoke with others, dispelling the presumption that Zoom town in-migrants are exclusively fully remote techies. But the point stands that, regardless of occupation, newcomers and existing residents shouldn't have to fight over a short supply of homes.

▲   ▲   ▲

Denver resident Maren Hamilton and her husband, Dustin, came to Bend in 2020 during an abnormally warm October. The two remote workers had driven from Colorado to Oregon to celebrate her brother-in-law's wedding in the Portland area and decided, since they were already making the trip, why not work from Bend? They stayed in a single-bedroom cottage on the edge of the Deschutes River. The cabin's scent recalled Maren's grandparents' Minnesota cabin. A grassy area and a riverbank let her two dogs, Bergen and Juniper, two Australian-shepherd-and-miniature-poodle mixes, go wild. Maren and Dustin took paddleboards onto the water.

Unlike Patty and John, Maren and Dustin had dreamed of moving to Bend specifically for years. Now and then, they'd kick around the idea, but job opportunities and housing prices weren't lining up. However, Maren was getting more serious. In October, she searched LinkedIn for jobs for them both and came across one similar to Dustin's work in Denver: Systems West Engineers, based in the Willamette Valley city of Springfield, had opened a Bend office. Maren flagged it for Dustin, who got in touch with the company. The first fit wasn't right, but next February, another job came up. "That's when we were like, 'Let's make this happen,' and we jumped on it,'" Maren said.

Dustin was Oregon grown. He'd wanted to live in Bend since high school, according to Maren. (He was busy elsewhere in the house while she and I spoke by phone.) He was raised in Eugene and traveled with family to Central Oregon to camp around Lava Lake, not far from Mount Bachelor. "It was always on his radar. But to be honest, it was this dream that was not real," Maren said. They met seven years ago in Seattle and went south into Oregon to camp with his family. "Immediately I was like, 'Wow, you're right. This is such a cool place. I would love to be a part of this community,'" she said. They stayed in Seattle a few years. As they prepared to leave, they considered Bend, Portland, and Denver—but there was no work in Bend. They moved to Denver and fell in love with their neighborhood. If they were going to move again, only a small Colorado mountain town near Denver could draw them away, or, finally, Bend.

Even so, when a Systems West job for Dustin came available, Maren grew stressed. She longed for Central Oregon. But around the same time, she was trying to land a position with The North Face, the outdoors gear maker. The North Face was part of VF Corporation, a global firm that had recently moved its headquarters to the Denver metro.[8] She interviewed for other jobs there before but hadn't gotten them. In February 2021, a hiring manager called to tell her one was opening up and to encourage her to apply. She assumed she would need to stay in Denver if the job worked out. She and Dustin both went through interviews at their prospective companies. Dustin got his offer first—and she got anxious. But then The North Face ended up being amenable to the idea of her working remotely. "I went from this high stress level to, Oh my gosh, it just felt like this couldn't even be real," Maren said. "How could all of these things be perfectly falling into place?" The couple hired movers to take their stuff from Colorado to Oregon, with Dustin's new employer covering some of the cost. They found a home to buy.

How'd that come about? Dustin and Maren had friends in Seattle who wanted to go to Bend, too. That couple found a real estate agent team on YouTube, worked with the agent and got the off-market house. Maren began watching their videos and contacted the Kromm Real Estate Team (we'll hear from John Kromm later). "As soon as we made the move, we hit the ground running with going to look at houses, and obviously saw that there was very fierce competition." They decided, "If we find what we want, we're going to do everything to get that." The right place came up. The real estate agents "knew that this house was going to be listed, and so they were able to get us in before it actually hit the market," Maren said. It was them against another couple, but the competition backed out. They walked through the four-bedroom, two-and-a-half-bathroom home and snapped it up.

"We paid $150,000 over list price for a house that was not even on the market and that had no other offers on it," Maren said. That statement may come as a shock, and Maren clarified that "our house appraised at what we paid." It just happened to be much higher than what the owners were listing it for. After Maren and Dustin did the walk-through, they basically asked, "We want this house. What do we have to pay for you to not list this house tomorrow morning?" Hence, the apparently inflated purchase price.

As we talked on the phone, Maren was just back from a hike to Chush Falls near the Three Sisters. It wasn't a long drive, better than the Colorado traffic to which they were accustomed. They got drenched at Chush from water spraying off the falls, but the dogs had a blast. "It feels like we're starting the forever part of our life. When we bought this house, we were like, 'Well, this is a lot of money, but we'll literally probably live here until we're dead,'" Maren laughed. Moving to Bend for Maren and Dustin was not a snap decision; it was something they worked toward for years. The fact that they paid $150,000 over list on their home exemplified how a market of severely limited commodities favored those with the means to compete and whose incomes were not fully tied to local wages. That was 2021; I reached back out to Maren in 2024 to see how she was doing in her forever home. Paying over the asking price was a big bet, after all. I wondered how she felt about the decision now, with the perspective of time's passage. Was it worth it? Had it been a strain on their finances? Had they needed to make concessions in other areas of their life to make Bend work out, or had it been relatively smooth sailing? "We feel confident it was the right decision for us," Maren reflected. "Although housing prices haven't continued to rise at the same rate they did when we bought, they still have increased. And we were able to lock in a low interest rate that allowed us to afford our dream home and not have to make concessions in other areas of our life."

▲   ▲   ▲

For Billy Duss, a longtime Seattleite, pounding the pavement in a pair of sneakers was meditation. He clocked "mental health miles." Running on the streets of Seattle proved a good way to clear his head in the chaos of the pandemic. He had control over the day, or at least a sense of it. But nature was better, he found. He set out for Cougar and Tiger Mountains east of the Emerald City, running the trails. Without the distracting noise from traffic, he heard trees and waterfalls. Even so, nine months into the pandemic, he found himself either running or staring at the walls of his and his partner Maggie's apartment. Maggie worked night shifts as a nurse. Billy worked for Hines, a global real estate investment company, where he managed an employee commuting program. "The city started losing its charm, in a way," Billy told me. "I'm a big Sounders fan. I had season tickets, but I wasn't going to any of the games. I couldn't go to Mariners games. I couldn't ride the bus. I couldn't do all these things that made living in the city worthwhile. So that started forcing me to reassess what I wanted to do and where I wanted to be. There was a growing importance of access to outdoors and nature." Already the common pull of somewhere less claustrophobic was tugging at him.

There were family considerations. Maggie's parents moved from Wisconsin to Bend to be closer to their daughter. The younger couple wanted to be closer to her folks than six hours by car. Billy had been a Seattleite for more than a decade. What would it meant to leave now? He could always keep staring at the apartment walls.

They left Seattle.

Maggie lined up work at a dialysis clinic. There were expectations for Billy to come into the office on short notice at his Washington job, though, so he left Hines and rolled into Bend unemployed, his "leap of faith," as he recalled. He cast a line on LinkedIn, telling everyone he was moving. He wanted to continue to work in transportation, either locally or as a remote employee. But he conceded he'd be open to a career change. He wrote, "If you're hiring, or know of anyone you could introduce me to, I'm all ears!"[9] One reason he posted online was, he reckoned Bend didn't have a wealth of transportation jobs available, so he networked with the utmost haste.

Someone local messaged Billy, asking for a half hour over coffee. The man he met for coffee was a manager for a transit company called TripShot. "Thirty minutes of coffee turned into a ninety-minute coffee interview and eventually led to this job," Billy said. He got a remote position as a "customer success manager." Billy was in Bend, and other employees worked in the Portland metro, the Bay Area, and elsewhere. Billy didn't need a return-to-office plan like so many other white-collar workers. His home office at his two-bedroom apartment was all he needed. "My return-to-office is walking down the hallway," he said.

When we first spoke in August 2021, Billy was only a few weeks into his TripShot job. He seemed to enjoy the work. His office in the second bedroom was sparsely furnished: desk in the corner, stationary bicycle behind it. Outside was a trail he could take into the forest, where he could run as far as he wanted without diverting onto a road. Fully remote work meshed with his personality. "I'm an introvert," he said, "and the open office environment that we were in before led me to a lot of distractions, and also led me to hiding in the phone rooms a lot to do my work."

While the apartment was suitable for the moment, they still wanted to own. They put in an offer on one house about $10,000 or $15,000 over asking. "We did that cheesy thing where we wrote a letter to the sellers to say why we wanted the house and everything like that, and they went with someone else," Billy said. They persisted. Billy didn't want to wait so long that they'd get priced out. "It looked like things were slowing down in Bend, but having lived in Seattle, having had a house with my ex-wife and seeing how much that had appreciated and how what we could afford one year we couldn't afford a few years later, I didn't want that to happen again," he said. He saw how quickly real estate prices had shot up and understood that if they wanted somewhere of their own, they'd have to jump on it quickly. He said, "It pushed me to be like, 'Okay, as soon as we both have jobs lined up, let's immediately start the search again.'"

I nudged him, "When it comes to jumping on big decisions like this, do you typically take charge, or was this out of character for you?"

"This was a little bit out of character for me," he reflected. "Usually, I am much more methodical and very, very cautious."

To find their dream abode, they looked at maybe six places over two days with their real estate agent. Location was important. They landed on a place in central Bend. Billy could bike to the store or into downtown. The couple only had one car and planned to buy an e-bike. Budget-wise, they wanted to keep the house under $600,000. The four-bedroom home they found had been on the market for more than a month, Billy recalled, and the price gradually notched down. He couldn't recount the amount perfectly but recalled that they offered $575,000, got countered, and settled around $580,000 or $585,000. In the end, their bid still came in under asking.

The search lasted all of three days: boom, boom, boom. This home was of newer construction, with a large kitchen, dining, and living area on the first floor. "My big thing was a gas stove, and Maggie's big thing was having a good tub," Billy said. There was room for a kid's play area for the future. Bedrooms were upstairs. At first it struck them as too much. "It's bigger than what we need and bigger than what we expected," he said. "Our first apartment in Seattle was five hundred square feet." But since they planned on having children, they knew they wouldn't have to worry about upsizing later, especially if Billy was still working remotely and needed an office. There was room to host his family members without everyone piling on top of each other. Maggie and Billy gambled by trading Puget Sound for Central Oregon. So far, the bet was paying off.

▲ ▲ ▲

The anecdotes from Patty, Maren, and Billy reflected how urbanites moved into Bend during the pandemic and purchased homes with a speed that would make many lower-earning locals jealous. They all came from western states, including Oregon, Colorado, and Washington. Private motivations propelled each one, but they cited the natural amenities of Central Oregon or, in Billy's case, how Seattle was losing its appeal. It was easy to wrap my mind around the draw of relative affordability, and my short catalog of interviews represented only a few newcomers. Could outside data say something meaningful about COVID-era relocators influencing the market in a way that was out of the norm for Bend?

When I contacted Damon Runberg in 2021 for the *Business Journal*, he was skeptical of the "Zoom town" narrative. The data didn't necessarily back the idea of historic growth as people left big cities for Bend. Instead, Runberg theorized, fewer people were leaving while a normal number of people were moving in. "The net effect feels like a lot of people," he told me then.[10] By early 2022, Runberg seemed even more wary. He published research in February for his employer, the Oregon Employment Department, illustrating how the growth Deschutes County experienced during the pandemic pretty much aligned with pre-COVID times. He wrote, "Bend became a token 'Zoom Town' as there was a perception that remote work led to a dramatic increase in population growth. . . . This was true for many places across the U.S., but much less true here in

Deschutes County." Drawing on statistics from Portland State University, among the most frequently used population-data sources in Oregon, Runberg reported that Deschutes County's population grew by just over 5 percent between 2019 and 2021. "That is fast growth for most normal places, but it is largely consistent with the pace of growth the county was seeing before the pandemic," he wrote. Still, he allowed that the types of people who moved into the region had probably changed in the last several years, likely shifting toward "more retirees and higher income workers who can afford the higher cost of living."[11]

National media made a lot of the Zoom town narrative, and Oregon reporters like Brenna Visser and I carried the story, too.[12] There was truth to the hypothesis. But the available data forced complexity into the picture. Calling Bend a "Zoom town" was labeling a preexisting trend. Remote work was already happening before COVID: census data showed the Bend-Redmond metro ranking among "the highest concentrations of home-based workers in the United States" at 9 percent in 2016, "behind only Lawton, Oklahoma, and Boulder, Colorado."[13] The groundwork was laid for Bend as Zoom town well before a pandemic set more urbanites bounding onto the high desert. Meantime, ECOnorthwest had pointed out the shortage of homes for low- and middle-income residents back in 2017.[14] That's not to say the COVID-19 rush had no effect. It magnified the post-Great Recession disparities between who could and couldn't afford to live in Bend. The entrenched nature of *that* trend put all the more pressure on government and the private sector to make room for everyone.

CHAPTER 4

The Vacation Rental Investors

Patty and John made good use of the vacation rental market on their first pass through Bend in early 2020, before they finally found a home of their own. Owners of Airbnbs and other vacation homes make good money by renting out their properties on a short-term basis to tourists and house hunters. But because they take up precious housing stock, they're also the subject of local acrimony. Once on the Bend subreddit, a user with the name "Hops_n_Boost" from Vancouver, Washington, said they and their girlfriend loved Bend and wanted to spend more time there. They asked for advice on buying a second home and renting it out as a short-term rental for supplemental income. Responses ranged in tone from educational to contemptuous. A sampling:

> davidw: With plenty of people in Bend unable to afford a *primary* property, this post is not going to get a lot of love. Your best bet is to speak with a realtor, probably.
>
> boosted_b5: GTFO
>
> GotMilkTZW: Just what Bend needs is another STR [short-term rental]. Do us all a solid and just get a hotel room when you come please.
>
> sunslinger: I thought this was satire at first. You should have added in From California also just to get some extra traction.
>
> bendguy123: Buh-bye![1]

The response to the Reddit poster reflected the frustration locals expressed toward vacation rental owners, just as they have in other cities where housing markets are strained. The user with one of the least vitriolic responses was davidw, real name David Welton, a local pro-housing advocate fond of fedoras (even his Reddit avatar wore one) and new-home construction. The exchange gave a taste of the local back-and-forth, but I wanted to learn more about the quantifiable effect these rentals, and the investors who owned them, had on the market. What did investors have to say for themselves, and what did the literature show?

One Central Oregon investor, Suzanne Moore, bought a two-bedroom house outside Bend in fall 2020. It was one of two short-term rentals she owned, each on at least a half-acre. While Moore didn't manage the short-term rentals directly, leaving that work to a local company called Central Oregon Vacation Homes, she told me her guests were the kinds of people who sought space and "that quiet, wooded cabin feel." Bend's reputation as a vacation paradise is well known. Mount Bachelor is great for skiing, the Cascade Lakes Scenic Byway provides the perfect get-out-of-town asphalt ribbon, and South Sister is a regular stop for hikers. Moore dropped about $28,000 on renovations, shelling out for contract labor ($10,880), electrical work ($4,244), interior paint ($2,465), appliances ($1,415), and many other upgrades to the two-bedroom home.[2] Moore had purchased it for $309,000 in October 2020. She and I connected in August 2021, so I asked what she thought the property would cost her as of that date. Without many available properties for comparison, she guessed anywhere from $450,000 to $475,000. "It's unreal. On the one hand, it's great to see that type of appreciation in less than a year. On the other hand, it's concerning, because that means that many people are potentially priced out of the market, who are looking for a two-bed, two-bath house, who maybe can't afford more than ($350,000)," Moore said. "I see both sides of it."

Moore ran the Central Oregon Investor Network (COIN), whose monthly investor meetups invited joiners to "get started making some COIN today."[3] A Portlander before she moved to Central Oregon, she grew up taking weekend hikes with her aunt around Mount Hood. When she was at the University of Oregon, Moore enrolled in rock climbing, and she went up Smith Rock. She saw how much Central Oregon had to offer. Dating a guy from Bend helped, too. In the late nineties and early aughts, the city was still about "big trucks," and "funky old diners," and it had "a much smaller-town vibe," as she described it. "I think it still does have that for people who are coming here from places like Portland and San Francisco. But for people who either moved here five–ten years ago or grew up here, it feels like a totally different place." I remembered those days clearly, like the trucks outside Jake's on Highway 97. Bend became her weekend escape. There was money to be made, too. She recalled still being in Portland and eyeing real estate in Bend when she thought, "Wow, you can actually find some deals there." Yes, she began investing, but she was also a classic second-paycheck case study. "It also fit the lifestyle that I love," she said, "which is more outdoors, more space, more interaction with wildlife, and just being on the mountain or at the lakes within twenty-thirty minutes." The east side of the Cascades beckoned, and she went to La Pine, a half hour south of Bend.

The money in vacation homes was good. "You can make upwards of $100,000 a year if you have a short-term rental in Bend," Moore claimed. Research in 2018 from the University of Oregon put the average revenue in Bend from short-term rentals at just over $17,000 a year, though the study found average yearly revenue could go as high as about $158,000. The study wasn't clear on how many short-term rentals you would need to own to make $158,000, and because the research was from 2018, it certainly didn't account for the pandemic real estate boom.[4] Nevertheless, it was a compelling narrative for investors, particularly at a time when COVID-era eviction bans remained in place for long-term renters. "If you think about it, your risk is minimized with short-term rentals because you don't have to worry about evicting people," Moore said.

Moore was a real estate agent, too, so she saw firsthand how bidding wars intensified in early 2021. In some instances, she put in offers for clients and got rejection after rejection. She recalled representing buyers who bid $150,000 over asking and wondering whether they'd get the place. "Those numbers are just unreal," she said. As a broker, she had represented clients who couldn't spend more than $500,000, and others who could shell out far more than that. "They're beating out a middle-class family who's maybe not making as much money," Moore said. As all this was playing out in the first quarter of 2021, she wondered how people earning less than six figures were supposed to buy homes. She pointed to restaurant and pub workers. "How do they afford to live here?" she said. "If we can't support the people that work for all the things that make this town cool, then we've got a real problem." Before she planted roots in Central Oregon, Moore heard one person describe residing in Bend for those workers "as being broke with a view."

"Now," Moore said, "it's homeless with a view."

I asked her, what's the top criticism of investors in Bend?

"Hmm," Moore answered after a pause. "I guess that they're driving prices up." Now there was about a ten-second pause. "But I don't know that that's all driven by just investors. We talk about all the people moving here from other, bigger places. And sometimes it's Portland. Sometimes it's other states. And I don't know that the criticism is any different for investors as it is for other people who are moving here to live here because they can, now that they don't have to rely on a Bend salary.

"On the other hand, investors, the thing that people have to remember and maybe don't is that investors provide housing stock, in many cases," Moore said. "Yes, there are people that are doing short-term rentals. But there's also people that are investing in long-term rentals here. And that means that we have places for people to live who work in the service industry, who work in other industries, who can't afford to buy. So if we didn't have investors, we wouldn't have any rentals."

▲   ▲   ▲

A YouTube channel can prove excellent marketing. Bend real estate agents John Kromm and his wife, Shannon, posted videos to their Kromm Real Estate Team channel with technicolor title cards. Many of the explainer-style videos feature John Kromm looking into the camera, casually riffing on the latest residential trends in Bend as upbeat music plays in the background. In one video about managing vacation rentals, he told viewers about the short-term rentals he and his wife operate in Bend. "To some locals, that makes us the bad guys," Kromm said, "but whatever."[5]

Locals harbored concerns about vacation rentals taking up housing stock, which explained why Kromm told viewers he felt like people would cast him and his wife as villains. Even though it took a detour into vacation-home chatter, the main point of the real estate agents' channel was to draw new homebuying clients. Among them was Maren Hamilton, the remote worker who moved in from Colorado. Hamilton directed me to the Kromm Real Estate Team channel, and I got a good sense of the flavor of videos they were doing. I got John Kromm on the line in January 2023, and he told me that in the few years since he and his wife started doing YouTube videos, they'd seen far more buyers. "That's the way the channel's designed: People find us from outside the area, because they're wanting to learn about the area," he said. "As they learn about the area, they call me. They say, 'Hey, we're relocating to Bend. We love your videos. We're moving there, and we want to work with you.'" (Many buyers who arrive are frustrated by the lack of options, Kromm said. "There isn't a lot of inventory. But they're desperate to move here, so they're willing to take and buy whatever they can get their hands on.")

The couple didn't just broker deals. The Kromms owned four short-term rentals. John Kromm acknowledged how badly the rentals displease neighbors ("it's the old NIMBY thing"), and how they don't like people partying next door. He said none of *his* neighbors had any problems with his rentals. Two other cul-de-sac homes by one of his places have tenants. "Our house is much cleaner, nicer, upkept, and better taken care of than the other two homes," he said. "It's frustrating to me, because you can get a bad renter into a long-term rent situation, and they can totally trash the house." He painted for me a mental picture of moldy, rotting furniture out front; of cars parked in the yard. "No one's trying to stop that," he said. But short-term rentals have arrivals and departures nightly. One bad guest, he said, will be gone soon enough. Getting rid of or restricting short-term rentals didn't make sense to him.

Kromm nodded to the argument that if some homes are Airbnbs, they're not available for long-term tenants. "I understand a small part of that," Kromm told me, "but they are definitely a really fantastic investment for people. And if they have the means to make that investment, then good on them." Kromm's remarks suggested a disconnect between frustrated residents and investors like himself, who entered the housing market, converted homes into vacation rentals, and generated profits from Central Oregon's natural beauty. But feelings aside over whether Kromm was the "bad guy," as he'd joked in his video, the most important question remained: to what degree did vacation rentals influence the housing market?

▲   ▲   ▲

The Bend City Council was grappling with that very question. In December 2021, residents brought their concerns about the rentals to city leadership.[6] A few months later, during a follow-up March 2022 work session, a licensing program manager named Lorelei Williams gave councillors the rundown. Williams's presentation showed the presence of around eight hundred "whole house STRs" in 2018, 2019, and 2020. Since Bend had approximately forty thousand housing units at the time, short-term rentals made up about 2 percent of the housing stock. That percentage was relatively stable because new development was still coming into Bend. A few slides later, Williams indicated just under 1,100 short-term rentals (presumably including the "whole house" rentals) remained active in Bend as of this presentation. The permits for whole-house short-term rentals were the most popular, but some permits let homeowners rent out bedrooms.

The presentation then displayed data drawn from an anonymous survey of STR property owners, thanks to the interest of a councillor, Anthony Broadman, who had wanted to know what the owners thought. The results, tallied from more than three hundred respondents, gave a general profile of the people running these rentals. They suggested that a quarter of owners lived out-of-state, while 41 percent claimed to live on their short-term rental property ("The owner-occupied room rentals may be a little overrepresented, but again it's an anonymous survey," Williams warned), 32 percent resided in Central Oregon, and 2 percent lived internationally. Most of them only owned a single short-term rental. Unsurprisingly, the survey illustrated that while all seasons were popular for the vacation homes, summer was the hottest time of year. According to the survey results, STR owners said they rented to vacationers, traveling workers, and people moving to the area. Williams described the last group as people who might need somewhere to stay temporarily while they looked for permanent housing. Once the presentation concluded, Councillor Melanie Kebler asked the most pertinent follow-up, "If all of the short-term rentals in Bend suddenly became long-term rentals and started housing people, how much of a dent would that put in our housing deficit?"

Housing Director Lynne McConnell took Kebler's question. "Certainly not enough," McConnell laughed. "That would not singlehandedly solve the housing challenges that we are facing in Bend. And the other thing that I think is important to recognize . . . is that the majority of these licenses are in homes that maybe are in the upper-income ranges. And that's not where we have the most pressing need for housing in this community. The concentrated focus really is that middle-income and lower-income sector. That's where the biggest pinch is being felt."[7]

Months after the council meeting, Kromm got a notice in the mail about an upcoming public hearing. Bend was considering moving ahead with changes to how it regulated vacation homes, including beefing up the buffer between many rentals. Clearly exasperated, Kromm started an August 2022 video with his face in his hands: "Look, not a real big video here, just a quick thing that I think investors and potential investors need to know." He then produced the rectangular city public-hearing notice for his YouTube viewers to see. He talked about how much money the rentals generated. "But at the same time, cities and municipalities don't like them, and they've been cracking down on them," Kromm said. "And that is certainly the case here in Bend." Under the current city codes—not to mention other barriers like homeowners' association rules—it was already tough to find eligible properties, he said. "Trust me. I know. I've been looking." Now, Kromm said, the city was trying to make it that much more difficult. Take, for instance, the city's proposal to widen a buffer between many short-term rental properties from 250 feet to 500 feet.[8] The city in 2015 adopted the 250-foot buffer to mitigate vacation rentals from concentrating heavily within certain popular areas, such as the Old Bend neighborhood downtown.

So far it had done the job, dispersing short-term rentals throughout town.[9] In his video, Kromm reckoned this latest buffer increase, to 500 feet, would mean the pool of eligible properties would be roughly halved.[10] City officials, however, estimated that with new buffers approved, the share of residentially zoned properties in town eligible to turn into short-term rentals would drop from 66 percent of properties to 46 percent.[11]

In October 2022, the Bend City Council voted unanimously to rework the codes, increasing buffer zones and allowing "short-term rental permit holders to rent out their properties as a long-term rental without losing their short-term rental license for up to three years." Under prior city code, your license would lapse if you went more than a year without renting your place out as an STR. The council's move was aimed at encouraging owners to rent to long-term tenants, granting owners room to maneuver, and meeting the council's own biennial goal of cutting "regulatory barriers for housing development, with an emphasis on incentivizing rent and price restricted affordable housing, middle income housing, and housing that serves vulnerable community members." New rules took effect in November.[12]

To understand why Bend councillors adopted the new short-term rental regulations over the consternation of property owners like Kromm, it's helpful to look back to research published a few years prior. In 2018, University of Oregon scholars published a wide-ranging study to understand how short-term rentals were affecting the state's smaller cities, including Bend, especially at a time when so much research had already been done on larger communities. They wanted to know how prevalent the vacation homes were in small cities, how much they constrained housing supply, what local planners thought of them, how much money they brought in for owners, and how they were regulated. They sent a survey to city staffers across the state and found that if short-term rentals exceeded 5 percent of a city's housing stock, that may affect housing supply. The UO team chose that threshold because before Airbnb opened for business in 2008, most regions had seasonal vacancy rates of under 5 percent.[13]

Rebecca Lewis and Robert Parker, two of the UO researchers behind the study, explained why that mattered. To be sure, having any homes sitting without full-time tenants or owner-occupants has an effect on the housing supply. However, Lewis qualified, the share of homes on short-term rental platforms was small. Even though their research was years-old by now, it appeared to track with Bend's pandemic experience. "It could have an impact on long-term housing supply," Lewis said, "but I think not to the extent to which it's perceived in a lot of cities." Added Parker, "Any impact on housing availability is an impact that cities should pay attention to, but my sense is that the concern has outstripped the issue." The possible effects of short-term rentals, even in communities like Bend, have been blown out of proportion, Parker said. A longtime housing researcher, he tried to keep things in perspective: short-term rentals were far down on the list of concerns compared to barriers such as infrastructure, land supply, regulatory constraints, and maintaining a construction industry that can pump out more homes. "STRs end up being a little bit of a blip," Parker said. Still, he allowed that "in the current climate, every unit makes a difference, and the solution is for (governments) to regulate and monitor what's happening with STRs." Bend was attempting to develop a meaningful short-term rental regulatory framework by expanding buffer zones and incentivizing property owners to rent out their buildings as long-term housing stock without compromising their STR permits.[14]

Still, a strong financial incentive powered property owners like Kromm and Moore, who chose to own vacation homes. Lewis and Parker's team found that in seven of ten cities they analyzed, including Bend, owners could generate more revenue from short-term rentals per year than they could by renting to long-term tenants. In Bend, the average annual revenue (they didn't list mean or median income) from short-term rentals stood at $17,184—with average annual revenue maxing out at $157,773 for the data researchers reviewed—while you could make $12,972 a year, on average, renting to a long-term tenant. (A shortcoming of the data: we don't get max-out rates for long-term rentals.) In Lincoln City on the Oregon Coast, short-term rental operators could generate an average of $12,494 in revenue every year, compared to $10,080 from longer renters. The upper end of Lincoln City's short-term rental revenue potential was $117,250. In Seaside, another popular coastal town known for its quirky downtown, short-term rental owners made $17,886 on average, maxing out at $198,425, and those renting to long-term renters averaged $10,704. The UO study said, "Therefore, in these cities, there may be motive for property owners to operate STRs rather than renting properties as long-term rentals."[15] Kromm confirmed as much over the phone: "The numbers are far more lucrative for short-term rentals." Investors like him were sure to stay in Bend. Aided by explainer videos and fellow professionals, would-be mountain-town investors had the means to educate themselves on the investment environment and network with like-minded businesspeople. But as of 2022, short-term rentals only made up around 2 percent of the total housing stock in Bend, for now running counter to the notion that vacation rental investors were the ones to blame for the city's housing woes, like them or not.[16]

Delivering remarks on residential investors in 2022, Marcia Fudge, President Biden's HUD Secretary, said that from Phoenix, Arizona, to Atlanta, Georgia, "Institutional investors are reshaping local housing markets and making it more difficult for first-time homebuyers to purchase a home. While single-family rentals are an important housing option for many households, the scales have tipped too far in favor of investors over owner-occupants. This hurts families seeking to buy affordable homes and renters looking for decent housing within their budgets. With rising rents, it exacerbates our nation's shortage of affordable housing."[17] It stands to reason that investors are certainly influencing housing markets, but are they causing shortages?

Journalist Jerusalem Demsas, writing in the *Atlantic* in January 2023, counseled that readers worried about the crisis should keep their eyes on the ball: instead of scapegoating investors as the main source of unaffordability, they should focus on the real problem of housing undersupply. "Investors are not *driving* the unaffordability; they are *responding* to it," Demsas wrote. "Many different investors are all flocking into the housing market; what is most relevant is the fundamental reason they are all being drawn there." Investors are attracted to single-family homes because shortages boost prices. Demsas criticized how elected officials had let homebuilding become bogged down by legal challenges and opponents who didn't adequately represent the interests of their communities. "If elected officials want to fix the problem, they should eliminate those constraints, such as bans on duplexes, triplexes, and multifamily buildings," Demsas wrote. "And they should curtail the various legal pathways that are used to obstruct new housing."[18] In Bend's case, research had years ago established the need for more middle- and low-income housing,[19] at least some portion of which would need to come about through apartments, townhomes, triplexes.

Bendites held justified frustrations over investors' willingness to benefit from vacation homes as the city endured a shortage of places to live, reflected everywhere from city council meetings to Reddit posts. Yet the evidence suggested vacation-home owners received a disproportionate amount of blame for Bend's housing crisis. Commenting on Oregon in general, state economist Josh Lehner once remarked that he'd been told time and again that investors had bought every home and crowded out prospective local owners. "The point isn't that those people are wrong (they are), but that in a supply-constrained world every little change feels problematic. Some purchases were investors. Some were out-of-state techies or whatever. They aren't the true issue, which is fundamental lack of supply," Lehner noted.[20] This line of argument underscored why, even though vacation rentals constituted a small percentage of the overall housing stock (at least in Bend), it still felt as though they were everywhere, taking up homes that should either go to long-term renters or owner-occupants—that is, people who'd live in them rather than use them as single-detached hotel rooms.

CHAPTER 5

The View from Stevens Road

One of Oregon's most consequential political fights centers on how much state lawmakers and local governments should restrict urban sprawl. Under state law, cities have what are called urban growth boundaries, which curtail growth and don't easily budge. Spurred by the housing crisis, state lawmakers in 2021 passed a bill to bring 261 acres on Bend's southeastern edge inside the city's growth boundary, with the potential for thousands of new homes, including income-restricted affordable units. The area was called the Stevens Road Tract.

Crisscrossing the undeveloped chunk of land was an extensive but informal web of natural trails. Regionally characteristic sagebrush, junipers, and ponderosa pines grew amid creeping understory vegetation. From the tract's higher elevations (they topped out at 3,714 feet), one saw Mount Bachelor, the Three Sisters, and Broken Top. As the "Stevens Road Tract Concept Plan" noted in June 2022, "The natural beauty of the site—key trees, outcrops, views—should be retained so they can be enjoyed by all in the future. . . . Locating multifamily and affordable housing in prime locations with close proximity and access to parks and open space ensures equitable access and opportunity for all to enjoy the natural features that make this area unique."[1]

The story of the Stevens Road Tract touched on decades of battles over how to conserve Oregon land. The state's storied approach to land management is part of what makes it special. The fight over building up or building out is just as important in Bend as it is in Willamette Valley cities, such as Portland. What's more, those thousands of proposed homes on the Stevens Road Tract could take decades to hit the market. It takes a long time for developments to go from planning to construction.

Expanding Bend's urban growth boundary, even by a few hundred acres, was a stressful ordeal. Oregonians have long opposed California sprawl, or anything remotely like it. While a rural-urban cultural divide splits Oregon like a fissure,

The Stevens Road Tract on the east side of Bend will be developed into housing over the coming decades. (Photo by Jonathan Bach)

the state is united through time in its love of beauty, from the cold, oceanfront sands of the coast to the sprawling forests of the Willamette Valley to the lonely high desert of Central Oregon. For decades, timber had formed the wooden core of the economy, while geographical diversity meant Oregonians could travel from west to east and see ocean, trees, farms, mountains, lakes, desert, and snow, all in the bounds of one state. But by the 1960s, the forests and farmlands had fallen under threat amid unconstrained real estate growth.[2] People grew concerned about losing ground to unmitigated urbanization. In one instance, an Oregon State University Agricultural Extension agent named Ted Sidor worried about the Willamette Valley because of its vast agricultural lands. Sidor calculated that every acre with a house on top translated to four acres of lost farmland. In the Portland metro's Washington County, he estimated annual losses of $35 million in farm income due to suburban sprawl.[3] This was near Portland, but distress over urbanization, and the laws that followed, affected all of Oregon, including the deserts at the state's core.

State lawmakers in 1969 considered Senate Bill (SB) 10, an early stab at protecting crucial farmlands and mitigating urbanization by requiring local officials to plan and zone (zoning being a process that mandates what kind of buildings are allowed in a given space) all the land under their purviews by January 1972. The bill had the ardent support and eventual signature of Republican governor Tom McCall, who believed that scattered urban developments were akin to "little cancerous cells of unmentionable ugliness" that could metastasize, decaying Oregon "into a land of aesthetic boredom." Importantly, McCall called attention to how sprawl burdened Oregonians with unnecessarily high infrastructure and service costs. Even after January 1972, few counties had followed through on the zoning and land planning required by SB 10, and those who didn't got extensions from the governor. Cities had a higher compliance rate, but still fewer than half of them got the jobs done by deadline.[4] The state sought a more rigorous law than SB 10 to shield its vital agricultural assets from being swallowed by expansionist subdividers.

McCall's statewide land-use doctrine was a flashpoint in the perennial grapple between state and local control. Local governments had a hard time saying no to developers, because fresh development meant fresh tax revenue, and when shopping malls and homes sprang up more jobs came with them. While zoning was America's favorite way by now to control development, it was frequently a tool for safeguarding property values rather than conserving land.[5] Racial bias permeated zoning. Starting in the early 1900s, officials at various levels of government in the United States began pushing zoning as a means to keep lower-income Black Americans from living in middle-class neighborhoods. Zoning ordinances were designed to keep other forms of construction—commercial, industrial, or apartment buildings, for example—from encroaching on single-detached neighborhoods.[6] This exclusionary zoning spawned neighborhoods heavy on single-family homes. Much has been written about the impact of exclusionary zoning on big cities, though it certainly affected communities such as Bend. As Lynne McConnell, Bend's housing director, told me, "Housing, once you build it, typically lasts for quite a while, and so these patterns are still with us today."

SB 10's lofty goals ran up against local officials, who often had little ability and little political will to follow the act's zoning rules. In late 1972, Central Oregon's Jefferson County, which didn't have a staff planner, asked Governor McCall to declare a ban on new partitions and subdivisions within the county until it had completed its local zoning and planning rules. Jefferson County officials felt like vulnerable prey at risk of being cornered by subdividers as some other counties instituted their SB 10 obligations. Urban studies professor Sy Adler wrote of the high-desert county's dilemma, "The episode supplied an exclamation point to the growing awareness of the limits of SB 10 and strengthened the support to address them during the 1973 legislative session."[7]

McCall, a former reporter who shifted into politics, felt unmitigated residential and industrial development were among the greatest threats to the state. In point of fact, he spent a good amount of his younger years reveling in Central Oregon's open spaces, exploring rimrock crags and wading a summertime Crooked River, which twists and ambles far north of Bend. "Years later, McCall traced his own love for Oregon and its land to his childhood days in the Crooked River country," reported his biographer, Brent Walth. As governor, McCall pursued statewide land-use planning with a vigorously deployed doctrine that growth for the sake of growth alone was irresponsible and foolhardy.[8] In 1973, McCall went before assembled lawmakers to decry "grasping wastrels of the land" who threatened Oregon. "There is a shameless threat in our environment and in the whole quality of our life, and that is the unfettered despoiling of our land," McCall declared. "Sagebrush subdivisions, coastal condomania, and the ravenous rampage of suburbia here in the Willamette Valley all threaten to mock Oregon's status as the environmental model of this nation."[9]

A new hope emerged in the form of Senate Bill 100. The man who wrangled a group to craft SB 100 in the runup to the 1973 lawmaking session was a dairy farmer and Republican, the freshman state senator Hector Macpherson.[10] Steeped in such works as *The Quiet Revolution in Land Use Controls* and the *Model Land Development Code*, the same documents studied by environmental activists, Macpherson believed that the state government, alongside regional agencies, needed to participate more directly to conserve farmland. He considered land more than just a private commodity; it was a resource in which members of the public held a significant interest.[11] The rural Linn County farmer became McCall's man on land-use, huddling with the governor's staff and others to dream up a new, better bill than SB 10.[12]

Under SB 100, a new state agency called the Land Conservation and Development Commission would come up with statewide planning goals. Drafters of the original SB 100 controversially proposed setting up "critical areas of state-wide concern," areas where state officials would hold the power to supersede local land-use decision makers. Macpherson understood this could become the bill's most divisive element. Among the critical areas would be scenic waterways designated by the state, state recreation areas and parks, locally managed parks inside unincorporated areas, every estuary, much of the land on the Oregon Coast Highway's west side, and the Columbia River Gorge. This was a sampling of the critical areas where the state would wield ultimate control if drafters had their way. The state agency would craft regulations for what could be done in critical areas. The first version of SB 100 reflected what environmentalists, planners, and the governor's office had aspired to.[13] It wouldn't make it through the statehouse unaltered.

By the time lawmakers enacted SB 100 in 1973, they dropped several earlier proposals, including the one to designate the critical areas of statewide concern. Lawmakers made sure local governments would hold considerable control to coordinate planning. Adler wrote, "The loss of an authoritative state agency role regulating critical areas and activities and the devolution of coordination authority to the counties meant that local governments would exercise a great deal more discretion than environmentalists thought appropriate, given their vulnerability to capture." Basically, local governments maintained a great deal of control within the nascent land-use system. Even so, the state had staked out the major components of its land-use system, and the newly created state-level land-use commission held ample sway in the years to come.[14]

With these two bills—first SB 10 and then SB 100—Oregon lawmakers began to squeeze out zealous developers and tighten the rope that would rein growth by, respectively, requiring local governments to put in place land-use plans that conformed to state standards, and creating the land-use commission and its associated Department of Land Conservation and Development.[15] Under the new system, local comprehensive plans, once approved by state commissioners, became documents to control how people utilized land in a given part of Oregon.[16] Bend's comprehensive plan was drafted in 1974 and gained the Land Conservation and Development Commission's approval in 1981.[17]

Statewide goals were imperative to the local plans. Once up and running, the commission conducted workshops around Oregon to learn what residents thought its scope should be. The department, based on what people said, made a first pass at goals and guidelines, which were subsequently put out for yet more public comment. It went on like this through second and third drafts, and in December 1974, with a final draft prepared, the state commission finally adopted initial statewide planning goals and guidelines, which became effective in January 1975. The initial fourteen goals related to all corners of Oregon's bounty and its needs, from agricultural and forest lands to housing.[18]

After McCall raged against "the ravenous rampage of suburbia"[19] in his 1973 speech to lawmakers, the most salient land-use goal for those watching the residential market was Goal 10: "To provide for the housing needs of citizens of the state. Buildable lands for residential use shall be inventoried and plans should encourage the availability of adequate numbers of housing units at price ranges and rent levels which are commensurate with the financial capabilities of Oregon households and allow for flexibility of housing location, type and density."[20] To unpack the quote: in all this goal-envisioning around appropriate use and conservation of land, the idea was to look after neighbors' needs to have a roof overhead, a roof they could afford. Be flexible about where to put homes. Be flexible about what kind are built. That was the spirit of Goal 10. As demonstrated in Bend and across the state in the decades to come, Oregon failed to meet Goal 10. Two agencies, the Department of Land Conservation and Development and Oregon Housing and Community Services, said as much when they delivered a critical assessment in a December 2022 report to the Oregon Legislature, noting that, "While the originators of Goal 10 intended for careful planning that would result in balanced, diverse, and affordable outcomes, implementation has fallen far short of that intent." State agency officials continued in their report:

> The historic implementation of Goal 10 has overemphasized "accommodation" of housing need by completing an accounting exercise of the theoretical capacity of land, while doing little to ensure that housing is built or address where it should be located and whether households are realistically able to access it. This has negative consequences for all Oregonians—with dramatic underproduction, rising rates of cost burdening and homelessness, and continued patterns of segregation and involuntary displacement. The state needs to make comprehensive updates to our planning systems to better produce needed housing.[21]

Agencies recommended "accurately identifying what housing is needed by income and holding ourselves accountable to action," "providing strategic, flexible funding for housing the market cannot build on its own," and "measuring and evaluating progress towards improved housing outcomes, especially for those who have been historically underserved."[22] The suggestions came amid a modern-day push for new construction. "Taken together," the report said, "these recommendations can transform our system from one that plans for and invests in too little housing to one that plans for and builds the housing we need, where we need it."[23] Oregon needed a system up to the task of delivering the housing so desperately needed by so many residents.

However much the land system might need future tweaks, McCall saw his vision through in Oregon. The governor's innovation became a centerpiece of environmental work in the state, even if it took almost ten years for all the various counties and cities to meet the planning requirements prescribed by

SB 100. "No other act in McCall's administration left such a profound impact on Oregon, nor was any other as controversial," Walth wrote in his biography. "Land-use soon became a booming business for lawyers as local governments and private interests fought the new law in court." Nevertheless, the new laws did what McCall wanted. "Oregon had a plan for growth," Walth wrote, "no matter how painful its enforcement."[24] The system, which preserved much of the beauty Oregonians relished, remained intact long after McCall's death from cancer in 1983.[25]

▲ ▲ ▲

While striving to keep farm and forestlands safe from urban sprawl to help the economy, the new land-use system had the added benefit of making Oregon, including Bend, one heckuva place to live.[26] On April 7, 1994, Oregon economist Ed Whitelaw, president of ECOnorthwest, went before the US House of Representatives Committee on Natural Resources at a meeting in Salt Lake City, Utah, to lay out a concept most closely associated with him: the second paycheck. The second paycheck was a way to understand how people were compensated for living in the Pacific Northwest, and as such became one way to see why they were drawn here.[27]

Born in Kansas in February 1941, Whitelaw considered smoke-jumping as a job but, acknowledging the danger, ended up in a wildly different profession: teaching at the University of Oregon. The economist started ECOnorthwest in his basement in Eugene in 1974. Whitelaw was by no accounts stodgy. He was the kind of man who would get his daughters into the family Volkswagen and find leafy blockages in the city streets that were causing big puddles to form, stop the van, clear the muck, and grow gleeful when the whirlpools sucked down the water. "He would call it saving the city," said Dana Whitelaw, Ed's middle daughter, who is now executive director of the High Desert Museum south of Bend.[28]

Invited to speak before federal lawmakers in Utah in 1994, Whitelaw promised to make his points quickly. He recounted for them a conversation he had with Eugene businessman Tony Reyneke, who led a video-game maker called Dynamix. Whitelaw asked Reyneke where he recruited programmers. Most came from outside Oregon, and they were often in their twenties. They were paid below the national rates offered by competitors, even. "Why is that?" Whitelaw recalled asking Reyneke. "Well, he says, it is an hour up to the Cascades for skiing, it is an hour over to the coast; some of them like to fish and so on." The programmer recruitment tactic perfectly exemplified Whitelaw's second paycheck at work. He explained, "The economics lesson from that is, each worker and, as it turns out each retiree in the West, gets in effect two paychecks: one denominated in dollars and the other denominated in forested mountains, clean streams, a low probability of getting mugged, scenic vistas, and so on. That is, the second paycheck is quality of life."[29]

Whitelaw's remarks came at a time when Oregon workers made, on average, about $25,000 a year, slightly less than the national average of about $27,000.[30] His federal testimony wasn't the first time Whitelaw had shopped around the double-paycheck idea, and it certainly wouldn't be the last. Whitelaw was known as the man behind the "two paychecks" when journalist Timothy Egan interviewed him for a 1991 *New York Times* story about how the Pacific Northwest's economy was, curiously, doing well while the rest of the country endured a downturn, with jobs being added at almost triple the US rate. A big part of the narrative was how Northwest states had come under pressure to shift their economies away from timber, long the mainstay product, following hard times for the timber industry during the 1980s.[31] Still, against this background of industry diversification, Whitelaw, teaching economics at the University of Oregon, issued a message with traces of McCall-era conservationism[32], warning against California-style overdevelopment and strongly echoing the governor who'd been dead nearly a decade by then. "An attractive environment is money in the bank, and that's what the Northwest has in great abundance now," Whitelaw told Egan. "If you throw it away during a quick binge, as California did, you are in for a long, long hangover. We have not yet spent our inheritance."[33]

Whitelaw died in the small Central Oregon community of Tumalo, north of Bend, in April 2021 at age eighty. He'd only been diagnosed with cancer in January. Damon Runberg, the Oregon Employment Department economist living in Bend, considered the ECOnorthwest founder a hero and a mentor. Whitelaw once told Runberg that even though an unemployed person was a statistic, they were firstly someone probably having a very rough day. Whitelaw's lasting lesson to the younger economist: "Don't lose sight of that suffering in your analysis."[34]

Runberg was among the Northwest economists carrying on Whitelaw's legacy. He adopted the second-paycheck term to describe people's lifestyle choices, including what draws them to this or that community and what they care about. The idea transcended Central Oregon. "I always try to say this to not be too Bend-centric, that if you really value theater, and you love seeing shows or live music or whatever it might be, then New York City has a huge second paycheck to you, because it's really hard for me to see live theater or high-class, world-class theater in Bend," Runberg told me. Bend doesn't check the box for those who need Broadway shows. However, many are attracted to the outdoors scene, so Bend issues hikers and skiers a big second paycheck. But in Oregon, the statewide land-use planning program that kept that second paycheck so hefty remained contentious.

▲   ▲   ▲

In 2022, as Senate Bill 100 neared its fiftieth anniversary, ex-Governor John Kitzhaber delivered a speech at an event for Thrive Hood River, one of Oregon's oldest land-use advocates.[35] Kitzhaber maintained a smidgen of his public profile since resigning in 2015 amid a conflict-of-interest scandal uncovered by the Portland alt-weekly *Willamette Week*.[36] In his Thrive Hood River speech, the former state leader asserted that many young people don't think about forest and farmland preservation when they think about land-use planning; they instead think about increasingly expensive and scarce housing. "They tend to view zoning regulations, which many now equate with land-use planning, as a method by which those who have a lot protect it and gain more at the expense of those who don't have very much, and there's some truth to that," Kitzhaber said in his speech. "To them, and I think to a lot of other people, it doesn't seem fair, and it doesn't seem just."

Kitzhaber said there are longtime and ardent defenders of the system who have resisted even the minor tweaks meant to make statewide land-use planning more effective as times have changed. "For some of those people, our land-use planning program and its current structure has become almost sacred and almost an end in itself, and they don't really want any changes at all to that structure," he said. "My concern is that the potential conflict between these two perspectives—between people who have a fairly rigid view on the structure of the program and people who view the program as a tool for exclusionary housing—could undermine the political support that this program has enjoyed for the last fifty years."[37]

Also in 2022, Rebecca Lewis and other University of Oregon researchers prepared a study for the Department of Land Conservation and Development, the agency created back in the 1970s. The school's report outlined what was hindering Oregon homebuilders as they tried to develop more homes. Per survey results, tight land supply stood out as a high barrier to new homebuilding, as did the common problem of expensive construction costs. Under Oregon's land-use system, cities had the urban growth boundaries (UGBs) encircling them. Even though the boundaries tend to get flak from some corners, the researchers found a small number of open-ended responses—ten of almost 1,300—specifically singled out UGBs when discussing the worst hindrances. "The results do not directly point at Urban Growth Boundaries (UGBs) as the primary culprit in land supply," university researchers found. There was nuance. Even if a large supply of land were considered for houses, that wouldn't automatically translate to more construction and cheaper dirt: "While some of the findings might be suggestive of a lack of overall land supply in UGBs, they point much more clearly towards moving land that is brought into UGBs to a development ready state."[38] In Bend, the undeveloped Stevens Road Tract would need to be brought up to this "development ready state."

Lewis and her fellow researchers didn't consider the growth-boundary process perfect. "The implicit assumption has been that if land is in a UGB and it is not constrained, that it is 'suitable and available' for development and has the appropriate characteristics to accommodate needed housing types," they wrote. But state-mandated analyses churned out by cities didn't take into account whether so-called buildable lands inside their boundaries could handle the homes those cities actually needed.[39]

That's an infrastructure problem. Residents typically want things like sewer lines where they live. But infrastructure is costly to lay down. University researchers drew attention to how the state land-use program had overlooked this important facet of the housing production pipeline. They wrote, "Despite myriad planning requirements, the statewide land-use program leaves land readiness to local governments with little guidance, support, or coordination to prepare land for development." Most cities in Oregon put it on developers to make infrastructural improvements to a site,[40] a status quo that has those developers splitting their attention between infrastructure and homebuilding instead of just zeroing in on the thing they do best: putting up walls, doors, windows, and roofs.[41] Nearly half a century after McCall rallied Oregon behind statewide land-use planning, Lewis said the statewide land-use system accomplished what it was supposed to vis-à-vis preserving farmland and forests and stopping sprawl from spreading into the countryside. It focused growth within urban growth boundaries, even as other places saw their populations diffuse across more space; Oregon's land was being used efficiently. The lack of infrastructure, however, was still a problem. "We don't have a way to pay for infrastructure in the land that's already inside the urban growth boundary," Lewis explained. "We have enough land, but we don't have a way to service it; to put roads and water and sewer within that land." Her UO report noted that, "As a baseline estimate, Oregon will need between 75,000 and 90,000 acres of *serviced* and *suitable* land to accommodate need for new housing, underbuild, and homeless individuals between 2020 and 2040." Much of that land already sat inside UGBs, researchers noted, but the challenge lay in getting it ready for homebuilding. Some evidence from the Portland metro indicates it takes at least five years from the time land is brought into the UGB to when it's developed.[42] There is always tension between whether to build up or out. As Lewis said, "Oregonians hate density and sprawl." She laughed. "I think that's a Kitzhaber quote." It is. "We don't want to expand our urban growth boundary. But we also don't want to densify inside our urban growth boundary, and you can't have it both ways."

▲   ▲   ▲

All this sets the stage for the Stevens Road Tract. The 2021 bill to bring the tract into Bend's urban growth boundary touched on the hallmarks of the land-use system. House Bill 3318 was cosponsored, among others, by Republican senator Tim Knopp and Democratic representative Jason Kropf, both of Bend. The bill stated:

> Whereas the Stevens Road tract is not zoned for farm or forest uses; and . . .
> Whereas the City of Bend in particular is experiencing an acute housing crisis and a need for affordable and workforce housing; and
> Whereas the City of Bend in particular has an acute shortage of large parcels available for subsidized affordable housing; and . . .
> Whereas sections 2 to 9 of this 2021 Act are intended to result in a dense, master-planned development focused primarily on providing affordable and workforce housing in a complete community context; now, therefore,
> Be It Enacted by the People of the State of Oregon . . . Sections 2 to 9 of this 2021 Act are added to and made a part of ORS chapter 197.[43]

Let's do a quick line by line: No forests or farms would be harmed. The fact that the Stevens Roads Tract wasn't zoned for forest or farm uses aided the argument that it won't affect potential agricultural uses. Check. The next line demonstrated the need for homes for people making different incomes. There was bipartisan agreement that Bend faced a substantial housing crisis.

Check. The line after that claimed there was not enough land for properly rent-restricted low-income housing, highlighting a need to bring in more dirt. All right. Sections two through nine dealt with the logistics of pulling the land into Bend's urban growth boundary in order to develop it. Lastly, Oregon Revised Statutes (ORS) are the state's laws. ORS chapter 197 deals with land-use planning.[44] The Stevens Road Tract legislation was going to become part of the vaunted land-use laws.

Lines of opposition and support formed as HB 3318 progressed through the state legislature in June 2021. One of Oregon's most influential conservation advocates, 1000 Friends of Oregon, worried the bill didn't require the typical housing needs analysis that takes place when a city considers expanding its urban growth boundary.[45] Bend and Deschutes County tried to change Bend's urban growth boundary during the Great Recession, but the Land Conservation and Development Commission sent the proposal back for more work. After going back to the drawing board, Bend managed to successfully expand the boundary in 2016 by nearly 2,400 acres. In the 2016 UGB expansion, it used the process prescribed under state land-use laws, including producing a housing needs analysis, the very same document of more than hundred pages I touched on at the start of this book.[46] This was the lengthy process that backers of HB 3318 were trying to shorten, as something of an emergency measure to make more land available quickly for homebuilding. Conservationists saw it as ignoring the rulebook. 1000 Friends of Oregon deputy director Mary Kyle McCurdy testified in June 2021 that HB 3318 "would allow this UGB expansion without application of Oregon's land-use laws. Those laws reflect sound policy. . . . Under HB 3318, none of this sound analysis will take place, which might be even more needed in a place like Bend that is growing quickly and must shepherd and phase investments in roads, sidewalks, pipes, etc."[47] Again, the argument centered on how to get infrastructure lined up.

Taking a harder line, conservationists with Central Oregon LandWatch stood in outright opposition. LandWatch staff attorney Rory Isbell indicted the proposal on several counts, from its alleged circumvention of state land-use law to what he saw as possibly the worst offense: how few of the 261 acres would be set aside for affordable housing.[48] Under the bill, twenty acres were supposed to have income-restricted affordable housing.[49] Isbell noted that "although the bill's preamble cites needs for 'affordable and workforce housing,' 'subsidized affordable housing,' and 'development focused primarily on providing affordable and workforce housing,' the bill proposes to dedicate only 7.6% of the land for affordable housing"; the rest would go to private developers to build "unaffordable housing out of reach to the neediest Bendites." Isbell excoriated the bill: "The declared aspiration of this bill is to provide affordable housing, but instead of meaningfully doing that, the bill squanders the opportunity to make a real dent in Bend's housing affordability crisis that could be made on this public land."[50]

Nevertheless, board members from Central Oregon FUSE, the nonprofit where Colleen Sinsky worked, joined Bend city councillors in supporting the urban growth-boundary expansion. "Central Oregon FUSE is a nonprofit organization working to address our region's growing homelessness crisis by developing supportive, affordable housing for people living with disabilities," board members Bruce Abernethy and Monica Desmond said in written testimony. "Central Oregon's shortage of affordable housing units leaves these community members stranded outside in survival mode, and will increasingly threaten our agency's ability to hire and retain qualified staff." Without reservation, Desmond and Abernethy praised the inclusion of affordable housing.[51] Another group, Kor Community Land Trust, testified in favor, noting that "Bend has grown to be an island in the desert so to speak, for the surrounding rural areas." Amy Warren was Kor's co-founder and land development director, and a Bend resident of twenty-six years. Warren explained to lawmakers, "This growth has come at the expense of housing though, particularly affordable housing for our local workforce." Setting aside twenty acres for affordable housing, Warren said, would "be significant in addressing the goal of providing stable housing for our community."[52] The bill cleared the legislature over conservationists' opposition. Central Oregon LandWatch published an online post about the Stevens Road Tract later in the year, warning, "These one-off waivers erode Oregon's world-renowned land-use system that prevents costly sprawl. . . . But, what's done is done."[53]

▲　▲　▲

These things take time. Even after state lawmakers rushed through an emergency urban growth-boundary expansion during the 2021 session, it would still be years before any roofs sheltered Bendites at the Stevens Road Tract. Possibly a decade or two because these things take time. It's another instance of hurry up and wait.

In September 2023, Bend city councillors approved their own urban growth-boundary amendment to bring the Stevens Road Tract into the fold. When I caught up with Bend senior planner Damian Syrnyk in October 2023, Deschutes

County commissioners were poised to pass an ordinance to make the UGB change official. It marked incremental progress toward developing the approximately 2,500 homes for which the Stevens Road Tract had capacity. Syrnyk told me 1,728 of the homes would go for market prices, while 759 would open as deed-restricted affordable units. But it would be years before anyone stepped foot through any of those doors. Syrnyk described the complicated maneuvering that needed to happen: there were so-called planning amendments that the city council had to adopt and that the Department of Land Conservation and Development needed to approve. The State Land Board needed to authorize placing the land on the market, because the property was technically under state ownership. That might take a year. Then it could eat up another one or two years for various city approvals of a master plan for the site, and its annexation. After *that*, timing would hinge on market conditions, a developer, supply chains, available laborers. Bottom line, Syrnyk estimated the buildout could take between ten and twenty years, "based on what we've observed with larger, master-planned communities like Northwest Crossing." Situated as the name implies on Bend's west flank, Northwest Crossing covers 486 acres, nearly double Stevens Road. It started as a kernel of an idea in the 1990s, and developers worked over the coming few decades to craft a mixed-use neighborhood that managed to see sales during the Great Recession, when buyer demographics changed from mostly young families to retirees and empty nesters from out-of-town with enough cash to still buy as lending tightened. These Recession-era cash buyers viewed paradisiacal Bend as a bargain. Homebuilding in the neighborhood wrapped up in 2018.[54] A *Bend Magazine* article from April 2021 (COVID times) offered the best accounting I could find of how many homes Bendites actually got out of the land. The staff-bylined story reported, "Today, the development is comprised of 1,175 homesites, with home sales over the past six months averaging around $900,000, according to Cascade Sotheby's realtor Lisa Connors, who has worked with buyers and sellers in the neighborhood since 2015."[55] Syrnyk told me of the gargantuan undertakings, "These areas are large, developed in multiple phases, and with each phase involving some land use, building, and private engineering development review. Projects of this size can also phase construction of key infrastructure."

Imagine the scale of time: twenty years to open the doors Central Oregonians need today. It's long enough for a newborn at St. Charles Medical Center to mature into a college sophomore. City officials would still need to find a developer to build the residences. There was no guarantee a developer would stick with the project, depending on the labor market, materials costs, and interest rates, not to mention any number of other crucial factors. All the while, Bend's population will continue to rise, straining the housing market even further. A draft report from the city forecast the population within the urban growth boundary could increase from about 111,000 in 2025 to 156,000 in 2045, a 40 percent jump in twenty years.[56] As for the infrastructure, such as water and sewer, needed to make the tract livable, "Future developer(s) of the property will primarily fund and deliver infrastructure required for development of the Stevens Road Tract," according to a 2022 concept plan.[57] Infrastructure costs money, and putting it on developers to come up with the cash to modernize the site most certainly factors into whether a builder takes on the project. Putting infrastructural costs primarily on the developers also acts as a force to push homebuilders or property owners to pass costs along to eventual homebuyers or renters. We start to comprehend why there's a push and pull between developers and government about the need for infrastructure spending: the money has to come from somewhere.[58]

The Cascade Mountains are clearly visible from the winding trails of the Stevens Road Tract. (Photo by Jonathan Bach)

If it takes, on the low end, ten years to get the first Stevens Road Tract houses open, it's not hard to imagine the housing shortage having intensified substantially by then. More service workers will likely have to commute into Bend. If homebuilding doesn't pick up broadly across the city and housing stock remains unbalanced, the market-rate homes making up most of Stevens Road Tract will likely debut at exorbitant prices, out of reach to teachers and restaurant workers.

Makenna and I set out to see the Stevens Road Tract for ourselves on a clear morning. I wanted to get a sense of where all these houses would be. We both expected a barren and dusty lot, and we couldn't have been more wrong. Pulling right onto Stevens Road in our pale blue Honda CR-V hybrid, we tried to find any indication of the state-owned land but, with no major visual cues, ended up flying right past it. Makenna, in the passenger's seat, pulled up a map from the city's website on her phone. We got our bearings, flipped around, and pulled off to a gated area, then got out of the SUV. A white, cracked Oregon Department of State Lands sign—no way we'd have read this from the road—was leaning against some rocks on the ground and showed this was, in fact, "Stevens Road Tract Deschutes County."

We'd found the contentious urban growth boundary, or its future edge. A beat-up pole gate stopped a couple of parked Subarus and our CR-V from driving into the tract. I situated the car out of the way of the gate, and we trekked into the tract's interior. My green waxed-cotton jacket was too heavy for the sunshine. Trail dust accumulated on my leather boots. What surprised me most as we walked the paths was how many trees there were, trees that would have to be cleared to make way for homes. This was a recreational site in its own right: mountain bike tire tracks were pressed in the dirt, and we passed a few trail walkers. On one offshoot trail, I engaged a woman in conversation about the housing that was to be built here. If she had any strong feelings about it, she didn't reveal them, but she directed me to where to look at the mountains and praised the "subtle colors" of the high desert. Colors were on full display now: blue sky against white peaks, pale brush against green trees. From many places it was easy to find the Cascades, a striking waypoint that made me certain the homes here would eventually sell for high prices. Developers and real estate agents would have a marketing field day with these views. Going into this research outing, I was excited to see where new homes would rise. Leaving, I was still enthusiastic for the homes, but my optimism was tempered by the realization that this is the exact kind of place where, because of the immaculate vista, prices will probably go through the roof. I'm open to being proven wrong. We got back into the Honda and pulled away, rushing along Stevens Road toward town, the snow-capped Cascades in full panorama.

CHAPTER 6

The Push for Middle Housing

Building homes on Bend's outskirts, on terrain in need of sewers and pavement, could take a decade or more—time that regular Bendites didn't have. Could filling the spaces already inside the city with townhomes and triplexes provide a quicker way to boost housing stock? That was the idea behind what's known as missing middle housing. But this middle housing no doubt rubbed up against preferences for beefy, single-detached homes. In real estate agent John Kromm's experience, buyers wanted three-bedroom spreads with offices—which made sense as work-from-home became more acceptable post-COVID (think of Billy Duss in his home office)—triple-car garages, recreational-vehicle parking, and yards. "It makes it really frustrating when everybody's trying to steer us to be more condensed," said Kromm. "That's just not what we hear people want." I believe him when he says that. But I can't help but wonder whether a worker presented with a potentially more attainable townhome in Bend would take the deal, instead of having to commute in from distant Redmond or Terrebonne.

Zoning made density more difficult. Architect Daniel Parolek is credited with coining "missing middle housing," three words that captivated pro-housing advocates after he started pushing the idea in 2010.[1] Parolek traveled the country, Idaho to Illinois to Oregon, to talk middle housing.[2] Speaking in Portland in 2016, he said obstacles such as zoning and reactive neighbors who prefer single-detached homes hindered the construction of duplexes and fourplexes for the past half-century or so. These units, along with triplexes, townhouses, courtyard apartments, cottage courts, and a few other housing types, sat between traditional single-detached homes and mid-rise apartment buildings.[3]

For decades, developers didn't have many options on land zoned for single-detached homes. Zoning that favored single-detached homes in well-off neighborhoods came with a racist history. The Supreme Court in 1917 struck down a zoning ordinance in the case *Buchanan v. Warley*, a case involving a Black resident's attempt to purchase property in Louisville, Kentucky, on a block already occupied by white and African American households. In overturning the rule, the court reasoned racial zoning rules got in the way of a property owner selling to whomever he wanted. Many cities, however, ignored the ruling. Others adhered to *Buchanan* on a surface level, but used so-called exclusionary zoning to keep middle-class neighborhoods reserved for single-detached homes unaffordable to many lower-income, non-white families. Richard Rothstein, in his book *The Color of Law: A Forgotten History of How Our Government Segregated America*, wrote, "Such economic zoning was rare in the United States before World War I, but the *Buchanan* decision provoked urgent interest in zoning as a way to circumvent the ruling."[4] In cordoning large swaths of land solely for single-detached homes, zoning rules constrained many of the denser housing options that Parolek advocated. In 2019, Oregon reformers sought to reverse the ingrained bias toward single-detached homes with upzoning, as proposed in House Bill (HB) 2001. Upzoning relaxes zoning codes to ease the way for denser development, with the goal of increasing housing stock and, the thinking goes, improving affordability.[5]

Instead of waiting for individual cities to upzone of their own volition, drafters of HB 2001 sought to implement the policies around much of Oregon. House Speaker (and future governor) Tina Kotek, a Portland Democrat, was largely responsible for the bill. In her years in the Legislature, Kotek, originally from York, Pennsylvania, would develop a reputation as a shrewd negotiator.[6] With a background in policy roles for the Oregon Food Bank and Children First for Oregon, she entered politics before the Great Recession, winning a state house seat in 2006. In 2013, she became the country's first openly lesbian House Speaker in a state legislature. She pressed issues from raising the minimum wage to sick leave. Housing became her cornerstone.[7]

The transformative HB 2001 started as four pages with only Kotek's name attached. In broad strokes, the initial legislation required "cities with population greater than 10,000 and counties with population greater than 15,000 to allow middle housing in lands zoned for single-family dwellings within urban growth boundary." At the outset, the bill defined middle housing as duplexes, triplexes, quadplexes, and cottage clusters ("groupings of no fewer than four detached housing units per acre with a footprint of less than 900 square feet each and that include a common courtyard"). The early bill included a provision to help protect developers against NIMBYs who dragged housing projects to a state tribunal called the Land Use Board of Appeals in the hopes of getting them axed:

"An applicant whose proposal to develop middle housing under this section is denied is entitled to attorney fees if the applicant is the prevailing party on an appeal to the Land Use Board of Appeals."[8]

▲ ▲ ▲

Tina Kotek was in a hurry. HB 2001 was making its public hearing debut before the House Committee on Human Services and Housing the afternoon of February 11, 2019. Kotek approached the microphone in front of committee members, who sat in a semicircle. She immediately started her pitch, talking about the housing crisis and the need to encourage more construction, her eyes trailing from her colleagues to some papers on the table in front of her, before she caught herself for skipping an important piece of decorum: introducing herself for the record. Kotek looked up, straightened herself, folded her hands. "Excuse me," she said. "Tina Kotek, State Representative, House District 44, Speaker of the House."

Some laughter broke out in the lightly packed committee room. Kotek apologized to the committee chair, saying she was pressed for time. In the span of a few minutes, she harkened back to her childhood in a neighborhood that wasn't missing middle housing. "There were duplexes next to single-family homes next to quads next to multifamily," she told lawmakers. "That type of neighborhood, I think, provides opportunity for all those folks, and we need more of that, in addition to maintaining our current land-use values and maintaining our urban growth boundaries." She discussed the need to change the pace at which Oregon was homebuilding. She tried to assuage fears that neighborhoods would rapidly change. She stressed that her legislation was not a single-family home ban. "I grew up in a single-family home. This isn't about single-family homes. This is about choice. This is about the future," Kotek testified. "This is about allowing for different opportunities in neighborhoods that currently are extremely limited, and it's about preparing for the future and providing more units, all of which we need to do if we're going to be successful in our crisis."[9]

HB 2001's zoning reforms caught the notice of Bendites like pro-housing advocate David Welton. He was a self-described YIMBY, a standard bearer of the "yes in my backyard" movement, a movement that started in Stockholm and gained traction in the United States.[10] In Bend, Welton was one of the most visible YIMBY adherents. He grew up in Eugene but had lived internationally. Welton met his wife in northern Italy, where he worked as a software developer. The Welton family decided to move back to the United States and, initially, considered Boulder, Colorado, another college town like Eugene, about forty miles from Rocky Mountain National Park. Boulder certainly checked the boxes for good schools and tech jobs. It had a vivid outdoors scene. There were job offers, but the sticking point was the price of homes. Fortuitously, Welton got a job offer in similarly sized and situated Bend, where the cost of living at the time seemed cheaper. The family made their Bend move in 2015. At first, finding a rental proved difficult, even though, with Welton being a software developer, the family didn't hurt for money. As he recounted to me later, there was just a lack of inventory. Even so, they managed to find a place and settle in.

In 2016, Welton saw a proposal that stood to build more apartments on Bend's west side. The pitch made sense to him, considering how difficult it was to find somewhere to live. The *Bulletin* reported in August 2016 that the idea, technically a rezoning proposal with the potential to ease the way for more apartments, was rejected five-to-one by local planning commissioners. Central Oregon Community College and a developer were pursuing a zoning change that would have let builders bring far more density to the land. But earlier that month, opponents showed up at a public hearing and testified about "changes to the character of the surrounding neighborhood" and the potential for more traffic.[11] By Welton's telling, the proposal "got killed by this angry mob of NIMBY neighbors."

Spurred to action, Welton in September 2016 launched Bend YIMBY, a website to bring the pro-housing gospel to locals. The crisis, as Welton laid it out in his first post, was a vacancy rate for rentals close to 1 percent.[12] Welton opined to one commenter, "The real problem is that we as a country are not building enough housing in desirable places, with ground zero being the California Bay Area. Bend is affected by this as well, though, and needs more market-rate housing to contain prices so as to not become another San Francisco or Boulder."[13] Welton's blog posts continued to populate the website: here he gave recommended reading for fellow YIMBYs, calling the journalist Conor Dougherty's *Golden Gates* an "accessible introduction to the YIMBY movement and the housing crisis it is trying to tackle."[14]

Welton later summed up the YIMBY philosophy to me: it was about developing an abundance of housing in all sizes and shapes. By the 2019 legislative session, Welton had been running his Bend YIMBY platform for nearly three years, and he was taking the pro-housing message to state lawmakers. Like Kotek, he noted the urgency of the housing crisis. Larger cities weren't the only ones with rent-burdened residents, he testified, characterizing HB 2001 as a "pragmatic, practical, and market-based" solution. Welton told lawmakers, "As a renter who has seen my rent go up year after year, it's urgent that we allow supply to catch up to demand, and this bill is a great way to do that."[15] Other Bendites backed HB 2001. Inge Fryklund, a longtime homeowner who'd lived around the globe and espoused the benefits of mixed-use and mixed-income housing, wrote in, "I would like to see more housing options available in Bend—instead of the monochromatic single-family housing that locks so many families out of housing and deprives all of us of the more vibrant neighborhoods that European cities have."[16] Another local, Katie Wilson, added, "By increasing housing supply in many shapes and sizes, we allow the market to catch up to our current migration patterns and expand opportunity for all by protecting the American dream for families of all incomes, especially young people and seniors."[17] Intentionally or not, Wilson was touching on some of the very demographics—millennials and Baby Boomers—that Bend's 2016 housing needs analysis specified as growing populations in need of denser housing options,[18] the kind perfectly aligned with the spirit of the "missing middle" movement.

Landlord lobbyist Deborah Imse, executive director of the influential Multifamily NW, had nothing good to say about a statewide rent control bill that would pass in the same legislative session, calling it bad policy that didn't work as intended. "However," Imse said, "efforts to increase supply will help address the housing shortage and help make housing more affordable in Oregon. HB 2001 is a start. By eliminating the restrictions on multifamily zoning in communities and cities throughout the state, we can continue to build houses and increase density in existing neighborhoods. This reduces infrastructure costs to local governments."[19] A lack of infrastructure continued to be a dominant problem in the homebuilding conundrum, and building dense middle housing in existing neighborhoods could lessen the need to build new sewers and streets in cities' outer reaches.[20]

In a February 25, 2019, email to Taylor Smiley Wolfe, Kotek's policy director, the planning director from the mid-Willamette Valley city of McMinnville asked for tweaks.[21] The planning director, Heather Richards, indicated the city supported the aim of the proposal but took issue with the population threshold of 10,000 people that would trigger cities being subject to middle-housing rules. "It is not clear to me why 10,000 was chosen as a population threshold for cities, but the type of planning needed to respond to the HB 2001's mandate is complex and resource intensive, and most smaller cities will not have the staff," Richards wrote. "McMinnville is a city of approximately 35,000 residents. We have three planners processing all of our current planning applications and long-range planning initiatives. Many cities smaller than McMinnville have one or two planners on staff. . . . I would suggest starting with cities of 25,000 or more."[22]

"Thank you very much for your letter," Kotek's policy director replied to Richards by email that night. "I appreciate the thoughtful suggestions and have passed them along to the Speaker for consideration."[23] By the time amendments started slotting into HB 2001, the population threshold was raised to 25,000 people, though there were requirements for smaller cities to allow at least duplexes in single-family zoned areas. The attorney fees provisions also wouldn't make it through.[24] In April 2019, Kotek returned to the Human Services and Housing committee to talk through amendments. She mentioned a report from the Sightline Institute think tank as a source on how building multiple housing units on a piece of land instead of one large home lowers construction costs.[25]

What's that? A way to lower construction costs? That was a report worth reading. I didn't immediately find the Sightline study in the official record, so I turned to Michael Andersen, a researcher I knew at the think tank. I told him I was looking back at old legislative testimony. I asked him what incentive a developer would have to build several units on a chunk of land and need to find multiple buyers (in the case of for-sale units) instead of just constructing a single dwelling on the property for a single buyer. I told him, "I'm curious how putting more units on a single piece of land pushes down construction costs, as Kotek said." Oh, and did he have the study handy? I fired off the correspondence just before midnight, and amazingly, Andersen responded within an hour. He linked me to the Sightline report. It was online after all. He gave me the backstory: "I worked with Kotek's staff to write this in response to questions she was hearing from legislators," mostly Democrats. "It's a collection of factoids strung into a series of narratives." Comparing missing middle to single-family homes, the report stated, "Most importantly, (missing middle) divvies up land costs among several households. Since land often accounts for half the value of a detached home, this is a big cost saver." On the other end of the spectrum, comparing missing middle to towering apartments, "Because middle housing uses low-rise, wood-frame construction, it has lower construction costs per square foot than taller apartment buildings. This can make family-size rental homes more viable."[26]

Andersen got to my question about why developers would build more homes on a single parcel. "For a for-sale product, I think the benefit to the developer is that it's much easier to find two families who can afford a $500,000 home than it is to find one family that can afford a $900,000 home," he said. "That said, I don't think that's always enough incentive to do a plex." Andersen directed my attention to the report, which stated, "Just making something legal doesn't guarantee action. For that reason, it is important for local jurisdictions to carefully design their middle-housing codes to encourage this type of housing development." Playing out the logic, the report continued:

> To illustrate the gradual result of legalizing middle housing: Duplexes have been legal on every corner lot in Portland since 1991, but only 3.5 percent of affected lots have redeveloped as duplexes in the 28 years since. Middle-housing legalization would let more housing diversity develop gradually, as structures reach the natural end of their lives and are replaced—not always by large one-unit buildings but sometimes by a few smaller homes instead. In other cases, HB 2001 would decrease the chance of demolition because it would allow large, old buildings to be internally divided into a few homes, bringing new life to classic structures.[27]

His comments underscored how government's role in the housing dilemma often comes down to the balancing act of offering incentives, approving permits, and tweaking laws. You can show developers a plot of land, but you can't make them build.

Still, the idea of choice played into proponents' arguments to sway Republicans to support HB 2001 during the 2019 session—and Kotek knew this. "Where we found traction with our Republican colleagues is, we talked about choice," Kotek recounted later, during a housing event called YIMBYtown at Portland State University. "We talked about having options. That idea that you have more options to live, for affordability purposes, because not everything was going to be either single-family standalone or a giant, multifamily apartment. There were going to be other options within something that really matters to Oregonians, which is our land-use system within our urban growth boundaries. And people were like, 'Yeah. We need more choice.'"[28]

Lawmakers in the house passed HB 2001 in June 2019 by a vote of forty-three to sixteen, with one excused voter. The same month in the state senate, the bill passed seventeen to nine, with two excused and two absent votes. Governor Kate Brown signed the middle-housing bill into law in August.[29] The watershed moment in Oregon housing politics didn't go unnoticed. The *Wall Street Journal* (WSJ) ran a Bend-datelined story a few months later with the headline, "Does Oregon Have the Answer to High Housing Costs?" Centering the article on statewide zoning reforms, *WSJ* reporter Will Parker wrote that Oregon was "a testing ground for a new approach to solving the nationwide shortage of affordable housing." The problem was apparent in Bend, where, Parker wrote, "New-home construction hasn't kept pace, and the vacancy rate for rental apartments has hovered around just 1%. Home prices have increased at more than triple the pace of wage growth over the past decade, data from Zillow and the Oregon Employment Department show." To illustrate, the *WSJ* included a graphic that compared the growth in home sales prices and wages from 2010 to 2018. The graphic looked like a wishbone balanced on one side, home prices sloping steeply up and to the right while wages moved along a flatter incline. The statewide law would pair with moves Bend had been making to loosen its zoning regulations for the past few years. Parker reported, "Early results there suggest the new zoning encouraged more building and could help start to alleviate the housing shortage."[30]

Kotek and her allies secured a housing reform during the 2019 session that stood to add density to Oregon's cities. Legislators reformed decades-old zoning rules to better allow compact homes to fill in the missing middle, hopefully at lower costs to developers and, in turn, residents. For her part, Kotek never forgot the middle housing of her childhood or what benefit it could bring to Oregonians, especially after taking office as governor in 2023. If Tom McCall was the land-use governor, Kotek was trying to be Oregon's housing governor.

In one piece of pro-construction public relations in March 2024, nearly five years after HB 2001 passed, Kotek's office posted a social-media video of her at her desk, sleeves rolled up, talking to viewers about why we needed so many different kinds of homes. Her teaching aids of choice were Lego homes and minifigures (or minifigs). She described the deep housing shortage, and how that shortage advantages wealthy minifig families who can outbid others. Other minifigs were left with nowhere to live. That's why we needed different types of homes in the Lego neighborhood, in addition to single-family. "How about a duplex?" She plopped down a duplex. "How about some multifamily apartments?" She dropped in blocky multicolored apartments. "And maybe some townhomes." Kotek slid a pair of townhomes down the middle of the neighborhood, its rainbow of options now ready. "Then everybody," said the governor as she moved her remaining minifigures into place, "has a place to call home."[31]

▲ ▲ ▲

The Bend City Council approved its House Bill 2001 code changes in 2021. Brenna Visser was on the story for the *Bulletin*. The city was charging toward being among the first cities across the finish line for complying with the new state law. Some of the most important changes included axing parking requirements at middle housing and limiting the number of short-term rentals at such developments to one. Visser explained to readers in a fall dispatch, "All of these changes are intended to help chip away at requirements that can add to the cost of development, as well as serve as barriers to getting the development off the ground in the first place."[32]

With the code changes going into effect that November, the city of Bend advertised the benefits of middle housing. Not every Bendite wanted or needed a big home. As such, the retooled codes would allow middle housing in every corner of its residential areas, no matter the zoning, with only some exceptions where covenants or conditions and restrictions, known as CC&Rs, blocked middle housing. The city made clear its intent to bet on the missing middle: "Middle housing is designed to be more affordable. Affordability is impacted by building requirements such as parking, height, and distance from the road and other structures. The new code reduces many of the requirements previously limiting the development (of) middle housing, helping to prioritize more units that are likely more affordable than large homes." The other argument the city harnessed was that new code changes would lead to "more housing for community members who live and work in Bend," because "the new code limits permitted short-term rentals for developments that have more than one unit. Previously there was no restriction on the number of short-term rentals units by property. Now, the code will allow only one short-term rentals unit per property in residential zones, as long as the property complies with all other requirements for short-term rentals. This change will further the goal of supporting the use of middle housing for people who live and work in the City of Bend."[33] The city was trying to spur the construction of homes for local workers, and it saw middle housing as a key means to accomplish the daunting task.

For many developers, considering whether to undertake a project is a balance of maximizing profits and mitigating costs. "The land value of any lot, it gets passed on through the eventual home cost when that's sold to a buyer," Lynne McConnell, the Bend housing director, told me. "If there's one house on a lot, that entire land value gets passed through. If you can put four homes on that same lot, then that land value is divided into four separate homes and spread out a little bit further, so that the cost overall is reduced. That is not a perfect solution but is one of many tools to try to help increase affordability." McConnell said, "We know that we can't subsidize our way out of the housing crisis. That's not possible. There's not enough subsidy available currently at any level." One prong of HB 2001, then, was to encourage developers to build lower-cost homes without government subsidies. "This type of density is a significant step over time towards reducing costs generally, and towards allowing households of lower income into higher-performing opportunity areas with better schools, better connections to employment, better social connections, which we know are a significant part of folks having an upward trajectory in their professional careers," she said. To better incentivize developers to build densely, city officials were trying to speed along permits for these kinds of buildings. "It's not just the ability to build it, it's the ability to build it quickly, without a whole bunch of discretionary review, and those things really make a difference (for developers)," she said.

The idea was to topple whatever was damming up new development following the long dry spell Bend and other cities had endured, while figuring out how to make middle housing more doable. "Anything we can do to help make that type of housing easier to build is worthy of consideration in Bend, and that's how we approach it," McConnell said. "It's not just saying, 'Yep, you could do this.' It's figuring out all of the other parameters that may act as a barrier to that type of housing development and evaluating whether we can move any of that out of the way."

Per usual, Bend required pipes and other infrastructure to undergird residential construction. It was much like what University of Oregon researchers found when they studied how important laying down infrastructure was to ensuring that vacant land became buildable land.[34] According to McConnell, the denser Bend becomes, the fewer sewer lines and roads need to stretch to reach outlying parts of the city.

Here's one unresolved point of contention I couldn't untangle. McConnell said the more homes a developer builds on one lot, the more money they can save in infrastructural costs. Deborah Flagan, a vice president with local homebuilder Hayden Homes, said the exact opposite when I asked her if middle housing is a little easier for a home builder to pencil out than a single-detached home, since you're splitting the land costs between units. That's when she brought up infrastructure. Flagan told me, "You're able to split that land cost and reduce that land cost, which is one of the biggest items. The challenge is that when you take an existing lot, or an existing home site, you typically only have one set of utilities. So you now are having to go in and figure out how to add a second set of utilities. Where is it going to be positioned on the lot?

And the cost of the infrastructure to do this is heightened drastically." She didn't say how drastically, but in general her comments didn't jibe with McConnell's explanation of middle housing lowering infrastructural costs. Flagan continued, "Although you're getting the cost savings on the land, you're making it up, maybe it's not 100 percent, but there's definitely additional costs on the infrastructure side, which I don't think was really thought through." The distinct takes from Flagan and McConnell on infrastructure and costs and middle housing highlighted how government officials and developers don't always see eye to eye on what it takes to build a home. I wanted to know about the end user, the homeowner. "On the net," I asked Flagan, "does it drive down the cost for your average Bend homebuyer who's looking to just get their foot in the door in the market, do you think?"

"This bill is for infill homes, so this is not for new development," Flagan said, saying this is the kind of attached housing that would go into downtown Bend. "What's ended up happening is, they're either demolishing that smaller home that would have been sold at a lesser price, because it was probably a smaller square footage. And now they're going in and putting two or three homes there on that piece of property. And they're increasing the size of those homes. . . . We're getting more units built, so that's a positive, because maybe you're getting two units or three units on this piece of property, which is great. But the cost of the home itself is more expensive, because it's a different type of product than what was there before."

If in the early days of middle housing some new homes were being priced high, that shouldn't come as a surprise given the deep shortage and voracious market actors. Yet the answer certainly wasn't to abandon new ideas and only build big single-detached homes. Locals already knew where slowing down construction led, and the city didn't have the land supply for single-detached alone. McConnell echoed a common adage in housing circles when she said, "There's no such thing as a silver bullet for housing affordability in the United States." House Bill 2001 represented one way to mitigate land costs and make different kinds of residences available. As always, the infrastructure problem needed a fix. Bend was a proving ground for ideas, and local leaders were willing to see what worked and what didn't as they chased their goals. McConnell said, "Our risk tolerance for new housing policy is higher than a lot of places because of all the factors that we're facing."

▲ ▲ ▲

In a city where size is prized, how do you make compact housing more appealing? Mary Hearn, a property owner who's helped get several compact-housing projects off the ground, is a true believer in density. She runs with David Welton's YIMBYs and praised city officials for recent zoning changes and their work to advance middle housing. Hearn harbored her own frustrations with the city of Bend's long permitting timelines—"Their turnaround time for permits has been lousy, which is time and money"—but she was willing to give some grace. "They've got their own struggles internally, trying to improve those processes and churn out permits faster, so it's just difficult on all sides."

Educated at the University of Colorado Boulder, Hearn moved around the country—Hawaii, Alabama, California—before landing in Bend with her partner. She used to do subdivision development, and she purchased her first Bend investment property near the Newport Avenue Market grocery store near downtown, with plans to construct a duplex. The land already had an old mill house. She wanted to get into infill development. But Hearn scaled back her plans from a duplex, which was becoming too expensive, to an accessory dwelling unit (ADU), defined by the American Planning Association as "a smaller, independent residential dwelling unit located on the same lot as a stand-alone (i.e., detached) single-family home." They are commonly called granny flats.[35] Still, the mill-house property was a good testing ground. "I really wanted to go through that process of building an ADU and just work with the city and figure out what that looked like," she told me. Hearn remodeled the main house, and her tenant ended up buying the whole property, ADU and all. That meant she got her money out of it. She'd also bought two other single-family homes, making her a landlord, a position she didn't want long-term. She sold them in off-market deals to tenants; they'd struggled to find anything else, she told me.

Hearn continued to hustle, finding more old homes that could either be rented out or torn down to redevelop the underlying land. She thought she'd either develop herself or partner with friends she'd made since moving to Bend. She ended up "selling" three parcels. One of the parcels, technically, she didn't purchase herself. She acted, effectively, as an intermediary to get the land to Hiatus Homes, which was putting forty loft-style apartments on the dirt. Located near the Midtown Yacht Club, the Hiatus Penn apartments would each measure about five hundred square feet apiece. "Whether you are a remote worker looking for a stylish and productive work environment or someone who just moved to Bend and is looking for community, Hiatus Penn has it all," the development's website advertised. "With Hiatus Penn, Hiatus Homes is delivering the dream of living in Bend to more people, thoughtfully increasing housing density in the region, and creating energy-efficient, sustainable living on a larger scale."[36] Elsewhere, property that Hearn offloaded was supposed to become a thirty-six-unit, energy-efficient development. Hearn said, "I found this weird niche of finding these properties, and then finding people that wanted to develop them, and whether I did it myself, or sold it to somebody else that was going to build something, I was happy either way that more housing was going to be built."

The growth conversation in town is "contentious," Hearn told me. "It's just a constant battle." What, philosophically, is at the heart of that battle? "Change is really hard," she answered. People who'd grown up or lived in Bend a long time—she termed them "the Originals"—didn't want traffic, exhaust, long commutes. They did, however, want for themselves and their children to be able to afford to live in Bend. And they probably arrived for many of the same reasons "all of us" did, she suggested. It's a unique place with much to offer. Hearn said, "You can't just wall up Bend and say, 'Okay, that's it. No more growth.'"

If anyone knows about anticipating growth, it's Anyeley Hallová, a long-time real estate developer and, in 2023, chair of the Land Conservation and Development Commission, the statewide land-use body created in 1973 under Senate Bill 100. Reporting on Oregon's land-use system in 2022, Jeff Mapes, a reporter for Oregon Public Broadcasting, drew parallels between Hallová and the late Governor Tom McCall. In his time, McCall didn't have to wrestle with climate change or overwhelming housing shortages, yet both he and Hallová "looked to the way we lived—to our physical surroundings—as they responded to the crises of their time. For McCall, it meant protecting Oregon's farmland and other open spaces. For Hallová, it means transforming cities." Mapes described her "as the 21st Century embodiment of the McCall way."[37] In addition to chairing the state commission, she runs her own real estate firm, called Adre, and when we caught up in 2023, she chaired the US Green Building Council, which is known for issuing the sought-after sustainability credentials for developers called LEED certifications. The approach she described for assuaging the housing crisis was straightforward: she saw value in reducing regulatory barriers to development and incentivizing new construction, not getting everyone stuck in the mindset of "zoning will save it all." In other words, local governments should talk with builders about how to build.

Those conversations would be different on the coast, in Portland, and in Bend, all distinct parts of the state. For one developer, density may be the answer; for another, it might be cutting back on the required number of expensive parking spaces. Hallová pointed me to a thirteen-page document from the Department of Land Conservation and Development called "Housing Production Strategy Program - List of Tools, Actions, and Policies."[38] She worked on this document by crowd-sourcing the list from people she knew: market-rate developers, affordable housing developers, policy wonks, and others in the know. There were other contributors to the government document, of course. But Hallová said if she hadn't been involved in producing it, the product would have largely focused on zoning changes. "There are certain things that might be good in a certain time period," she said, "but at another time period, they don't do anything at all based on the market."

What Hallová and the document were really discussing was less about just boosting density and more about boosting homebuilding in general. Production tips were vast and customizable to local governments, who could pair different ingredients to cook up the best solutions for their distinct corner of the state. The list was comprehensive, but also didn't shy away from how certain strategies may heighten the risk for gentrification and displacement. Enacting housing rehabilitation codes to encourage renovating older buildings and turning them into multiplex housing, for example, could come with risks. The document suggested, "Where naturally occurring affordable housing is being lost to rehab; add incentives to maintain affordability to increase anti-displacement impacts." The document discussed code changes and culling regulatory impediments, but it went into financial incentives for developers, too—the kind of thing Hallová had stressed. Among those incentives were reducing or exempting so-called system-development charges to lower builders' development costs. In addition, according to the document, local governments could try to publicly fund infrastructural improvements—such as street intersection improvements—when affordable or workforce housing is built.[39]

While the recommendations for increasing the general supply of housing were notable, a question remained: how do you make people *want* to live in middle housing at a scale large enough to make a difference? Hallová, who went to Harvard, pointed out that townhomes in Boston sell for $6 million, so clearly some wealthy people want to reside in them. To that end, a Beacon Hill rowhouse recently sold for more than $28 million, a local record.[40] Fair enough. There was of course demand. Plenty of communities have massive supplies of brownstones and other attached housing. But this wasn't New England. Her next point struck truer to the Oregon story. "We're at a point in every major U.S. city where single-family homes and other, larger homes are not financially viable for most folks, and so I think one of the drivers will be the affordability," Hallová forecast. Good architectural and interior design has a part to play in making middle housing more attractive to Oregonians, too. People want back-yards, space, to feel they have privacy. "Those are concepts that you can embed design-wise," she said. "You can give some of those qualities of single-family in missing middle housing if it's designed well."

CHAPTER 7

Getting a LIFT

Bend's housing director, Lynne McConnell, had made clear to me that government subsidies alone wouldn't save the city. But could subsidies—where taxpayers cover some of the costs of housing development—offer some relief, especially if state lawmakers had already authorized them for that purpose? Specifically, I turned to gauge the effectiveness of a newish program into which lawmakers had sent hundreds of millions of taxpayer dollars, with the goal of spurring more low-income rental (and to a lesser extent for-sale) construction. The Oregon legislature established the Local Innovation and Fast Track program, commonly referred to as LIFT, in 2015. LIFT was empowered with $40 million in so-called bonding authority, a funding mechanism, in 2016.[1] But it proved nearly impossible for me to judge how well the program had served Bend residents: while some money had gone to Bend for the homeownership side of the program, no Bend project, I would learn, had received any rental housing subsidies from LIFT until years later. What gives? I asked the state agency that ran the program. A spokesperson confirmed that Oregon Housing and Community Services (OHCS) hadn't received any LIFT rental program applications from Bend until 2023.

Was this a failure of local builders to tap into LIFT? Or was it a failure of state officials to promote it adequately and actively to applicants in Central Oregon's most populous city at a time when it was clearly—and had been for years—struggling to house its most vulnerable residents, many of them renters? A mix of both factors? It was difficult for me to say. I'd been covering LIFT since its very first project opened in the Willamette Valley in 2018. So why did it take until 2023 for Bend to submit a proposal, and what was that project? Digging deeper, how was LIFT any more innovative than the next government strategy? Curiously, in deep blue Oregon, the promise of LIFT was inextricable from Reaganomics.

▲ ▲ ▲

President Ronald Reagan told Americans that the Tax Reform Act was more revolution than reform. On the White House's South Lawn one day in October 1986, Reagan declared the act a job generator and tax break for the poor. "Now that we've come this far, we cannot—." An awkward clap from someone nearby cut the president short. Reagan grinned. Rampant applause let loose. He finished his thought, "We will not allow tax reform to be undone with tax rate hikes." After his remarks, he sat down to a small outdoor desk to sign the big act. As part of this "revolution," the president unleashed one of the most consequential and confusing federal homebuilding programs still operating today: the Low-Income Housing Tax Credit (LIHTC).[2] With one hand, his administration instituted a new tax credit for low-income housing, but with the other it slashed funds to assisted and public housing, a move that, as the Urban Institute put it, "contributed to the crisis that left public housing authorities unable to provide decent, safe, and affordable housing."[3] Still, the tax credit lived on as a housing production tool. In 1996, Michael Stegman, a high-ranking housing official in the Clinton administration, called it "the most important resource for creating affordable housing in the United States today."[4] By the early 2020s, as it neared its fourth decade, the program cost the government on average more than $13 billion a year.[5]

Under LIHTC, shorthanded in housing circles as "lie-tech," states now issued federal credits for real estate professionals to acquire, rehabilitate, or build affordable rentals. Here's how it works: Let's say you own property and want to build affordable housing on it. You apply for federal tax credits (they come as 4 or 9 percent credits), which can reduce your income taxes. But here's what typically happens: instead of taking the tax break yourself, you sell the credits to an investor, usually a financial institution, for the money you need to build your building. The equity financing you get becomes a layer of funding needed to make your development go from architectural rendering to reality.[6]

The program has flaws. Supporters say LIHTC helps revitalize low-income neighborhoods and gets people to invest in rentals in those places, but skeptics argue other federal programs, particularly housing vouchers to help tenants pay rent, can assist low-earners without being so expensive.[7] The libertarian Cato Institute in 2017 urged President Donald Trump and Congress to repeal LIHTC, saying it "produces costly low-income housing" and "complicates the tax code." Cato authors underscored how complex LIHTC deals tend to be compared to market-rate transactions, as LIHTC projects typically pull in several state and federal subsidies, each with different rules to follow. The Cato Institute said states should reduce zoning and building regulations if they wanted to spur housing production.[8] The group makes some accurate points, in terms of deal complexity, but dismantling LIHTC with no alternative federal financing source could destabilize what's become a key component of the affordable housing pipeline, however flawed: but for the program, it is unclear what motivation developers or the investors who buy their tax credits would have to build homes for America's poorest, besides another government incentive or sheer good will.

Oregon used the tax credits over the years to build and preserve homes for the poor. But after the 2008 financial crisis, the state's legislature, acknowledging a worsening housing crunch, began investing millions in an ambitious production initiative, testing the theory that if they shoveled enough money toward the problem, they would see big returns. To get the most out of that money, they'd need to figure out a way to make LIHTC do more heavy lifting through what's known as leveraging: using one source of money to pull in even more, like, well, a lever. This new test bed was the Local Innovation and Fast Track program (its acronym, appropriate to the lever analogy: LIFT). What differentiated LIFT was not only how it served as so-called gap financing to help get projects over the line, but that it also helped developers better utilize the 4 percent federal tax credits. The idea for the program started while Governor John Kitzhaber was still in office, as part of his 2015–17 proposed budget, according to a former state housing agency official who was there at the time. It wasn't called LIFT yet; the name came later. Kitzhaber resigned in February 2015 before the program got its legs beneath it. "My sense (from the outside) is that today it bears little resemblance to what we had in mind eight years ago," Kitzhaber told me in February 2023. "It is neither fast nor innovative." He made the point that "the reality is that, from both a practical and political standpoint, the statewide housing crisis cannot be solved by focusing solely on low-income housing. The lack of workforce housing is a growing barrier to job creation in many parts of rural Oregon."[9]

To speak with someone with direct knowledge of how LIFT's early years played out, I headed to downtown Portland to meet with the woman who used to run the state housing-finance agency. Margaret Salazar, an activist turned government administrator, played an integral role in LIFT's rollout. She spent her early career working for the US Department of Housing and Urban Development before leading Oregon Housing and Community Services, the housing-finance agency. In 2022, she left the state to return to the feds, bidden by President Joe Biden.[10] She was the perfect person to question on LIFT. No longer with the state, but still well positioned in the field, she might speak candidly.

In mid-December 2022, I entered the ground floor of the Edith Green-Wendell Wyatt Federal Building in downtown Portland, a good twenty minutes from my apartment, and shuffled through the metal detector just past the entrance. Vanessa Krueger, the HUD spokesperson, was waiting for me past the tower lobby's checkpoint. I had arrived early for my 2:00 p.m. appointment with the boss, HUD Regional Administrator Salazar. The spokesperson and I chitchatted a few minutes, before Krueger escorted me up the elevator to the fourth floor, passing cubicles and hanging a left into Salazar's well-kept and, in federal fashion, unflashy office. I'd return to the HUD field office on unrelated business in 2024, after Salazar left for a nonprofit job, to find her space turned into a conference room. That day, I settled into the blue chair adjacent her and Krueger, who took the blue couch under an appropriately broad map of Oregon. Though Salazar's job was regional, this was still the Beaver State.

Salazar was raised in Hood River, the seat of Hood River County set between the dramatic sweep of the Columbia River and Mount Hood along Interstate 84. Makenna and I regularly zip by Hood River in our Honda on our way through the Columbia River Gorge and into Washington, where she has a regular gig as a cellist with the Yakima Symphony Orchestra. We stopped once to get photos and check out the lovely, hilly Hood River downtown. It's easy to imagine Salazar growing up there, shaped by a rural upbringing but still within proximity to urban life. By highway, her hometown is an hour east of Portland. As a young woman, she left for the East Coast, going to Wesleyan University in Middletown, Connecticut, to earn a bachelor's in anthropology before returning to the West, landing in California's Bay Area, where her parents had grown up. She wanted to work in the nonprofit sector and, like many who choose that line of work, she thought she could make a difference.

Salazar's time as an activist laid the foundation for her work for the government. This was a period of her life when, in the late 1990s, she was tapped to work on a just-cause eviction campaign, walking door-to-door to meet with families who stared down losing everything. "Being a twenty-two-year-old activist, I was like, 'Hell no, we need to protect these families,'" she recalled. The work fired up her passion for housing, and from 2004 to 2006, she studied at the University of California, Berkeley, obtaining her master's degree in public policy.

Margaret Salazar led Oregon's housing finance agency through a turbulent period after the Great Recession as state officials were trying to boost affordable housing supply, with varying levels of success. (Photo by Jonathan Bach)

Salazar didn't plan to work for the feds. She'd wanted to go the nonprofit route. But others recommended she sign up to become a presidential management fellow. Her résumé explained what the role meant in a level of detail better deciphered by a policy wonk, but in broad terms, it entailed "engaging nonprofit developer partners to resolve complex program and financing issues."[11] In real terms, it meant getting her foot in the door at our nation's housing department. She took the chance. If anything, it'd be a good learning opportunity. The young Democrat was off to HUD's San Francisco office. Despite her reservations about working under Republican President George W. Bush, she quickly came to believe that the scale of resources the federal government had at its disposal was so immense that someone could have an impact no matter who they were. (Years later, she still had a program plaque on a shelf in her Portland office.) What she couldn't have predicted in 2006, though, was that within two years, the world of housing turned upside down. In 2008, she became a production chief with HUD, running a team as the financial markets crashed all around them. This was the moment for HUD's Federal Housing Administration to lean against the economic cycle, a role it had taken over and over thanks to its ability to stimulate mortgage lending during hard times. The FHA, established in 1934 under President Franklin D. Roosevelt as a means of low-barrier home lending, was by the early twenty-first century considered a New Deal antique. By 2006, it was all but missing from America's hottest residential markets. In California, FHA-backed loans accounted for only about one in 260 sales. But after housing prices crashed and the financial crisis spread, the FHA's market share skyrocketed to a full quarter of US home sales for a brief moment as it became a lender of choice.[12]

From Salazar's vantage point, up to then officials had largely been working on refinancing existing low-income housing, but dealmakers all of a sudden came to them for hefty market-rate transactions in places like San Francisco and Las Vegas. Complex affordable housing transactions are not for the squeamish, she told me. Subsidies mitigate some financial risk, but the real danger lies in the prospect of never finishing the project. "On the market-rate side," she said, "we had staff that had never underwritten new-construction market-rate deals, and suddenly we were getting deals in a really sketchy, shaky time." It was a crash course in housing finance. Salazar subsequently went to the District of Columbia during the Obama administration to work on affordable housing preservation. In 2014, she and her husband discovered she was pregnant with twins. Living thousands of miles from family wasn't going to cut it. Also, her husband didn't love the District. "He doesn't own a suit, and he couldn't get a decent latte, so he was like, 'I need a microbrew. I need a latte. I need to wear my fleece,'" Salazar ribbed him. He was from the Bay Area, and she was from Oregon. As much as she loved DC, they moved back west again. As it happened, a job as HUD field-office director in Oregon opened. She took it in 2014. While she was glad to come back home to make a difference after logging so many professional miles, this wasn't California. To her, Oregon didn't have the same saturation of developers and financial partners. But she was undeterred, setting her eyes on rural Oregon as the place HUD could make its impact felt. Communities outside the Portland metro were short on homes. HUD officials made themselves known, going around the state to work on veteran homelessness and manufactured housing. But Salazar didn't stay with HUD in Oregon for long.

Kate Brown rose from secretary of state to the governor's office upon Kitzhaber's resignation in 2015. All of Oregon's problems suddenly confronted her. Among its most pronounced was housing. In 2016, Brown wanted someone to take control of the state's housing-finance agency. A different Margaret— Margaret Van Vliet, who left the Portland Housing Bureau in 2011 to run Oregon Housing and Community Services at Kitzhaber's request[13]—had put in her resignation as agency head, effective May 31. As an interim director, Brown tapped a newer agency official named Claire Seguin, who'd joined the year prior in an assistant director job.[14] But Seguin wasn't meant to lead long-term. Brown's office looked for an outsider. The governor's office called Salazar, who had coordinated with Van Vliet on other projects, to gauge her interest. She was in. In September 2016, Brown appointed Salazar the new OHCS director, stressing her broad experience and the urgency of the task ahead. She'd start in November. The state needed to increase housing stock, said Brown, who was effusive as she described her new agency leader to Oregonians. "Margaret has extensive leadership and expertise in housing issues, at the local, statewide, and national levels, and I am pleased she will join me in addressing the unprecedented housing challenges Oregonians face."[15]

Her second day on the job, Salazar received a call from the office of Oregon's secretary of state. Once Brown left that office to become governor, she brought a longtime aide to Oregon senator Jeff Merkley, Jeanne Atkins, out of retirement to serve as secretary of state.[16] Atkins's office was now telling Salazar that an audit of OHCS was about to go live. In addition to accepting business filings and registering people to vote, the secretary of state's office regularly audits agencies as a government transparency measure. Anyone can read the reports. OHCS's number was up. With Van Vliet out, Salazar had to issue a formal response.

Released in December, the audit made public a top-to-bottom scrutinization of the agency. With vacancy rates low and poor Oregonians struggling to find homes they could afford, OHCS officials in turn struggled to communicate with developers, straining relationships with the people who build homes. Oregon lagged other states in getting developers the money they needed to ensure projects penciled out. Rising costs, paired with flattened wages following the 2008 crisis, meant that staying housed was costing residents a greater share of their earnings. Auditors stressed the importance of OHCS shaping up: "The loss of even a single (affordable) rental unit could mean one more Oregon family may not be able to find a home."[17] In addition, by increasing gap funding, auditors suspected Oregon could broaden the impact of the tax credit program administered by the agency, which could preserve more low-income housing.[18] After all, Oregon needed to maintain what it had already built.

There was more. State auditors criticized OHCS for not having a comprehensive statewide housing plan in place, a plan required under state law since 1991. The plan was supposed to include affordable housing inventory, population trends, market conditions, and other important indicators. It was supposed to give a sense of what homes people experiencing homelessness and income-eligible families needed. OHCS leadership countered that a "consolidated plan" represented its effort to follow the law. Auditors parried that, even though the consolidated plan showed how the agency used HUD money, it didn't give any reader the full view of Oregon's housing resources and needs. Therefore, auditors concluded, the report OHCS leadership was talking about didn't qualify as the "comprehensive state plan" defined and required under state law.[19] Auditors recommended the agency draw up the right plan and make sure it included all the necessary information.[20] In her formal response on November 29, one of her first acts as OHCS boss, not even a month into the job, Salazar told auditors that work had actually begun to develop the statewide housing plan in 2015: "It is not lost on anyone at the agency that Oregon faces a housing crisis and that a plan that will use data and research to guide the investment of our scarce housing dollars is top priority."[21]

A new face in a high-visibility posting, Salazar needed to get the housing plan out. Work on it started full force in 2017 as officials traversed Oregon to listen to people across the state. They headed to the watery coast, to the wheat country of Eastern Oregon, to the crowded Portland metro, to booming Central Oregon. In each and every corner, with ears to the pulse of the state, they heard of housing distress.[22] As officials were wrapping up their statewide housing plan in late 2018, Brown seized on one of the report's big data points: Oregon had nearly eight thousand affordable homes under development, a figure the governor claimed was a record, albeit with bated optimism. "We are serving more people that struggle with homelessness than ever before, and we're helping more Oregonians buy their first home—yet much more is needed," Brown warned in a video released online in November 2018. She emphasized that the data-driven, five-year plan would guide Oregon toward fixing its problems.[23]

OHCS made bold promises through its director and the plan. "We have a record number of affordable homes in the pipeline," Salazar reiterated in the same video, posted to YouTube. "We're opening doors all over the state. But our goal is to triple that and over the next five years (by 2023) to have a pipeline of 25,000 affordable rental homes. It's a drop in the bucket when you think of the overall housing supply, but we know that the market will simply not produce homes at a level of affordability that will reach vulnerable Oregonians, low-income Oregonians, and folks that are on a fixed income."[24]

Among the most salient findings of the legally required statewide housing plan was this statistic: Oregon would have needed more than 155,000 additional housing units to keep up with population growth between 2000 and 2015, a timespan that included key Great Recession years, underscoring how construction had failed to match demand for at least a decade and a half. The new treatise spelled out the effects with the deadpan line, "This imbalance is reflected in today's home prices." All the while, the share of Oregon renters considered severely cost burdened (spending more than half their earnings to pay rent and utility bills) was on the rise, hitting 27 percent, up from 19 percent in 2000.[25] The economics were supply and demand. Adding more doors to the rental market should ease the pressure on people's paychecks, the housing plan said: "Rents and housing prices continue to rise relative to incomes, resulting in more of Oregon's households experiencing cost burdening. . . . Without additional production of affordable and market-rate units, this (low-vacancy rate) situation inevitably leads to increasing rates of homelessness, increased housing instability, and cost burdening." Low-income Oregonians—people making 80 percent of the area median income or less—were unsurprisingly experiencing cost burdening with much more frequency than people at moderate incomes and, of course, the wealthy.[26] That's where the Local Innovation and Fast Track program came in, as a way to boost affordable housing supply for cost-burdened, low-income residents. By the 2017–19 budget cycle, state lawmakers had allocated $120 million toward LIFT to spur residential development: $40 million during the 2015–17 biennium, and $80 million in the most recent budget cycle.[27]

When the video about the statewide housing report appeared in late 2018, Oregon's first LIFT affordable housing development had just opened in the mid-Valley city of Salem. Doing a story with photojournalist Kelly Jordan, I went across town to the Cornerstone Apartments for the *Statesman Journal* during the complex's opening week one day in August.[28] This was a model for the kind of low-income apartments Bend could see in the future if more LIFT money flowed there. The 180-unit Cornerstone Apartments complex was blocky and sprawling, its apartments sequenced on multiple levels across multiple buildings, with ample parking. Buildings alternated between a moderate shade of green and a lighter one.[29] To the outside observer, this would come off as another bog-standard, late-2010s complex. But for residents like Susan Qualey and government leaders, it represented so much more: somewhere for hard-pressed Oregonians to live and for officials to show their expensive bet with LIFT was paying off. Children in tow, Qualey toured the apartment for the first time with Kelly and I there. To refresh my memory, I recently looked back on Kelly's photos from the day and saw the mom and kids in a state of joy. Their smiles lit up the walls. A tub of toiletries held a note that said, "Thank you for choosing Cornerstone Apartments as your new home! Welcome home." One of Qualey's kids, eight years old, quickly claimed one of the rooms for herself and her younger sister. Qualey did not know where her family would stay without the apartment, she reflected later. "I feel it's truly where God wanted me and my children, because everything just worked."[30]

Brown and Salazar were on-hand at an official opening celebration. The governor's speech struck a hopeful tone. Brown keyed in on the importance of having rents that let working families not have to worry about deciding between which of their bills to pay and what to go without in a given month. Salem's white-bearded mayor, Chuck Bennett, nodded along next to her. "When we can do this for one family," Brown said, "children do better in school, and parents do better at work.... When we can do this for 180 families, a community grows stronger." Salazar, in thick sunglasses behind the outdoor lectern, declared a win. "The Cornerstone grand opening is a momentous occasion for us at the agency and for so many of our partners, because it is the first community funded with LIFT to be completed and have residents moving into their homes. Today, we're not just celebrating the success of this incredible development here at Cornerstone," she said, marking "incredible" with a gesture, "we're celebrating the success of the LIFT program."[31]

▲   ▲   ▲

As lawmakers pumped helium into the LIFT balloon, OHCS needed the federal Low-Income Housing Tax Credit program and its underappreciated 4 percent credits. Unlike the 9 percent credits, the 4 percents weren't competitive and, per Salazar, didn't appear to be used much for new construction outside of Portland. The caveat with 4 percents was that at least half a residential develop-ment had to be funded with what are called private activity bonds, and apart-ments typically stayed affordable for thirty years. Apartments with competitive 9 percent credits remained affordable for sixty years.[32] (Private activity bonds are a kind of bond "used to attract private investment for projects that have some public benefit."[33] One state housing official, Natasha Detweiler-Daby, put it succinctly: "You don't get a 4 percent unless you have private activity bonds.") Salazar, with her reserve of California deal-making experience, envisioned using LIFT to leverage 4 percents and private activity bonds for new construction in rural Oregon. State auditors had pointed out, and Salazar recognized, that Oregon was leaving federal funds on the table. "We saw it as an enticement to get Low Income Housing Tax Credit investment into Oregon that would oth-erwise, frankly, go to another state, and I think people need to understand that: that when they try to push the LIHTC program to do something different, that capital can go elsewhere," Salazar told me at HUD years later. She was clearly proud of unlocking the noncompetitive credits for new construction, pointing out an award in her downtown office from the National Council of State Housing Agencies (NCHSA). She said, "It changed the game."

The housing agency's NCHSA award entry from 2019 told a similar story, down to describing LIFT as a "game changer." As of 2019, LIFT had produced more than two thousand fresh affordable homes throughout Oregon, nearly seven hundred of them within rural parts of the state. The agency likewise stressed its ingenuity in leveraging 4 percent credits and bonds to get more rural housing up. As in other states, Oregon officials had failed to see the potential of the 4 percent credits, usually closing only a few transactions with them every year and only getting new construction in the Portland metro. "With LIFT, we saw an opportunity to leverage the state funds with the 4% program to unlock the new construction potential of small towns and rural communities," the agency boasted in its award entry. Officials also saw a way to help communities of color. "This funding strategy has unleashed the 4% LIHTC program as a powerful new construction tool for rural Oregon transactions that would never have penciled out without LIFT." OHCS closed four 4 percent deals in 2016, twelve during 2017, and another dozen in 2018. The agency expected to close twenty transactions in 2019.[34] State housing officials were pulling that federal money off the table.

State lawmakers continued giving more cash to LIFT. By 2019, Brown had proposed sending another $130 million to LIFT, more than doubling its up-to-then investment of $120 million.[35] But instead of $130 million, lawmakers stepped up with $200 million in the 2019–21 cycle,[36] testing the idea that funneling large amounts of money toward the housing shortage would produce the results they wanted: more homes. The pressing question was how much LIFT could accelerate OHCS toward its lofty statewide goal of tripling the affordable housing pipeline to 25,000 housing units. In a 2019 update, agency officials wrote that, with just over 10,000 units, they were on track to reach their five-year goal.[37]

One thing jeopardized LIFT and LIHTC's happy marriage. LIFT and LIHTC were supposed to make magic to turbocharge residential construction. But for LIFT to connect with the 4 percent tax credits, it needed two things: investment from the Oregon legislature (check) and federal private activity bonds (check). Bonds were running dry, which threatened to untether LIFT and LIHTC for many pending projects. OHCS put developers on notice in October 2021, explaining in a public memo how over the past few years, affordable housing production gained momentum thanks to the boost in state resources and other regional funding. But the success meant they had reached capacity and had to pause 4 percent LIHTC and bond applications. "Pausing applications will allow OHCS to manage our existing pipeline," Director of Affordable Rental Housing Julie Cody pronounced.[38]

As the state invested more money to build homes, more developers wanted to get in on the 4 percent tax credit. Where there had been little interest previously, a blizzard overloaded the system. "It felt really critical at that moment in time to say, we need to let everybody know that we can't continue to collect applications, because then we are going to be too far over our skis. We're going to be too overcommitted to provide certainty," explained Natasha Detweiler-Daby, the OHCS affordable rental housing director who succeeded Cody. OHCS placed several Oregon developments "under review" because private activity bonds ran out. The agency planned, going forward, to make builders compete for the previously noncompetitive 4 percents, a switch that reflected how tightly constrained bonds were.[39] Officials had long operated their program from savings, so they didn't have to utilize their current-year bond allocations before, said Detweiler-Daby, who had clocked more than a decade and a half at the agency. Officials were caught by surprise. "It sneaks up on you," she told me.

The gravity of the moment was apparent. Some developers who had Portland-area projects (voters in the region passed a measure to pay for housing in 2018[40]) or worked elsewhere counted on the 4 percents without having to question whether they'd be able to get them, since they'd been noncompetitive. "It was really navigating a lot of difficult, hard conversations," Detweiler-Daby said. While leveraging the 4 percent credits was never a requirement to use LIFT, most developments did. Now, she said, officials had created a lane for "LIFT-only" developments without the tax credit. "We'll see smaller projects through that," Detweiler-Daby predicted. Just like that, the LIFT-LIHTC romance went *kah-thud*. Limited federal resources hampered the funding strategy lauded for unleashing the 4 percent credit as a construction tool. To be sure, many projects would still get funding with 4 percent credits and LIFT. But the episode showed the tactic only went so far as newfound demand outstripped Oregon's bond allocations.[41]

Detweiler-Daby put forward one remedy: change the formula by which the 4 percents are generated. As it stood, half a project needed bond funding to trigger 4 percent credits. Even reducing the requirement for private activity bond funding to a quarter to generate the 4 percent would do, she reasoned. Her boss, OHCS executive director Andrea Bell, similarly advocated a compromise 30 percent bond-financing threshold in a January 2024 op-ed.[42] By my reading, that would mean 4 percent credits would occur with more frequency and bonds would go further. Both Detweiler-Daby and HUD's Salazar pointed to the Portland-area housing bond from 2018 as another curve ball: projects funded through that assumed they would get the 4 percent credits, which strained the separate, federally allocated private activity bonds. "They made production goals and targets that were explicitly connected to using that resource, and together, that was too much," Detweiler-Daby said. In downtown Portland, Salazar confirmed, "When we put out the statewide housing plan, we did not know that the Metro bond measure would pass, which put that real crunch on private activity bonds." She knew OHCS wanted to see the 50 percent test for projects change so private activity bonds could go further. But people were trying to figure out whether the current surge would subside or if it represented a new normal for housing production in Oregon, Salazar told me.

Housing officials had certainly demonstrated they could use the 4 percent Low-Income Housing Tax Credits to great effect. But in the excitement that followed, and with the Metro bond projects counting on them, there was too much strain on the system. "Somehow, folks forgot to check into the availability of PABs before they finalized their plans," Salazar said.

Not long before I visited the HUD office, I had dashed off a short article for the *Portland Business Journal* about new state estimates that showed Oregon needed roughly 554,000 housing units for the next twenty years, an estimate that factored in expected population growth, a lack of homes for the homeless, and underproduction; that is, the homes we already needed now but hadn't been built.[43] The overwhelming numbers were fresh on my mind when I put the question to Salazar: can we meet the goal?

Salazar inhaled, let out a big sigh, and didn't directly answer in the first go, instead talking about how it's "a striking number" and how people can't afford to bicker over which is the best tool ("we need them all") and how commercial space can be converted to housing. She talked about utilizing land trusts, manufactured housing, tiny homes, home-sharing, housing vouchers. It was a good response, but not quite responsive to the question I asked. I restated, "Do you think we can meet that goal?" A few seconds passed.

"I don't think I can give you a yes or no. I think that the way to meet that goal is . . ." Salazar restarted, "One of the things Oregon needs to do is to start operating with a large-state mentality and be open to creating a welcoming environment for developers of all sizes." She acknowledged the need to be careful about displacement, gentrification, and racial equity, but market-rate developers need to be ushered in, she said. "One thing that I think has been good about LIFT, just to return back to that conversation, is that I think we brought in private developers that had not been active in the affordable housing space. And believe me, I was not popular for doing that." Yet, she said, people need to understand that with so much need and so much money flowing, we must bring aboard national investors, developers, and banks; elected officials need to call in corporations and philanthropists alike. "Just like Bend, we're having growing pains," Salazar said. "Who do we want to be? How do we want to get there?" Her mind went to her own children. "Their uncles are both homeless. I have one brother-in-law living in his car, and another brother-in-law who's living in a skilled nursing facility after suffering a breakdown and living in a homeless shelter," she confided. "That's the world they're living in. My mom's life was saved by moving into affordable housing at the end of her life. There are too many people at risk. We cannot keep playing the same games because we're afraid of evolving."

LIFT was effective in bringing thousands of new low-rent homes to a variety of communities across Oregon. But the complexity of how housing officials used it revealed deeper problems with how difficult our society makes affordable housing financing in general. But what did Oregonians get for their investment in the program? By the end of 2022, LIFT had paid for more than six thousand new rental apartments across the state, utilizing over $483 million in funding, an OHCS spokesperson told me in March 2023. That penciled out to an average subsidy per door of about $80,000. For owners, there were 468 LIFT Homeownership homes thanks to over $39 million in state funding, or an average subsidy of about $83,000 per unit. As for Bend, "OHCS has awarded funds to eight LIFT Homeownership projects in Bend since 2017. This has amounted to $6,197,297 in funds for the development of 74 affordable homes for purchase," the spokesperson, Delia Hernández, said. "No LIFT Rental applications have been received from Bend since 2016."[44] Indeed, it took until 2023 for LIFT rental money to trickle into Bend.

▲ ▲ ▲

Jackie Keogh and David Brandt were two business partners working to bring the transformative Rooted at Simpson and College View Apartments developments to fruition. Keogh is executive director of Rooted Homes, a land-trust nonprofit making a statement with inexpensive housing options in and around Bend. Brandt is, similarly, executive director of Housing Works, the housing authority for much of Central Oregon. Housing authorities administer affordable housing programs for a city or region. Their organizations joined forces to buy property from Deschutes County for an impressive ninety-nine total homes: fifty-nine rentals from Housing Works, combined with another forty for-sale cottages from Rooted Homes.

Rooted at Simpson and the College View Apartments offered a case study in how Bend builders could harness LIFT. In fact, Brandt's Housing Works was the first local organization to obtain LIFT rental money. Mind you, Brandt has voiced his own frustrations with the way the state program was set up, telling me in a June 2023 note, "Bend's very high development costs still make Bend's projects less competitive than other projects competing for those funds."

Despite these headwinds, on July 4, Brandt let me know that Housing Works was seeking $8.3 million from LIFT for College View. It needed the 4 percent LIHTC and the private activity bonds—a prime example of Margaret Salazar's LIFT-LIHTC matchmaking—as well as $5 million from what's called the Oregon Affordable Housing Tax Credit. Total expected project cost was $23.5 million.

What made College View so necessary was its price point for residents. The *Bulletin* editorial board pointed out on July 6 that College View residents would be those earning, at most, 60 percent of the area median income, equaling just over $57,000 for a four-person household. Crucially, as the editorial board argued, "These are the kinds of projects that allow people who are working in jobs that are necessary and important for Bend's economy to live and work in Bend."[45] The need for worker housing was clear, not just in Bend but throughout Oregon. OHCS got nearly two dozen applications for funding that totaled more than $222 million, far more than what was in the coffers. On July 7, ten projects across the state (five urban, five rural) obtained some $104 million in LIFT funding, including College View, which went home with its planned $8.3 million.[46] Housing Works planned to start construction in 2024. On the site's other end, Keogh's nonprofit was busy at work on Rooted at Simpson for prospective homeowners. How does a land trust save the end user—the homebuyer—money? Keogh explained, "With market rate homes, the most expensive part when you purchase a home is the land. If you remove the land cost, and you separate it from the home, the home becomes much more affordable. Never mind if you use House Bill 2001. . . where you're putting more homes on the same size land that you historically would have only put one home on. So the land trust essentially is a policy tool that separates the land from the home to not just ensure affordability for this generation, but in perpetuity, because what we have is an underproduction problem in this country of affordable housing.

And that underproduction problem is also emphasized by the fact that, if homes are not currently affordable, they are selling on the market, and we are losing affordable homes at a faster rate than we can build them." She said, "The land trust model looks at that problem, and uses essentially a social construct to say we want to have permanent affordability so that—let's use the city of Bend—city of Bend has an asset of X units of affordable homes that will always be affordable in their city and therefore always house lower-income households. . . . The way we do that is a deed restriction. So Rooted Homes stewards the land, and the homeowner owns the home outright."

How does Rooted Homes stay in operation, though? "At the end of the day," I suggested, "you need to take a salary, your employees need to take a salary."

"The best nonprofits have business models like a for-profit, but have a social construct within that," she said. "So yes, Rooted Homes charges a developer fee, on average 7 percent of the total development costs, for each project we complete. The goal is not just to use that to pay for staffing and operations, but if you do it right, is to be doing enough of those projects with a very expert but small team, so that you're able to use a portion of that developer fee to seed your next project."

As for its recent project, Rooted at Simpson, there are advantages to having rentals and for-sales homes within neighborly proximity. "Moving forward, our model will put rental and ownership on the same site," she said. The idea was that people who are living in the Housing Works apartments using Section 8 vouchers should find themselves buying a Rooted Homes cottage, attaining the dream of homeownership. "We want to motivate them to move out " of the rentals, Keogh said, "but they can't because especially in Central Oregon, they're displaced, and they're going to be like an hour-plus away from even any resources."

I hastily interjected, "Unless you want to spend like $700,000 on a house, which—."

"—Which you can't if you're living in a Section 8" rental, Keogh fired back, good naturedly.

Redeveloping the seven-acre site that Housing Works and Rooted Homes acquired from the county, a site that used to be a pumice mine, brought challenges. Somehow, I ponder, it always comes back to big bad infrastructure. Keogh said, "It costs us more to get the infrastructure—buy the land, get the sewer and water, and the site developed—than it does to actually build the homes in Central Oregon." Her team was spending more on infrastructure per square foot than on vertical construction. She said, "That's a huge issue, and the bigger issue is that no one funds that in Central Oregon, so I'm using low-interest loans to support that work or private money." Rooted Homes did have its system-development charges waived (those are the charges assessed by a city to pay for infrastructure), but that presented another problem: Keogh's organization is still on the hook to pay for any big improvements she undertakes to get the site primed for people, such as widening streets or putting in more water and sewer lines. Again, the money had to come from somewhere. "We need to start having a better conversation of, if we want affordable housing, we need to invest in infrastructure," she said. She doesn't care if the money comes from the city or state. "It's a huge gap." Why should Bendites care about the woes of a developer and something as seemingly benign as who pays for *infrastructure*? Because, as Keogh disclosed during our meeting, "This project almost fell apart because of the infrastructure challenges." No infrastructure, no inexpensive homes, even from do-gooders like Keogh willing to put their professional life into finding every which way to make low-cost options for Central Oregon's working class a reality.

In 2022, consultancy ECOnorthwest issued a report for the Bend Chamber of Commerce examining how the affordable housing shortage had stifled local economic growth. ECOnorthwest laid out the broad sweep of the issue: employers struggled to find workers in part because of a labor market that allowed workers to be choosy as many businesses reopened following mass COVID closures. "That's a cyclical issue problem that will ease with time," ECOnorthwest reported. "But the region simultaneously faces a structural problem that adds to the hiring challenge: the high and rising cost of housing."[47] According to employers, who might have underreported because workers typically don't tell their bosses everything about their personal lives, some four in ten employees had a hard time paying for everyday needs including housing, food, transportation, and childcare. Clearly disturbed by the mismatch between housing need and supply, one employer was quoted as commenting, "There needs to be a big push for more affordable housing in all new developments. It's sad when we see people who have $200k in their account and yet still can't afford to purchase a home with a large down payment."[48] Good luck if you were a middle-class worker trying to buy your first home. Citing data from the Central Oregon Association of Realtors, ECOnorthwest wrote, "Median prices of homes sold in Bend increased 75 percent between 2019 and the second quarter of 2022, from $441,000 to $770,000, making it difficult to purchase a home when earning in the middle-income group," defined as those earning 80 to 150 percent of area median income.[49]

Companies tried to boost pay and offer childcare stipends, but homebuilding was never far from the conversation: "Some businesses have considered providing workforce housing through supporting residential development on organization-owned property or acquiring rental properties for their employees."[50] This wasn't pure sunny altruism. There was a business case for getting serious about the dilemma. Nine in ten businesspeople agreed high housing costs adversely impacted not only their workforces but their "growth as a company."[51] Since commerce flows on the sweat of workers, business leaders needed to keep them housed. Katy Brooks, CEO of the Bend Chamber of Commerce, told me that for employers, putting money into worker housing represents an "attraction and retention strategy. It is not the company store." The calculus for employers, per Brooks, is more like, "Holy crap, I am competing for this labor pool that's incredibly small. I need these folks to be here. I'm going to look at this as an investment rather than a moneymaker for me."

For her part, Keogh painted a remarkably optimistic picture of the future: what makes Central Oregon and its local governments—namely Deschutes County and Bend—unique is that they've recognized the importance of affordable housing. Elsewhere, she's had to convince people of the need, which takes away precious time. Keogh previously worked in Portland and in Massachusetts. "Here, we've been able to grow because we were supported by these agencies who know that this is important," she said. "Instead of me coming in on my soapbox explaining why they need this, we can just go to the project."

Rooted Homes had more projects in the hopper besides Rooted at Simpson. One, in fact, was a workforce housing development. It was called Rooted at Poplar. It obtained $600,000 in LIFT Homeownership funding and consisted of seven houses on Southwest Poplar Street, four of them belonging to local workers. Each was 1,300 square feet in size and had three bedrooms and two bathrooms.[52] Just as government officials like Margaret Salazar were sparking innovative ideas for how to get more money into homebuilding, so too were local business leaders in Bend. In that spirit, the Bend Chamber of Commerce and Rooted Homes worked together to launch their "employer subsidized housing pilot." Through the pilot program, employers would help pay down closing costs for the cottage homes being built by Rooted Homes. To be eligible to enter the lottery from which lucky local employees would be chosen, entrants needed to be first-time buyers making 80 percent AMI or less. Entrants needed to have worked within the city at least a year.[53] Imagine you're a worker and this is your new setup: you get an electric bike to zip around town, courtesy of utility provider Pacific Power and Rooted Homes. There are pleasant trappings of a smallish community, such as community gardens and a common area. But the most important thing is the monthly bill. Your mortgage comes in around $1,400 a month.[54]

Demand for what Keogh's land-trust group is selling—not just homeownership, but attainable and personally sustainable homeownership—is overwhelming. In the summer of 2023, when the seven Rooted at Poplar cottages came available, more than three hundred people applied.

CHAPTER 8

Beyond Bend

Pressure was building hundreds of miles from Bend, in some of the most recognizable cities of the West: Boulder, Colorado; Boise, Idaho; and Bozeman, Montana. There were more reasons to compare members of the cohort than the fact that their names formed a nice alliteration.[1] Like Bend, Boise and Bozeman got significant play in the national media as Zoom towns. Newcomers pushed in from larger urban centers.[2]

Boulder stood out as a germane case study. The college town and Bend shared a similar population of about one hundred thousand residents, and both were set close enough to skyscraping peaks: much like the Cascades towered within easy reach of Bend, Rocky Mountain National Park was an hour-long car ride from Boulder.[3] Boulder and Bend had household median incomes between $74,000 and $75,000, by recent census figures. By land area, they each measured about thirty square miles in size, plus or minus a few squares.[4] Also familiar were the housing troubles of Boulder and the surrounding region. Local renters tended to experience cost burdening more frequently than homeowners, according to a regional analysis by Root Policy Research. Survey data collected from February to March 2020 showed thirteen thousand Boulder renters were cost burdened, and 8,500 of those were severely cost burdened, paying more than half their gross income on housing. As the study reinforced, severe cost burdening was "linked to a high risk of eviction or foreclosure, and homelessness."[5]

As elsewhere, part of the problem was a lack of available homes across different incomes. Apartment vacancy rates had dropped to historic lows because, although people wanted to live in the Boulder area, builders hadn't constructed enough rentals following the Great Recession.[6] Middle-income workers felt the crunch. Boulder deemed this its own "shrinking economic middle." The city's share of middle-income households fell by 6 percent from 1989 to 2017, while high-income households rose in correspondence. As the city noted on its website, "Detached single-family homes are increasingly only affordable to the wealthy," and "a large percentage of Boulder workers live in surrounding communities."[7] Bend parallels were clear.

Kurt Firnhaber, Boulder's housing and human services director, described a "barbell effect." The city had notched some wins with its affordable housing program over the years, getting low-income individuals housed, but wealthy residents took many remaining homes. "The folks in the middle, those that make, let's say, between $80,000 and $150,000 a year, can't really afford to live here," Firnhaber told me. "They don't qualify for affordable housing. They don't make enough money to purchase homes in the city, and that's the segment of the housing market that's unfulfilled." Firnhaber first arrived in Boulder in 1981 and studied environmental design at the University of Colorado (CU). After graduation he traveled internationally but returned to Boulder in the 1990s and started a local Habitat for Humanity affiliate. Then he went back abroad, working for Habitat as a country director for South Africa. Firnhaber stayed away for years, working this and that job, before his return. He took a post as deputy housing director with the city, moving up the chain of command to direct a merged housing and human services department. As such, he was well positioned to speak to Boulder's changes over the decades.

Modern Boulder is a hub of learning and research, but like Bend it has roots in extractive industries. Miners settled the area, named for a nearby canyon, in 1858. Several prominent developments, namely the construction of railroads and the University of Colorado in the 1870s, expanded the town. While Boulder became a gateway into mountainous mines, the late twentieth century brought new character. From the 1950s onward, a so-called government-industrial-educational complex coalesced, with the city emerging as a leader in environmental and scientific research. Among the most prominent examples of that complex is the National Center for Atmospheric Research, established by the National Science Foundation in 1960.[8]

The entrepreneurial spirit emboldened local businesspeople. Burt Helm, an editor-at-large with *Inc.*, christened Boulder "America's startup capital," citing a study from the Kauffman Foundation showing that, "In 2010, the city had six times more high-tech start-ups per capita than the nation's average. . . . and twice as many per capita as runner-up San Jose-Sunnyvale in California." But more relevant to the residential question was another theme: the open space encircling the city, which placed Boulder, as Helm illustrated, "in a bucolic bubble, with the Rocky Mountains on one side and parkland on the other."[9] Open space is tied to a "Blue Line" established by city charter amendment in 1959 to stop the city from piping water uphill.[10]

One evening in the 1950s, a man named Albert Bartlett was walking home from CU's physics building. Mathematics Professor Robert McKelvey cycled by, and the two began to chat. They would sometimes talk about Boulder's burgeoning population. In an essay decades later, Bartlett recalled McKelvey telling him, "Al, we have to do something about all of the houses that are being built up in the foothills." Bartlett thought, "Bob, you're out of your mind. What can we do? We are just a couple of nobodies, and the home builders are rich and powerful, and are working closely with the City Council." Their evening thought experiment led to a public campaign. In his essay, Bartlett wrote that he wasn't sure exactly how the Blue Line idea came to be, but the notion developed to draw a line and stop Boulder from supplying city water anywhere west of that line. The campaign for the effort only pulled in $500 in funding, yet voters liked the idea enough to pass their charter reform in July 1959, with 2,735 votes in favor and 852 against. Bartlett and his allies were ecstatic. "We had taken on the City Council and much of the Boulder establishment, and we had won," Bartlett wrote in his essay.[11] One Colorado journalist, Laura Snider, described the Blue Line as "the first sweeping protection for Boulder's mountainous backdrop."[12]

In 1967, Boulder residents went a step beyond the Blue Line vote with a historic sales tax to buy and manage open space, marking the first time local voters of any American city had chosen to tax themselves in the name of preserving open space. Today, Boulder's Open Space and Mountain Parks Department oversees more than forty-five thousand acres of protected landscape, with more than 150 miles of trails.[13] As in Oregon, Boulder residents said a hard no to sprawl. But on the record, the city noted that with regards to affordable housing, there is "high demand, with limited space available for new homes."[14]

While Boulder's land-use decisions weren't one-to-one with Oregon's statewide system, it was true they both conserved land. "You can't go up, you can't go down, and you can't go out," Firnhaber told me. He was trying to sum up to this outsider what hinders development within the city, from the open space limitations to strict building-height limitations (thirty-five feet throughout much of the city) to the fact that, with frequent flooding, many people don't have basements. "The urban growth boundary is really established by the open space, which has encircled the entire city," Firnhaber said. "You can't go beyond that. And so, there are still minor annexations that occur, but they're typically small." In turn, the market pumps out dense apartment structures. Because of the height limits, the apartment buildings can't be that tall.

I asked if a particular apartment complex or development sprang to mind when he thought of density. Firnhaber responded with a project called 30Pearl in what's known as Boulder Junction. More than a decade ago, local officials bought an auto sales property, but the business left only within recent years. "We started redeveloping the land, and some of it had already been parceled off and (redeveloped), but what's there today is three- and four-story housing," he said. A rapid transit center is close by for commuters, with buses driving in and out, rolling passengers around town or even out to Denver. There were some letdowns. "The train was supposed to come there from Denver. It never did. And the train station from downtown, the historical building, was moved there, and so it's a real transportation hub from a bus standpoint," Firnhaber explained. "The train just never got there, and possibly never will."

Pulling up the 30Pearl web page on my laptop while we talked, I absorbed the details quickly. The development sat on the corner of Pearl and 30th Street. The page advertised Boulder Junction as "a 160-acre redevelopment area in Northeast Boulder that is being transformed into a mixed-use, pedestrian-oriented neighborhood with regional transit connections and public spaces that benefit the entire community." It was the same kind of development that you'd easily find in far-larger Portland, albeit perhaps not on a stunning 160 acres within city limits. That is a lot of land. At 30Pearl, which was just one part of the broader Boulder Junction, city officials provided land and money to the local housing authority, Boulder Housing Partners (BHP), so there would be affordable housing. BHP built 120 apartments with the works: free Wi-Fi, energy-efficient heating and cooling, landscaped courtyards, and in-unit washers and dryers.[15] It had paseos and a creek corridor running through, with a pedestrian path to other parts of Boulder. It sat close to shops and groceries. The city had undergone a years-long planning process to take in feedback from residents about how the project could look. It was well received by neighbors, according to Firnhaber, who offered a hint as to why: "It's not close to any single-family neighborhoods," he said. "It was a commercial area."

Firnhaber took the view that, in the past ten to fifteen years, Boulder had undergone the metamorphosis from a town into a small city. As Colleen Sinsky had pointed out in Bend, growth forced Boulder to wrestle with big-city problems. In this context, Firnhaber was adamant about his professional objective as the housing director: "My mandate is to create affordable housing, and we do that. That can only really be accomplished through densification and redevelopment of our community." In some respects, his job became at least marginally easier of late. "When I first got here, affordable housing projects took twice as long to go through entitlements. . . . Now, when an affordable housing project comes through, the majority of the voices are people coming out in support and very little opposition, and the folks that support affordable housing have actually really gotten organized," he said.

It sounded like the YIMBYs had made inroads. In fact, YIMBYs swept into Boulder in 2016 when their first national conference landed there and drew some 150 attendees. Among them was Josh Stephens from Affordable Housing Los Angeles, who reported, "It served as a pep rally, brainstorming session and call to arms, all with the goal of making cities more affordable, equitable and even greener." YIMBYs didn't want indiscriminate new construction. The Boulder sessions focused on the nuances of environmental responsibility, social justice, property rights, and forging coalitions—all important components of a burgeoning, conscientious movement. There was also, as Stephens put it, "the delicate challenge of advocating for development without coming off as shills for for-profit developers."[16] The summary of the first meeting meshed with my experience covering a later YIMBYtown conference for the *Business Journal* in downtown Portland in April 2022. Adherents wrestled with where they fit in the complicated realm of housing advocacy. Still, the early bit of energy in Colorado appeared to have helped steady the glide path for housing advocates like Firnhaber, who said of the proponents and opponents, "It's more balanced now."

▲   ▲   ▲

Nicki Olivier Hellenkamp is quick on the draw with her Boise bona fides, telling people she's "a St. Luke's baby." The codewords mean she's from Boise. St. Luke's is the local hospital, and Hellenkamp has reason to make sure people know her roots run deep. Even though she was a Boise baby, raised in Idaho's biggest city, she moved away as a young woman and worked in neighboring Washington. Just before taking her job as the Boise mayor's housing adviser, she worked in Seattle government as a civil rights analyst. Does dropping in from Seattle tarnish her Boise credibility? Probably not. But growing up, she heard others grouse about "damn Californians" enough to think better of advertising that her parents had, in fact, relocated from the Golden State.

It was a February morning in 2023, and we were talking Zoom towns. "With COVID, you no longer had to make a decision like my family did," Hellenkamp told me. Her folks didn't make a drastic move by distance when they relocated from California to Idaho, but they committed to working for local employers.

"We made the decision to tie ourselves to the Boise labor market," she said, still referring to her family. "We have Boise jobs, and what the mayor here refers to as 'on Boise budgets.'" The dynamic changed for many workers during COVID. As she put it, "You no longer had that decision point of going, 'Uh, yeah, okay, we could sell our house in L.A., and we could certainly buy a nice house in Boise. But then we have to find a job in Boise that's going to be commensurate with our lifestyle in L.A.' You could just do it, and so suddenly, it was a much more attractive, I think, option for a lot of folks."

I had asked Boulder's Firnhaber about Zoom towns, too. He was at first stumped by the question. "I'm not sure I know the term Zoom town," Firnhaber said, surprising me. His uncertainty was a reminder that think pieces and twenty-four-hour news hadn't claimed everyone. I described the rough strokes, and it seemed to click for him. Firnhaber explained, "We've definitely seen that. It would be hard for me to speak to the scale or impact of that. But I do know, even in my department, and even in the city, people that used to live in the city of Boulder, or just outside the city of Boulder, some of them live, well, even up in Fort Collins, or thirty miles away, or even fifty miles away. It's given them more flexibility to move to a place that is more affordable."

Boise had its own affordability issues with which to contend. A December 2021 housing analysis by consulting firm Agnew::Beck told local officials and residents what they probably already knew, just in finer detail. With rising rents and appreciating home values, "The City of Boise is facing an unprecedented housing crisis," consultants wrote. Boise needed to add more than 2,700 housing units a year for a decade to match demand. That'd translated to more than 27,000 homes all told. Most of these new homes would need to be for people making at or less than 80 percent of the area median income. But 27,000 new homes seemed like a tall order at a time when homebuilders already hadn't been keeping up with demand. Over the previous three years, builders had constructed 4,100 fewer homes than Boise needed—so they were already building too slowly. The cost was great. Consultants estimated that solving the affordable housing deficit over the ten-year span would require some $4.9 billion.[17] The report pushed neighborhood density, big-time. On average, Boise neighborhoods needed to become 26 percent denser to meet housing demand within the coming decade, as the amount of vacant land to build new homes was severely limited.[18] There was some good news: although they hadn't delivered enough homes overall, builders had been leaning into multifamily construction. According to consultants, "This is a positive sign for meeting housing demand, given that multi-family construction is a denser housing form that uses less land to produce more units."[19] Agnew::Beck consultants were pushing for more apartments, because builders could fit more on the limited land available, rather than fewer sprawling, single-detached homes.

In early 2023, Boise was in the midst of rewriting its zoning code to allow greater density. Like Oregon, the idea was to stem the flow of suburban sprawl before it was too late. Hellenkamp said, "We don't want to just have suburbs all the way to Mountain Home," a community about forty minutes southeast by way of Interstate 84. The code rewrites were supposed to allow more of the vaunted missing middle housing and higher building heights along transit corridors. She said even though they're called transit corridors, they're more like "aspirational transit corridors" because they're underfunded. The looming question was, even if zoning changes passed and zoning no longer stopped construction of missing middle housing, would developers go ahead and *build* it? "If we're going into a recession," Hellenkamp wondered this early 2023 day, when the economy's prospects were uncertain, "are we actually going to see these additional homes that we really need?"

Big economic picture aside, something had to give: There were consequences to inaction. People were commuting from several towns over to get to their Boise jobs, Hellenkamp said. "It really has had a really significant impact on our residents and their ability to stay in the communities that they have helped build and are an important part of."

I asked her how she'd compare Seattle and Boise on housing, as someone who'd lived in both cities. She began with Seattle, where homelessness was far worse. That city had grappled with housing affordability for decades. Support systems built up over time to address the problem, although neither the homelessness nor housing conundrum had been solved in Seattle. And in Idaho, there hadn't been enough time to grow a similar ecosystem of coordinating groups, she pointed out.

As in Bend, Boise was fighting the big-city fights. "Do you feel that Boise will be able to build up that infrastructure quickly enough?" I asked Hellenkamp.

"It depends on the day," she laughed. "It depends on how optimistic I'm feeling that day."

▲   ▲   ▲

A few months earlier, in October 2022, Hellenkamp shared similar thoughts during a panel put on by the Osher Lifelong Learning Institute at Montana State University. It was called "Crisis! How Low Rental Inventory and High

Rents Impact Us All, Part 2."[20] Also on the panel lineup were Bend housing director Lynne McConnell and two Montanans, Emily Harris-Shears, a housing policy specialist with the city of Missoula, and Bozeman city commissioner Christopher Coburn. Using statistics pulled together by Montana-based Headwaters Economics, moderator Philip Bain highlighted how even though the four cities had differences, their rent burdens were similar. Bain asked viewers to think about half their income going toward rent.[21] This came at a time when Americans had been toughing it out with the worst inflation in four decades.[22]

Bain pivoted to Hellenkamp, who told listeners she was "a little bit of a boomerang situation": she'd grown up in Boise but had only moved back about a year prior. She contrasted being a Boise kid who didn't pay rent versus returning in adulthood to a vastly different housing market. The two biggest problems, she confirmed, were falling vacancies and rising rents. "It's been a very intense time to come home, but also a really important one."

Bend housing director McConnell was up next. McConnell was another California transplant who came to Bend. She had grown up in the Bay Area but moved to Oregon as soon as she had a say in where she could live, attending the University of Oregon to study sociology and diving into outdoor education. A winding path took her to Florida and beyond, but she returned to Oregon to attend Lewis & Clark College for law school. She worked for Multnomah County and, after some more travels, worked for NeighborImpact, a community action agency that offers struggling Central Oregonians, especially those facing homelessness, with services including rent subsidies and help paying their power bills.[23] Among McConnell's responsibilities at NeighborImpact was its homeownership program. It was a logical transition in 2017 when she took a job with the city of Bend as its affordable housing coordinator and was subsequently promoted to housing director. So when Bain asked McConnell to outline the top housing problems, her answer was simple. "For us, it is absolutely lack of supply as the number one crisis," she said. "That is true in Bend for both ownership and rental product, but rental feels like the biggest pinch often." The shortage pushed prices up. "We're not able to meet the demand of our community. Like Bozeman, we had a lot of folks in-migrating over the last few years, which was wonderful for revitalizing our community in different ways and bringing different folks. It's fun to have this much activity and growth going on, but it has really challenged us in terms of our ability to permit and create housing as quickly as we can."

"Any home runs?" Bain asked.

McConnell said the city's pipeline of affordable housing had surpassed eight hundred homes. She characterized the completion of those homes over the coming years as a huge accomplishment, especially since the city council's goal for the biennium was one thousand affordable homes. This followed Bend meeting its three-thousand-unit goal for the prior two-year period, a goal that wasn't restricted to affordable housing. Hitting the earlier target, McConnell said, reflected how strongly officials were pushing for new construction.

Two representatives from Montana echoed the Bend and Boise stories. Harris-Shears said officials in Missoula strove for every resident to have a home they could afford; that is, one where they weren't spending more than 30 percent of their monthly income on housing costs. That was a tough goal to meet with extraordinarily limited housing stock. "Our vacancy rate is over 2 percent for the first time in three years, which is really exciting," Harris-Shears told fellow panelists. "We measure a healthy housing market above 5 percent, and so we still have a ways to go, but we have a lot in the pipeline."

Coburn, the Bozeman city commissioner, was nodding along to others' testimony. Coburn was raised in Missoula but moved to Bozeman about six years ago for a job and so his partner could attend Montana State University. As a city leader, he spends most of his time thinking and talking about housing. "Oftentimes people are framing this issue around housing availability and the crisis that particularly renters are experiencing as a supply-and-demand issue, and that's true, to some extent," Coburn explained. "But I think I'm working to push the conversation further and say, this is really about a change in ideals, a change in perspective; going from one that was rooted in the ideals and the hopes and the dreams tied up into a single-family home and transitioning into the realities of denser multi-family, multi-unit housing."

The topic turned to developer incentives and how much they represented corporate welfare, one of the eternal arguments in local government. As Hellenkamp explained, "People hate to see developers get what they want in many communities, and so they're like, 'These are giveaways to the developers!'" She shook her fist and pitched up her voice for full effect, as if to evoke a grouchy city council meeting attendee. But it's normal to feel that way, she assured. "It is a real challenge. Especially in our market, even our affordable developers are almost all for-profit. We have very few nonprofit developers in our area." This was the tightrope: Many builders are out to make money, and it's left to government officials to try to get them to provide low-cost housing via incentives.

One of the ideas kicked around in Boise was improving so-called density bonuses: The trade would be that if a developer set aside, say, a quarter of their project as affordable housing in designated parts of the city, preferably near public transit, then the city of Boise would permit the developer's building to stand taller than usual. The thinking was, a taller building would have more units and the builder would make more money, meaning the affordable units inside might become more cost efficient. "Whether that is the right incentive, whether it's going to move the needle, we don't actually know," Hellenkamp said.[24]

Roping experts from Oregon, Idaho, and Montana together to talk housing made sense. In August 2021, the *Guardian* swung its international spotlight onto Bozeman via a story from Montana journalist Kathleen McLaughlin. Her compelling and incisive dispatch, down to side-by-side photos of a man living in a camper and an image of a swank women's clothing boutique called Luxe Society, reflected class contrasts between "haves and have-nots." With rents and for-sale prices on the rise, McLaughlin found that on one street, service workers lived in trucks, in trailers, and they pitched tents on the grass. Elsewhere she met a woman in her sixties who lived in her car and worked as a janitor by night. "They're the picture of displacement out west, the collateral victims of an affordability crisis created by Montana's booming popularity as a place for people with money," McLaughlin reported. One factor of the problem in Bozeman and Missoula is that Montanans have little in the way of bedroom communities to absorb residents pushed out of cities by high housing costs.[25] There are plenty of suburbs around places like Portland, but much of the West is without commuter towns. Big Sky Country is full of long, empty drives, I remember well. My family once hauled out to a whole other city (I recall it being one of the B's—maybe Bozeman, maybe Butte) to adopt a dog, a cheerful red golden retriever named Wiley, who hopped into the Land Rover as soon as we swung open the back hatch. He was our trusty pup for some time after we returned to Central Oregon.

McLaughlin interviewed sociologist Ryanne Pilgeram, whose book *Pushed Out: Contested Development and Rural Gentrification in the US West*, examines the small community of Dover, Idaho, and how a high-class six-hundred-unit development approved in 2004 came to exemplify historic themes of extraction and communal demoralization as residents lost access to a long-beloved beach. Pilgeram positioned rural gentrification as a phenomenon that should be viewed as a natural capitalist byproduct and "the expected outcome of a social system that privileges the economic growth of the few over other ways of organizing social life."[26] Pilgeram's ideas on rural gentrification reflected the tension between the need for more housing, the ways in which rural Americans are often left in the dust, and the knife-edge role developers play in either helping or hurting communities. She wrote that people scapegoat developers as profiteers who have little concern for communities' well-being—the same phenomenon that Hellenkamp had observed in Boise. Pilgeram took the broader view, positioning them as actors within a system that results from policies and laws that favor property owners' rights over those of communities. The results of that system, in Pilgeram's telling, are communities divided by economic and social class.[27]

She characterized modern rural gentrification as a continuation of historic extraction and exploitation in the West, from how Indigenous people maintained "a complex and reverent" relationship with the environment of the region but were exposed to disease by colonial settlers; to the ways in which well-heeled businessmen benefited most from the West's settlement. "The settlement of the American West is often romanticized as an era of democracy and opportunity, where diverse groups of Euro-American settlers could create new lives and new prosperity for themselves in a space freed from the social and economic structures of more developed spaces," Pilgeram observed. "But the settlement of the West was not open and free to all, and the primary beneficiaries of this process were not hearty settlers and their families but already-prosperous businessmen, who were essentially given millions of acres from the U.S. government to expand their wealth."[28] She drew parallels between expansionist timber barons and modern property owners while stressing their place within a system that, by its nature and across decades, disadvantaged community members with less economic might. It followed that, in the *Guardian* story about Montana, Pilgeram told journalist McLaughlin, "The way we allow development to happen is developers come in with plans that get approved by the city. What if, instead, we asked all the people who make minimum wage 'what do you want your community to look like?'"[29]

I put the housing question to Pilgeram myself in an email, starting with sincere praise for her book, a tome that shows how regular people get left behind. As a storyteller, I appreciated her tight focus on one community as a proxy for others in the West. In her book and the *Guardian* interview, she appeared skeptical of new development in rural communities. Perhaps I should have said she appeared skeptical of *high-profit* development, but either way: what solutions did she propose for cities and towns of the West that may very well need new housing stock in order to accommodate everyone? You can't legally stop anyone from moving in, so what's the balance these communities can strike between adding needed housing and not displacing existing service workers? Pilgeram wrote back acknowledging that new homebuilding needs to happen. Even so, she told me, "it needs to be based on the community needs and not what is going to generate the most profit, and frankly building housing that people working in communities can afford is generally not super profitable." By way of possible solutions, she directed me to an example in Idaho, where the Kaniksu Land Trust floated an idea for a community land trust. Like Rooted Homes in Bend, this was a private nonprofit that would own the land underneath homes. Owners could trade structures on the land, yet the trust maintained ownership of the dirt itself, the idea being to keep the real estate relatively affordable but still letting homeowners accumulate equity.[30] Pilgeram added, "Personally—speaking only for myself—communities need to plan for their growth and think about comprehensive zoning at the city and county level, and I think increasing density and protecting open spaces and agricultural land should be prioritized. That is a can of worms, but one communities in this situation should consider opening."

Governor Tom McCall opened that can of worms in Oregon a half-century ago, but time would tell if our 1970s innovation in urban sprawl mitigation might rub off on more states. Any governments that found effective solutions should borrow liberally from one another. The upshot from my conversations with Pilgeram, Hellenkamp, and Firnhaber was that, whether in Bend or similarly positioned cities, land trusts and increased density were gaining more recognition in the mainstream as plausible ways to ease the pressure.

CHAPTER 9

Who Gets to Live in the American West?

On an early fall morning in 2022, few people were walking the sidewalks along Northwest Wall Street, one of a pair of one-way roads that bisect the Bend core and pull drivers past low-slung shops and coffee houses. Sidewalks were quiet. Makenna and I parked the car and padded along in the October sun. We had driven over the Cascades to meet our baby nephew in Redmond. It was a new time for my family. My father sold his isolated home on the Terrebonne rimrocks in 2021. I didn't miss its cold hardwood floors. Dad moved into my sister and her husband's two-story townhome on Redmond's southwest edge. I was also in Bend to do some book research. Because of the logistics of getting there from the Valley, I needed to pair personal and reporting trips to make sure everything got done.

At a residential real estate firm, Cascade Hasson Sotheby's International Realty, row after row of home advertisements hung in the windows of the small, sleek office. A woman in a black cap peered inside. The agency was near the vaunted Tower Theatre, which was built in 1940 and used to play host to vaudeville shows. In 1996, the theater closed, but community members came together to raise more than $4 million, and the venue underwent renovations before reopening in 2004.[1] A white Chevrolet pickup lumbered by the theater. On Northwest Minnesota Avenue, a cross street, was Dudley's, the two-story bookshop café where I used to make lattes and work the register as a lanky teen. Once the clocked ticked 10:00 a.m. and the shop opened, Makenna and I poked inside. It looked good, clean. When I worked here under past owners, it appeared lovingly disheveled. I smoked cigarettes for the first time by the trash bin in the back alleyway. Customers played the beat-up, brown baby grand piano that once dominated the downstairs, volumes piled haphazardly on its aging lid. Now the room had shaped up. Books were neatly arranged for sale upstairs and down. Maybe some mess remained, and I had become too much of an outsider to see it anymore. More than a few wisps of the old spirit lingered, while something new and vibrant was taking hold. The new owner was doing good by this local landmark. Before long, it was time for me to leave Makenna to shop. Appropriate to the season, she bought a copy of Shirley Jackson's short stories and went up the stairs to read with a cup of coffee. I left to catch up with Colleen Sinsky, whose rental was minutes away.

I steered over a small bridge that briefly crossed the Deschutes and turned onto the neighborly Northwest Federal Street, parking on the other side of the lane from Sinsky's aquamarine home. The house, with its deep red door, sat in the shade of sky-high pines. Every indication of the November general election blared in the yard. Signs pushed a progressive slate: high on the ticket was, for mayor, Melanie Kebler, an attorney and city council member I'd met in passing at the YIMBYtown housing conference at Portland State. David Welton, with whom I hung out briefly at the conference, introduced us. Kebler was friendly. Our brief side conversation was insubstantial. More consequentially, her subsequent mayoral victory in the November general would underscore that Bend voters wanted someone to tackle housing head-on. One question in a DHM Research survey that December asked four hundred locals to rank priorities for the city of Bend with regards to housing affordability. Respondents could pick two answers. The most popular choice was "Provide housing for lower- and middle-income Bend residents," with 34 percent of respondents opting for that answer. Tying for second place were, "Provide housing for specific vulnerable groups of people, such as senior citizens or families with children" and "Create programs and services to help middle class residents better afford housing," at 31 percent. "Make it easier to build more housing in Bend" garnered 22 percent, and "Provide financial support for new affordable housing developments" got 16. Choices for "None of these" and "Don't know" came in last, with 15 and 2 percent, respectively. [2] The survey results showed that residents were anything but ambivalent; they wanted decisive action.

At Sinsky's rental in October, a Bend YIMBY sign stood on the other side of her front yard, pledging, "In our neighborhood, density means diversity, more neighbors = more fun, ADUs are awesome, characters make up the neighborhood character, renters are welcome, triplexes & fourplexes are pretty, Bend is for everyone." She greeted me at the door. I entered, and my host offered coffee with oat milk before showing me the place. This would make, no overstatement, the *perfect* starter house if it were for sale, though hopefully it'd list for less than a million. A living room and dining room, a petite kitchen, and two bedrooms constituted the main floor. In the living room was a couch, an armchair, a corner bookshelf. A guitar and ukulele hung from the walls. Art depicted plants and desert scenes. The backyard corralled chickens and a garden. Sinsky's calm voice juxtaposed against the barking of her fussy Australian shepherd, Danner, who followed us on the tour. With a stranger wandering through, Danner made clear to me this was his domain.

Sinsky and I sat down at the front-room table to talk. She and her partner had been in contact with Cascade Sotheby's, the real estate agency. They were prequalified for a mortgage. This was big news, an about-face from 2021, when she forecast leaving altogether. Any mortgage payments would be steep with interest rates so high. The Federal Reserve was trying to fight rampant inflation,[3] and before October was over, the average rate on a thirty-year mortgage would hit 7.08 percent, breaching 7 percent for the first time in twenty years.[4] But with the market's unpredictability and their lease expiring soon, the couple had decided it was time to buy and planned to stay in this house perhaps another six months. Sitting there, Sinsky told me, "I feel like housing prices are going to continue to fall, interest rates are going to continue to go up, and (I'm) trying to figure out, when is the least-bad time to jump in?" She was speaking for an entire generation of frustrated homebuyers who are trying to pinpoint "the least-bad time" to get into one of Americans' dearest ambitions: power over your own domain and financial future.

Sinsky thought back to her newspaper op-ed. Maybe it was time for an update. She and her partner couldn't agree on anywhere else to live. Their families were from different states, hers from California, his New Mexico. Neither of those states seemed attractive—and out-of-control prices put California definitively out of the running. In contrast, Bend sat squarely in the middle of their personal Venn diagrams. They wanted to live here because they both worked here. Their friends were here. After all, Sinsky had moved on from being a part-time program manager at Central Oregon FUSE to the nonprofit's executive director. "We've both for the past five years worked at local nonprofits, gotten our graduate degrees, done all the right things," she said. "We're both earning twice as much as we had been when we met each other." They both advanced in their careers and secured raises, though inflation and the cost of living deflated some of the enthusiasm. Even so, "this is really the only place that I've been an adult, so I just can't imagine choosing a spot on the map to go move," she said.

They'd consider Deschutes River Woods. Of course, I knew plenty well the heavily forested area south of Bend. Dad, Kati, and I used to ride our bikes to the Riverwoods Country Store, a roadside gas station cloaked in trees, for snacks and thick, sweet raspberry iced tea. We rode to Elk Meadow Elementary after school hours to hang out at the playground, close enough to the country store and our house for a kid-friendly route. The meadow across from the school had since grown housing. Sinsky didn't want to stay downtown. She had lived in central Bend for nearly six years, but it never felt like her neighborhood, because she knew the homes would be out of reach for her when it came time to buy. She got lucky with the rent but didn't find anything on this side of town in her roughly $400,000 to $500,000 price range. But it wasn't just a matter of capital. Deschutes River Woods promised what the two also wanted: space. "A quarter-acre would be amazing, just for gardening and chickens and having the raft," Sinsky said. The desire for acreage clashed with her support for housing density, sure, and the tension made her feel like a hypocrite. She told me, "That's something that my partner and I talk about a lot, just the fact that we want the single-family home that has contributed historically to so much of the lack of opportunity for so many people in the U.S."

Should she and other Bendites feel bad for wanting to buy single-detached? One research group said playfully and pointedly, "Everyone wants to feel like the king or queen of their own castle, and there is no other type of home that makes one feel this way more than a single-family house." More to the point, roughly eighty-two million of America's 129 million occupied homes in 2021 were single-family houses.[5] As of now, troublesome feelings aside, until Bend becomes properly dense and single-family stops dominating the market, the reality is single-detached homes make up most of what's available. That doesn't make advocates' push for densification any less worthwhile.

That said, money was a hurdle. Frenzied buyers earlier in the pandemic benefited from low mortgage rates, often below 3 percent.[6] Sinsky and her partner were in the class of workers unable to partake then; but now, home prices were dropping, which somewhat offset the sting of rising mortgage rates. Even in a cooling market, Sinsky knew they might have to either get a roommate or block off the largest bedroom for a renter in order for them to buy—this despite her anti-vacation rental instincts. Still, because it would make buying possible, and it'd be part of their home, "I feel like I'm not entirely joining the dark side," she said.

In some instances, Sinsky and other middle-class residents like her must make these kinds of compromises if they hope to stay in Bend. That makes it all the more frustrating when industry professionals don't seem to understand how excruciating navigating the homebuying process is for many of their potential clients, whether they're cobbling together down payments or praying for good loan terms. The day before, Makenna and I had driven along Southeast Third

Street, a main north-south road, when we passed a sign outside a home lender's office that asked in black-and-white, "What is stopping you from becoming a homeowner?" In a city experiencing its own version of gentrification, projecting the question to countless drivers seemed unnecessarily flippant. Sinsky knew exactly what sign I was talking about when I brought it up. She told me she had to stop and snap a picture and admitted she considered vandalizing it with an answer, but she didn't want to go to jail. "Then it would be, 'My recent felony is what's stopping me from being a homeowner,'" she joked.

One of the strongest tailwinds speeding her journey toward homeownership was, as she had recently discovered, that her father Jerry had socked away money and planned to help the couple with their down payment. "I honestly didn't know that I was in that class of privilege until the past six months," she said. Parents have been helping their kids buy homes for decades. It's part of intergenerational wealth. A YouGov poll in 2022 found just over one in three Americans who'd owned a home had parents who provided them with financial assistance when they were first-time buyers: 10 percent of respondents said their parents got the property for them or gave it to them outright, 7 percent said the parents paid the full deposit amount, and 18 percent said their parents either helped with the deposit or by some other means financially.[7] This isn't an American phenomenon. YouGov conducted a similar survey in the United Kingdom and reported, "Prior to the pandemic, the proportion of those getting help from the bank of mum and dad was double that of the 1990s." While the share of first-time buyers getting help from their folks shrank in the pandemic, it remained at more than one-third of Britons who bought from 2020 onward.[8] Of course the bank of mom and dad isn't open to all house hunters. Sinsky said even though getting assistance from a parent is common, she still felt guilty about it. She acknowledged that without her father's help, there was no way she'd be able to buy. And yet, it made it possible for her to see a future where she owned a home.

One morning the following month, Sinsky texted me with a Zillow post for a three-bedroom, one-bathroom home in northeast Bend. List price: just north of $500,000. Photos showed off the home's deep blue exterior, a twisting apple tree out back with a children's playset attached, garden space, all within an immense backyard. The living room and kitchen were wood-floored. Rustic, modern, just under 1,100 square feet. A perfect first house. Sinsky was exuberant. "Hi Jonathan, I'm excited that we just had our offer accepted on this house!" she texted. "Fingers crossed everything goes well in the next 30 days, and we'll be doing a chilly, mid-winter move!"

"Wow!!!" I responded. "That yard!"

She said the apple tree was a century old. "We're really excited. I didn't expect to ever live in such a nice house. I was expecting a fixer-upper, at best."

"Ended up doing Pilot Butte area instead of Deschutes River Woods it looks like?"

"Yeah, we were trying to find a balance between price-location-house-yard. This one definitely pushes the upper limits of our budget, so we'll be house poor for a while, but long-term I think this area will appreciate a lot."

Hard work, help from a parent, patience, and a cooling housing market culminated to give the couple the opening they needed to become Bend homeowners.

▲ ▲ ▲

I hoped to touch base with one of the remote workers who moved in during COVID. When I reconnected with Billy Duss in September 2022, he and Maggie had gotten married. They held a small ceremony at Mount Rainier in Washington. For their honeymoon, they road-tripped from Bend to Yosemite National Park in California, coming back up along the Oregon Coast, cutting across to Eugene, then heading home. But there was still more of Oregon he wanted to see, like Joseph and the Wallowa Mountains to the east. When Duss lived in Seattle, he maybe got as far as Newport on the Oregon Coast. He still wanted to attend the Pendleton Round-Up, the world-famous rodeo in Eastern Oregon. Bend to Pendleton is a four-hour drive; perhaps it'd be a nice day trip to take with the family: wide open vistas give way to lively arenas and downtown shops that welcome rodeo patrons in the late summer.

Duss and his wife were forging ties within Bend, developing a community of friends through run club and work. "We're starting to feel connected to this group of people a lot more, which happened a lot quicker than I expected," he said. He was still fully remote, working out of a home office in the house they bought, instead of having to work from the kitchen table. They had gotten a dog named Checo, named for the lightning-fast Formula One driver Sergio "Checo" Pérez. The pup was old enough that Billy wondered whether he should start commuting to a coworking office or coffee shop just to be around other people. He still found himself out on the trails on weekends. He ran one local outdoor loop a few weeks back with friends. He's doing "all these things that I don't think I would have been able to do as easily in Seattle, so the gamble paid off." There was also, of course, the cost advantage compared to Seattle. "The big thing of

Bend was, it was more affordable," he confirmed. "We were able to buy a house that we wouldn't have been able to in Seattle—certainly a much bigger house than we would have been able to afford in Seattle."

I wondered how much culture shock he experienced by moving. "There's definitely some," Duss said. "The biggest thing I miss about Seattle—and it's the thing I knew that I would miss about Seattle—was the amenities of a city. Bend is smaller than Seattle. The restaurants aren't quite as good. There's a little bit more car dependence. There's no transit really to speak of here. Buses run every thirty minutes. They're not super useful. I've adapted to that. We bought an e-bike, so I can get around town without us needing to buy a second car. (I'm) learning which restaurants are good and which ones are maybe not as good. But yeah, there is culture shock for sure. But it's the adjustment that I expected coming in and have worked on adjusting towards."

Bend's slower pace constituted part of the original curb appeal. Yet for Duss, learning to match the local speed took time. He offered an example by way of cooking: Seattle had more variety of higher-quality goods for sale, he said, whether from H Mart or the neighborhood grocery store. Now, he had to recalibrate. "It's level-setting and resetting my expectations, knowing I'm not going to have amazing tomatoes all the time," he told me. He came off as conflicted about ordering dry goods online: He said he tried not to, because he wanted to buy local. But if a business didn't have what he wanted, he'd look online for specialty items. "Fred Meyer only goes so far," he said of the Northwest retailer, which is in Seattle, too. "Fred Meyer's great to get stuff, but it's not super high-quality. Those sorts of things have been a little bit more of an adjustment than I expected: Just going from a large city and a large metro area to, I guess Bend is, what, a mid-sized city in the middle of nowhere?" On balance, it seemed like Billy and Maggie had done fine for themselves after moving to a new town. From experience, I know it's tough. Some friction is inevitable. Billy said: "I see us settled here and in it for the long haul."

Bend had a history of welcoming newcomers. The Duss family was among the latest. Just like my parents, Billy and Maggie were trying for the best life they could afford. They hit the roadblocks one might expect for people moving in from a larger metro (my folks were from Los Angeles), but overall they were acclimating to the new pace. Bend needed to ensure it had room for in-migrants like Billy and Maggie who were sure to continue moving in, while balancing the needs of existing residents. It came down to increasing housing stock across the spectrum of income, through missing middle housing and new apartments. That's not to say there shouldn't be any new single-detached homes. But those that are built, as local officials suggested way back in 2016, should be more compact.[9] This back-to-basics approach stood to help lift Bend from its housing shortage.

▲ ▲ ▲

For Brenna Visser, the *Bulletin* reporter, housing and homelessness came to dominate her coverage. She wrote about the rising homeless population.[10] She profiled a forty-six-year-old man who was "one of dozens if not hundreds who live in the wilderness off China Hat Road in Bend. He said he goes by the nickname 'Rev,' because he considers himself a reverend of a religion he refers to as 'Parkerism.' The basic tenets: Don't be rude and stay happy."[11] She wrote about a state-of-the-city meeting in October 2020 where Bend city manager Eric King, pointing out skyrocketing home prices and low inventory, declared, "Zoom town is a reality for Bend."[12] The stories were so all-consuming that she restructured her beat, giving away coverage of the Bend Park and Recreation District to another reporter. "Bend became a Zoom town, and people were moving here and buying up real estate like crazy," Visser told me. All the while, she and her partner were trying to lock down housing for themselves. In 2020, they wanted to move in together. Visser had been waiting on finding her own place but didn't want to waste time if they were going to go all in together. She said, "We were looking at stuff in February of 2020, and then March of 2020 hit, and we were like, 'Oh my god, what is going to happen? What is this going to do to us? Should we try to expedite this? Should we wait? What's the right move here?'"

The two caught a lucky break, getting moved up a housing waitlist because the people ahead of them bailed for reasons unknown. It was a minor miracle. They moved into a two-bedroom townhome close to Pilot Butte in the first months of the pandemic, renting it for about $1,250 a month. "We're paying $1,450 now here, which is still way lower than a lot of places new here," Visser said in 2022. "If we tried to move somewhere else with the same square footage, we would not find anywhere close to that price." She left the *Bulletin* in June 2022 for a land-use communications job with the city of Bend, posting a Twitter thread to tell everyone about the change:

> Why leave journalism? There's a long answer to that short question, but succinctly: burnout and finances. My soon-to-be wife and I can't make Bend our home on what I get paid as a reporter. And frankly, the last two years have been emotionally draining (other journos I'm sure

can confirm this). At the same, it has been an honor and a privilege to do this work through all these "unprecedented times."[13]

David Welton tweeted his congratulations a few minutes after Visser posted her thread.[14] Like other Bendites, he'd watched local reporters come and go. But the home angle struck a nerve. "Her announcement immediately jumped out. It's like, that's what we're talking about. I can't control the earnings of the newspaper. I subscribe to it to support their efforts. But I can't do too much more than that," he told me. "Housing is something that we all have a little bit more control over in terms of the political process." Visser felt she'd stalled with the local journalism pay scale. She said, "The thing that is frustrating and what ultimately ended up prompting my leave of journalism (with) what I was getting paid at the *Bulletin* was a sense of feeling stuck, like I won't ever be able to advance out of my position if I stay here."

The news group was trying to raise wages for its reporters. Gerry O'Brien, editor of the *Bulletin*, told me that at the start of 2023, company leaders increased reporter pay by $2 an hour across the board. A subsequent increase depended on achieving a companywide digital subscriber goal. (The *Bulletin* is no island: online subscribers have become vital to many newsrooms' bottom lines amid an industrywide decline of ad and classified sales.) O'Brien said, "The reason reporters leave due to the high cost of living in Bend is exactly why leadership and the owners of EO Media Group have made the commitment to reinvest all digital subscription growth revenue back into raising wages in our newsrooms across the company over the next two years, with a target of paying journalists at a level commensurate with a similar skill set in other positions." EO Media later sold the *Bulletin* and its other Oregon papers to Mississippi-based Carpenter Media.[15]

The story of the *Bulletin*'s attempts to keep up with the rapidly rising cost of living was the story of Bend businesses at large. Visser's departure from the paper and newsroom leadership's maneuvers on the wage issue—reporters eventually organized a union[16]—exemplified the very dilemma in which many locally based employers found themselves: how do you retain employees when their price to stay in town defies sense? Katy Brooks, CEO of the Bend Chamber of Commerce, spoke with me in November 2023 about the labor market for service sector jobs, but her words applied seamlessly to any number of industries. When employees "can't live close to where they work, this is a problem—and it's big," Brooks said. "I think that a lot of businesses are looking for solutions. A lot of businesses are opening their pocketbooks."

In a pipedream of a functioning world, where wages match the cost of living, and housing is affordable to the hard-working local employees who earn a range of different incomes, Visser and her fiancée, a therapist, should be able to move out of their townhouse into something they own, freeing up their rental for someone else who needed it. That just wasn't so in their present predicament. Said Visser, "We do not have a middle housing place to go, and so that was one of many reasons that prompted me to be like, you know what, I need to change the amount of money I'm making, because it's like, I may be okay now, but if I ever want to get out of this current phase of my life, we need to substantially make more money than we're making now."

▲　▲　▲

Greg Delgado left Cait Boyce's house in Terrebonne shortly before Thanksgiving 2021. His departure saddened his erstwhile roomie: she missed him at big events at her place. "He wasn't at my table," she lamented. Delgado's mother died in November, and he went to Arizona to help his aging father. His parents were married more than sixty years. "It's really hard for him," Delgado explained. With the coronavirus still a threat, the family made use of a tent and held a memorial service outside.

In January 2022, Delgado wished to come back to Oregon. With his past in social justice circles, he'd picked up a remote job in diversity, equity, and inclusion (DEI) work with Energy Trust of Oregon, a Portland-based clean energy nonprofit. He worked with the nonprofit but technically was a subcontractor with a group called TRC Companies, which managed a commercial-building energy-efficiency program for Energy Trust. Bottom line, he was in a cohort of consultants working with Energy Trust to better reach traditionally underserved customers, including small businesses and businesspeople of color.[17] Delgado had been under contract with TRC Companies since late 2021, working remotely.[18] So for now, instead of trying to find a place to live in Bend, Delgado decided to stay a while on the family property in Arizona.

Thanks to Energy Trust and the fact that he was with his father, he managed to pull together some money to buy a shuttle bus. Delgado wanted to convert the bus into someplace to live. The roughly twenty-six-foot white Ford had rectangular, vertical windows and storage space in the back. "It's got high ceilings," he explained later. "I'm going to rip the A/C unit out of the top. I'm going to put, like, a loft apartment (inside). It's just going to have a murphy bed and a desk. On the sides, it'll have benches, and I'm going to put in a very primitive ice chest, one burner stove, and one big, deep sink." He envisioned a shower and, likely, a compost bathroom. One website, HomeBiogas, described waterless compost toilets as perfect for mobile homes and reducing one's carbon footprint. The process works as "a small compost chamber collects the solid waste, while the liquids are either directed to a separate container or evaporated."[19] Delgado added, "I'm not plumbing this thing out." He envisioned a solar water heater and solar array on top of the shuttle bus. The vehicle was in good enough shape, so he figured he could make a small studio out of it, hopefully within a year. He'd find somewhere to park it, he reckoned. While he expected to one day inherit the Arizona property, Delgado said, "Owning property and owning land, especially at this point in my life, I don't see that as a possibility." Thus, his goal this January was to get the shuttle bus running.

The Greeley Avenue apartment worked because the rent didn't get jacked up exorbitantly, but he conceded he didn't want to live in an apartment again. And if he were still in Bend, he figured he either wouldn't manage to find anything, or it'd be "some tiny cubicle apartment" on the far end of town. "People who live in Bend can't afford to live there anymore. Working-class folks are having to move to Terrebonne. They're now having to move to La Pine. They're having to move to Redmond, and commute," he said. "The Terrebonne commute opened my eyes to how bad the traffic gets on that 97 going back and forth." Still, even when he had a cheap apartment, Bend wasn't always a breeze. During his 2016 state senate campaign, he'd done janitorial work at night and cooking jobs during the day when he wasn't knocking on doors. He said, "It was a hand-to-mouth living."

The Energy Trust work afforded him the ability to think longer-term. He seemed eager for the stability. He wanted to start his own business for DEI work. In his mind, it was yet another reason to fix up the bus: if Energy Trust needed him to go to rural Oregon and advocate for its energy-efficiency programs, he'd drive where he needed to go. But the idea of owning a business struck at a deeper issue: When you don't own a home or a business somewhere, it makes it more difficult to stay tied to the community, he said, which is especially challenging for people of color. "One of the challenges that we face as minorities (is that) access to ownership has been a challenge," he said, adding later, "These are the things that we want to try to change." In February 2022, Delgado established a limited liability company called Delgado Consulting LLC with the state of Oregon.[20] He now had a business of his own, fulfilling a goal.

When we spoke again in August 2022, Delgado had moved back to Oregon. He was still with Energy Trust and having fun with the DEI work. He still hadn't fixed up the shuttle bus to his specifications. Once he returned to Oregon, he first rented in Redmond, which worked for a while because it was month-to-month. "The lady was really nice, but she had lots of cats, and it was not the best living space for me," Delgado said. A few months afterward, he got into a rental in Bend, but in the way of dwellings, it was rough: "I'm scared that there's black mold in this house," he said, also describing the "the roommate situation" as tense. His roughly eight-by-ten-foot room leaned to one side. "It's really, really old and kind of sketch, but it's a house," Delgado said. He still wanted to remodel the shuttle bus waiting for him in Arizona so he could live in it. But he hadn't finished that project. Fortunately, when he and I checked in again in early 2023, he'd moved on, this time into a much nicer house in Bend.

Delgado probably would have needed to go to Arizona to help his grieving father regardless of whether the landlord evicted him from Greeley Avenue. But let's imagine he hadn't been pushed out. Theoretically, he could have tried to continue to make the rent payments from afar to keep ahold of his home if he found a job in Arizona or remote work with Energy Trust, depending on how much money he could pull together. But because he'd been evicted, he had to live for several months in a town, Terrebonne, where he had barely any community ties. Then, once back in Oregon from Arizona, he had to live in a couple of uncomfortable (to say the least) rentals, including one that seemed to need serious repairs, before landing in his current situation. He wouldn't have needed to ricochet around Central Oregon. Many Americans lived some version of Delgado's story, including but not exclusively during the pandemic. From the beginning of the pandemic in March 2020 to March 2023, landlords across the nation filed for more than two million evictions, according to the best available data from Eviction Lab at Princeton University. That was just across the states and cities Eviction Lab tracked with its limited resources, and the data was far from all-encompassing. When I checked the numbers, for instance, Oregon wasn't even on the list.[21]

Delgado made another run at politics, applying for a vacant seat on the Bend City Council in January 2023. It wasn't clear if he could take the appointment if he won it because he had moved around so much since his eviction. The city charter required twelve months of immediate past local residency for the post. Delgado countered by telling me, "This is my home. Just because I'm away from it for three, four weeks, or a month at a time, doesn't make it any less my home." Be that as it may, his interview with the city council, conducted by video call because he was in Texas for a funeral, got him in front of Bend's politicians for a few minutes. Delgado thanked them for the opportunity and told them about his past in immigrant rights advocacy and his Energy Trust of Oregon work. He got across why he wanted the seat. He told the council members that he thought this was a good chance to make not just his voice heard, but others' as well. He described his relationships within the Latino, LGBTQ, and faith communities. "I want to make sure that we all share in a collective voice, and bring it collectively, and respectfully, to the table," Delgado said. "So that was the reason I decided to run." Before the meeting was over, the City Council appointed another applicant, one who worked at a homebuilder.[22]

Delgado of course still had his company. He described himself to me as "a hired gun when it comes to doing diversity and equity work." He had the tools and the time as he puzzled over how to make Bend a fairer place to live. On the city's east side one day, he saw schoolchildren getting off a bus, and he guessed most were Latino. His hope was that they would feel like they belonged here, because when he began in advocacy, kids used to say, "I'm joining the military, because there ain't shit for me in this town."

CHAPTER 10

Toward Solutions

Are all the innovations and momentum in housing enough to lift Bend and its peer cities from deep residential shortfalls? I swing between optimism and pessimism. Evidence gathered over the course of my reporting suggests many are embracing the notion that, as goes the credo of the Bend YIMBYs, "everyone who works in Bend should be able to live in Bend—and to do that, we're going to need more housing of all shapes and sizes."[1] You can insert your city of choice between the quotation marks, but the full shape, size, and effectiveness of their movement will be better known in decades to come. Spend enough time reporting on housing, and you'll hear the same adage: there is no panacea. I used to take it as a cliché. By the time my research for this book concluded, I came to believe small solutions accumulate.

In the spring of 2023, Makenna and I attended a close friend's wedding at the Sunriver Resort. We stayed in a lovely room very much like those my sister and I used to clean. One evening, clouds glowed orange over a snow-covered Mount Bachelor and trees crowded in the foreground. I found a copy of *Western Home Journal (WHJ)*, a glossy real estate magazine, in our room. The cover story told of a couple who moved from Portland to the Bend area during COVID-19 after vacationing in Central Oregon for fifteen years. The pair had purchased twenty acres just outside Bend before the pandemic and "envisioned a modern yet warm home and had plans drawn up for a 3,800-square-foot house with four bedrooms, an office, a bonus room, and an outdoor kitchen," according to the story by *WHJ* editor-in-chief Cassidy Mantor. Said the husband of his new spread, "Pulling up to the house, you see three or four of the mountains that are part of Bend's landscape right through the windows."[2] The market would continue to support the construction of luxury homes like this wherever it could.[3] What did need help getting built was the low- and middle-income units for hotel and ski resort workers.

In the late fall, Mount Bachelor and the Campfire Hotel teamed up to subsidize housing for seasonal workers. This wasn't quite building new units, but it was a stopgap. Mount Bachelor employees would apply to live in hotel rooms at the Campfire Hotel on Northeast Third Street, and their payment would be subtracted through biweekly payroll deductions. Daniel Elder, the Campfire's general manager, told the *Bulletin*, "It takes places like Mt. Bachelor and Campfire Hotel to think outside the box and come up with a solution."[4] Bendites were testing solutions of their own. Shortly after news of the Campfire Hotel deal broke, I got back in touch with Katy Brooks, CEO of the Bend Chamber of Commerce. I asked her a question about the Valley–Central Oregon divide: "Do you feel like Bend ever has a hard time being heard in Salem?"

"Oh yeah," Brooks said. "We have in the past. It's improved a great deal over the last several years." She described Bend's culture. "We're very bootstrap-y. It's like, 'Ah, nobody's coming to help us—again.'" Thus, locals test out ideas for themselves. "I think that that has gained us a lot of notoriety in Salem. I think they're paying a lot more attention." Those in the capital were paying Bend more mind because of the recent population gains, she assumed. "It's really been a benefit to the state to look at how innovative we've been." She continued, "In the past, yes, I think we were very much ignored, because we're east of the Cascades. And the Valley and the Portland area is the great sucking sound of attention and money. But I think things are starting to change with that, but it's always a challenge to be heard when you're the biggest population center east of the Cascades," she said. "It's difficult to get here. It's very rural outside of Bend. And it's *tough* sometimes to get attention and money, frankly. But it has been getting better."

Brooks's remarks made me think of the LIFT rental subsidies. It would still take years to judge properly their effects in Bend because of the long lag in funneling that money into the community. But again, locals had been taking action of their own. One night in the spring, Sinsky sent me an email unexpectedly. She wanted to share info on a new Central Oregon FUSE pilot program called the Barrier Busting Fund, which helped pay some of the expenses that tended to stop people from getting into housing. Typically, money went toward security deposits, but the fund was flexible enough that people could rent moving trucks, install wheelchair ramps, or order identifying documents. "It's a pretty cool model that's already generating great data," Sinsky said. Funders were interested. Sinsky signed off on a personal note: "Our house is going well—feeling pretty strapped for cash, as expected, with this interest rate. But we're optimistic that it'll just be a few years before we can refinance at a lower rate."

Cleveland Commons and Rooted at Simpson broke ground on the same day: October 16, 2023. Sinsky, as well as David Brandt's Housing Works, had worked on the thirty-three-unit Cleveland Commons permanent supportive housing development. Simpson was the project, with its forty for-sale cottages, from the Rooted Homes land trust. Housing Works's rental side of the Simpson project would start later. Andrea Bell, director of Oregon Housing and Community Services, was on-hand for both the day's groundbreakings. Bell said Simpson would become "the largest permanently affordable and sustainable homeownership community in the city of Bend." At Cleveland Commons, Bell emphasized, "every home in this complex is for those who have experienced homelessness for many months and even years in some cases." Construction had commenced on seventy-three low-cost homes.[5]

All this was happening after Tina Kotek, the former Oregon House Speaker, was elected governor in November 2022. As an early order of business in January 2023, Kotek established the goal that builders should construct 36,000 new homes per year, up from the typical 20,000. It was a bold target from the state leader. Given her pro-housing history and the depth of Oregon's housing shortage, it made sense.[6] While some statewide initiatives were yet unproven, they showed Oregon's general trajectory was, potentially, toward building more homes at prices people could afford.

Soon after Kotek set her goal in January, researchers in February kicked around ideas for how to reach it. Researchers Michael Andersen and Jay Lee of the Sightline Institute argued for boosting apartment construction to come closer to the governor's goal. There was a historic precedent: when Oregon added hundreds of thousands of homes during the 1970s, half of them were apartments and similar attached housing. "Oregon added almost 330,000 new homes during the 1970s, almost three times as many as it built during the 1960s or 1980s," Andersen and Lee wrote. "That's not far off from the 348,000 homes that Governor Kotek wants the state to add by 2030." The Sightline writers continued:

> In the 2020s, Oregon will have some new advantages. For one, Oregon now has a private residential construction workforce almost three times the size of 1977's: 20,227, as of 2021. Oregon's total population is 4.2 million, more than double the 2.1 million residents the state had fifty years ago. It's true that a lot of work needs to be done. But if Oregon could bring the barriers to housing back down to the level of

the 1970s, its current and future workforce could find the time to do the job.[7]

Apartments were one way to do it. The state was also integrating a new system, called the Oregon Housing Needs Analysis, into its land-use laws to better understand how many homes each city needed. This new system would account for things like past underproduction of homes and housing needed for people experiencing homelessness, which were factors cities hadn't previously considered under the old methodology. Speaking with me in the Portland suburb of Beaverton, Ethan Stuckmayer, housing services division manager at the Department of Land Conservation and Development, said the upshot was that "local governments are planning for a lot more housing, just by nature of the math, than they were in the past." Bend housing director Lynne McConnell opined, "The way land-use law is evolving will give us a much more realistic picture of the need we have and the challenges we'll have delivering the quantity of affordable housing units likely to be shown as our need."

In Bend, the need for low- and moderate-income housing persisted with just as much, if not more, force in 2023 as it had when ECOnorthwest issued its 2017 report. I could imagine a future where the Stevens Road Tract on the east side became a subdivision thick with apartments and missing middle housing instead of only scads of single-detached homes. Any solution came with compromises and caveats. The resistance some of those I spoke with had to living in tightly packed homes—Delgado didn't want a "cubicle apartment," Sinsky went for a single-detached herself, real estate agent Kromm was clear about his clients' preferences—reflected how demand for detached homes remained entrenched. But let's say we build ample apartments and townhomes starting now. Who lives in the single-detached homes and who moves into the attached housing? Will young people use townhomes as starter homes with the intention to, with whatever upward mobility they can muster, one day level-up into detached? Possibly. No matter what, the city needed to rebalance its supply of housing in a way that allowed economy-driving workers to live in Bend without sacrificing their own economic health.

Makenna and I were ambling through our local Fred Meyer one night when an *Outside* magazine cover pulled me in: "The Future of Mountain Towns: They're great—They're also under siege. We can help." Lofty promise. What was most appealing was the solutions section spread across the inner pages, where *Outside* conjured its vision of (made-up) mountain utopia Bluebird Valley, population 7,500, designed for sustainability and affordability. Experts in fields as varied as climate and development weighed in to fabricate Bluebird Valley with *Outside*. It was dreamlike, from the gear co-ops and daycare centers to the parks, ponds, and greenbelt. Most salient were two ideas to keep housing costs under control: "The streets around downtown are dense with new apartments," and, "To avoid a housing crunch, officials built dorms and other rentals for seasonal employees. They also funded deed-restriction programs, creating a pool of houses that can only be sold to someone who works in town and needs a hand."[8] Downtown apartments. Workforce housing. The kinds of new supply that could lift larger (and realer) Bend from its trough of frustration.

What of the YIMBY argument of adding abundant supply across income levels? The journalist Jonathan Thompson wrote persuasively about the shortcomings of this "housing supply-side theory" as it pertained to amenity-driven communities of the West. In a pair of dispatches in September 2023 for his online newsletter the *Land Desk*, Thompson outlined how simply adding more housing supply in these areas doesn't fix their problems. He noted in the first piece that these communities' residential markets have become distorted by "wealth inequality, which manifests as some folks' willingness and ability to spend gobs of money to own their own little—or vast—piece of Jackson, Aspen, Moab, or Durango, versus everyone else's inability to do the same. The problem then is not a lack of housing, but rather a lack of *affordable* housing. And solving that problem is far more complicated than simply building more market-rate housing."[9]

The idea that wealthy individuals would spend lots of money to stake a claim in these communities had to do with the commodification of various corners of the West. Examining what some scholars have termed a "New West," Ryanne Pilgeram, in the book *Pushed Out*, asserted towns that formerly thrived on resource-extractive industries, such as timber or mining, remodeled themselves by realigning with tourism dollars, in turn commodifying the views available within the West. Instead of forests in the Pacific Northwest, for instance, being viewed for the economy-fueling raw materials they once provided, the region's spaces became commodities in which people could "demonstrate wealth and bourgeois values by recreating in nature rather than razing it." The New West emerged as a place where you could escape from somewhere else that was, either in perception or reality, less safe and more crowded. Pilgeram wrote, "In this postextractive economy, the natural landscape itself is the product (not the trees that might be harvested). Packaging that landscape for maximum profit becomes the primary goal in the New West. . . . Trees are still commodified in the New West, but in very different ways."[10] Pilgeram's argument aligned with what Thompson published a few days after his first piece:

> Demand in Durango or Moab, Telluride or Boulder, Tahoe or Bend, is not driven by concrete factors like local jobs. Nor are the prices folks are willing to pay limited by the salaries those local jobs pay. Demand in these cases is driven by a certain cachet of Place, or a desire to live (or own property) there. There is no concrete limit to this kind of desire unless, say, you put a toxic waste dump in the town square. Same goes with prices, which are driven not solely by scarcity (though that may have an effect), but by how much wealthy folks are willing to pay to satisfy their desires—which, apparently, is unlimited.

Thompson told readers he was a passionate YIMBY for new affordable housing. He said dense, mixed-use, and infill projects should move forward. He encouraged streamlining the permitting process for rent-controlled or deed-restricted affordable homes, "but not for huge developments that include just a couple token affordable units."[11] I remembered the Stevens Road Tract, and the conservationists' argument that it only had a small spot of required affordable housing. Was this a missed opportunity? Could, at the very least, building missing middle on the tract be one way to make those units *more* affordable than land-swallowing single-detached, even if they weren't all deed-restricted "affordable"? Thompson's writings aligned with half of what ECOnorthwest had already made clear: the need for more low-income homes. I felt conflicted about the sole focus on deed-restricted affordable units. On one hand, yes: they were precisely what the city required. Conversely, I appreciated from talking with sources that affordable rentals tended to be some of the most complex to get financed. "The most mind-numbing part of these projects is the capital stack," a veteran developer once told me, referencing the many layers of financing required to get these projects under construction.[12] Bend needed more low-income, affordable rentals, no shadow of a doubt. It also needed to add doors now. Those goals weren't in direct opposition to one another. Harnessing all available energy to build moderate- and low-income housing—forget swank luxury homes, they'd take care of themselves—seemed like a worthy compromise in the long run.[13]

There is growing recognition among federal lawmakers that workforce housing is an issue with which the United States will need to contend. Starting in 2016, Senator Ron Wyden, an Oregon Democrat, began pushing Congress to pass a tax credit similar to the Low-Income Housing Tax Credit, which President Reagan brought into being in the 1986. Wyden's idea was the Middle-Income Housing Tax Credit, and it would do what the name implied: subsidizing the construction of units for renters who earned up to 100 percent of an area's median gross income.[14] By late 2023, Congress still hadn't approved his legislation, but the name changed to the Workforce Housing Tax Credit (WHTC). In an emailed statement, Wyden said, "Housing is so expensive in places like Portland and Bend, but also in Tillamook and Ashland," cities on the coast and in Southern Oregon, respectively, "that folks closer to the median income need help affording it, too. WHTC would help finance construction of hundreds of thousands of units of rental housing affordable at a wider variety of income levels." At the heart of the bill was the acknowledgment that the federal government had a role to play in spurring new home construction across many incomes as a way of keeping communities intact. As Wyden put it, "Folks want to get more housing built for everyone who needs it." The senator, full of trademark enthusiasm, comes off very much a YIMBY. "The U.S. needs a supply-side response to this severe lack of housing. We need to get this country building new housing again!" he said. He projected a level of optimism uncharacteristic of the DC rancor that often seethes from news headlines, saying, "I believe with cooperation and collaboration we can meet the challenge here, on behalf of low- and moderate-income households in dire need of affordable housing."[15]

Harvard's Joint Center for Housing Studies in July 2024 released a study on middle-income housing programs that had appeared in various forms around the nation. A main theme Harvard researchers took away after examining eleven local and state programs was, "Nearly all use a percent of AMI [area median income] threshold to determine eligibility, rather than employment status, occupation, or some other criteria, even when they are specifically billed as 'workforce housing' programs." Income thresholds varied widely. Kansas's Moderate Income Housing Program, crafted in 2012, was aimed at people making 60 to 150 percent AMI. Georgia's Rural Workforce Housing Initiative from 2023 was geared toward those earning as much as 100 percent AMI. "While a different program in terms of structure, the Georgia Rural Workforce Housing Initiative provided an estimated $24 million in infrastructure grants for local governments across three funding rounds that will enable the construction of just over 1,000 units, at a cost of roughly $23,000 per unit," the Harvard housing researchers found. "Through the Moderate Income Housing Program, Kansas provided about $27 million in funding for the development of 992 for-sale or rental units in 2023 alone, at about $27,000 per unit." These programs were getting some results at relatively low per-unit subsidies.[16] On the topic of in-come thresholds, Brooks, the Bend chamber leader, commented on a LinkedIn post about the Harvard study that she thought "the AMI range will vary with the market. In Central Oregon the land and home prices are so out of alignment with incomes that a wider range of AMI is needed - for sure up to 150%." Carly Colgan, the Bend-Redmond Habitat for Humanity CEO who had posted the study to LinkedIn, noted that middle-income housing was important for several reasons. Among the reasons: "A diverse community enriches our social fabric. Ensuring housing for middle-income families promotes a balanced and inclu-sive community where everyone's experiences and perspectives are valued." Colgan's point: Everyone needed somewhere to live.[17]

I found more potential solutions by looking to smaller corners of the West. Moab, Utah, had transformed into a tourism hub and, increasingly over the past decade, a place from which to telecommute. Housing pressures had borne problems much like Bend's. A group of researchers spent part of the pandemic studying so-called gateway communities: towns of, at most, 25,000 people and close to a national park or similar landmark. Researchers found that in Moab, "An acute housing shortage, especially workforce housing, means residents are being priced out of homeownership; new members of the community struggle to find adequate affordable housing; and tensions in the community arise when wealthier new residents, often remote workers, displace lower-income workers, triggering income inequality."[18] Moab's population was just over 5,300,[19] so it was well within the qualifications of a gateway community. One of the research-ers, the University of Arizona's Philip Stoker, told me some of the best ways to provide and protect affordable housing are usually top-down approaches such as implementing rent control and mandating that developers build a certain amount of affordable housing. He conceded the top-down tactics don't tend to play well in rural areas because people don't want to be told what to do with their land. And yet, he said, bottom-up market forces will often push sales to the highest bidder. Stoker said, "That's going to be a massive political challenge in all these communities is, reconciling the desire to protect community character, allow affordable housing, and decide between whether we want to set new poli-cies that are enforced at the municipal or county level that impose regulations on development. Or if we don't want those regulations, how on Earth are we going to get market forces to provide affordable housing, as opposed to devel-oping high-end condos that they can sell at a premium?"

Bend already had rent control thanks to Oregon's statewide law. But an-other novel approach by the Moab city council was worth flagging. Moab felt so squeezed that councillors in 2022 approved a regulation to ensure a third of homes inside proposed apartment projects within certain residential zones would, in essence, be set aside for local workers, just like in *Outside*'s fantastical Bluebird Valley. It was another instance of needing to wait to see how it turned out, but it also showed western governments' ability to pivot. One Moab council member, Kalen Jones, said of the so-called active employment household ordinance, "We need to use every arrow in the quiver, and then some, and hope that in thirty, fifty, or a hundred years, Moab still has the vibrant and diverse community of residents that makes it what it is, and isn't streets of dark houses, like so many other, similar communities that have had their real estate converted from homes into simple investment vehicles." Jones emphasized how the mandatory set-aside struck a balance between the different needs of different stakeholders, saying, "We can't solve this problem without the participation of the development community, and this change to our zoning code is a reasonable compromise between the needs of the community and developers, allowing high-density redevelopment to profitably continue while making a moderate contribution to the needs of the community."[20]

As winter approached, I contacted Lorelei Juntunen, who had put together the original 2017 report on Bend by ECOnorthwest. She was now the consultancy's president and chief executive. I called back to her 2017 report on the shortage of low- and moderate-income homes and asked what solutions she thought could work today. Her reply didn't take long. "I have a lot of thoughts on this, but the short version is that Bend should aggressively put its resources toward low- and moderate-income housing," she wrote in an extended email replete with bullet points and thick paragraphs. "Developers (and financers) will build to the price points that the market will bear—these units are going to get built without public support. These high-end homes are helpful to the overall market and are needed in Bend. If they weren't built, those households would instead occupy a home that might otherwise be affordable to a (slightly) lower-income household, creating a pinch all the way down the income chain. However, they don't need any help to get built."

Policy analyst Juntunen then addressed another concern I'd raised: the need to build quickly. "There are options for the public sector to work on building affordable units that are less cumbersome than the rent-restricted regulated approach that we are familiar with. Most of them require partnerships with non-public sector partners." She raised the prospect of utilizing an inclusionary housing policy. "Because of the nature of the market there," she said, "I'd guess

that Bend is one of the rare situations where some version of inclusionary housing could work—the market will build high-end homes all day long, and Bend
is in the position to ask for some giveaways (land, fees, several options) that
can go toward more affordable units, without affecting feasibility for the higher
end homes. Devil in the details of course. Another approach achieving the same
outcome is through public-private partnerships. In their urban renewal area, for
example, if they own or acquire land, they could put out an RFP [request for
proposals] to attract a developer but condition the development on the provision of some units that are affordable." Land trusts could also be a go: "Another
form of a partnership—work directly with a nonprofit land trust to get more affordable home ownership product built." Juntunen said such partnerships tend
to be best suited to moderate-income homes. I think of Rooted Homes, Jackie
Keogh, and the few workforce homes her organization developed in city limits.
And in fact, when Keogh and I caught up again in March 2024, she informed me
that Rooted Homes was planning to shift its focus outside of Bend and double
down on cities within the tri-county area.

"After we complete our sixtieth home in the city of Bend, which will be
done within the year, we have chosen to look outside of Bend to areas that are
more diverse, are more affordable to build in, and have limited other affordable
housing options. Think Redmond, Prineville, Madras, La Pine," Keogh said,
"and we've targeted those communities for those three reasons. . . . For us, it's
expensive and hard to build affordable housing, and we are going to work in
cities that make it less expensive and less hard, simply put."

I asked Keogh, "What do you think that says about Bend right now, and its
future?"

She said, "As a resident of Bend, it honestly concerns me about the impact
of the culture and the accessibility of the city. And if you take away accessibility
of all incomes that, to me personally, negatively impacts the culture, right, from
artists to local restaurant staff, folks who have made Bend desirable. And I am
interested to see in twenty years or even ten, what Bend looks like and who it's
accessible to. Because even me as a privileged, white, heterosexual woman, had
I not purchased my house when I did, I would not be welcome or able to be
working in this community."

ECOnorthwest's Juntunen had argued that the private market would inevitably build high-end homes, and those did serve a purpose: to ensure, at
least theoretically, that high earners weren't crowding into the middle- and
low-income supply. Juntunen said Bend should set its financial resources
toward middle-income housing while leaning on federal and state dollars

to build deeply affordable apartments. Rooted Homes' shift toward other Central Oregon cities underscored why Bend needed to focus its attention on the low- and middle-income subsets, and find ways to make those projects easier to transact. Striking, too, was the notion that, as the University of Arizona's Stoker had suggested, inclusionary housing could work well in destination towns. While private developers will churn out high-end housing left and right—the demand is clearly there from newcomers seeking trophy homes—could city or state leaders order builders to set aside some units as formally affordable?

Portland has tested inclusionary housing (IH). Under the policy, developers "include a certain number of affordable units in new residential buildings with 20 or more apartments or pay a fee." It's been contentious, with detractors saying it hampers new construction and the Portland Housing Bureau saying that without the program, we wouldn't have upwards of 1,100 affordable units going into private developments.[21] Juntunen's take vis-à-vis IH and Bend: "I'm not saying it would be more palatable to developers. They'll still hate it. I'm saying that market prices might be high enough that you could encumber development with some additional requirements without it tanking feasibility and killing the project. But the Oregon-specific approach," where the building must have twenty-plus units, "works less well in Bend—there just isn't that much development at that scale occurring in Bend. If you could have a more flexible approach to inclusionary like, for example, one that could apply in a master-planned community, in a way that might apply to homeownership, it could be worth considering."

The reporting from this book reveals a few key takeaways. Bend and cities like it could find themselves better positioned to meet the demands of burgeoning populations of mixed incomes if they lean into constructing deeply affordable housing and middle-income workforce housing. To spur homebuilding, government officials can continue to look for innovative ways to leverage state and federal resources, much like Oregon Housing and Community Services did with LIFT and the Low-Income Housing Tax Credit, in order to use taxpayer money as efficiently as possible and to the greatest effect. Officials can forge better channels of communication between state and local jurisdictions, especially across the Cascades, so resources and ideas flow when needed. Apartments, townhomes, and other missing middle housing can become regular in our land-constrained state, alongside smaller single-detached homes.[22]

▲ ▲ ▲

The places in which I've lived are the terrain of my mental geography. I think about them when I'm not thinking about them. They are images in the amber of my mind. One example: the 7-Eleven near Pilot Butte. My dad and I used to go there all the time to grab snacks and chicken wings. But the encasement cracks when I'm confronted with all the changes the city has undergone. Even before we came back to Bend the second time, when Kati and I went to high school, Jake's Diner moved from its truck stop on Highway 97 to the city's eastside in 2005.[23] The old space turned into a shopping center. Wheeling through town in 2023, I witnessed other transformations. There were a ton of roundabouts. New homebuilding appeared prolific as I drove over the pavement I'd known for years, to a point such that, on first blush, a casual observer might think Bend had enough homes. Some might go as far as to think there were too many. But the evidence I'd gathered over the past few years told a darker story.

I rolled past city limits and outward to Barlow Trail. From the driver's seat, parked on the roadside, I barely made out our old two-story home through the scraggly trees on the lot. But there it was, a dull and beautiful yellow. I wish every family who couldn't yet afford to buy could still afford to rent a single-detached place like my parents got for $1,200 a month, an absurdly low price these days. Honestly, the owner was probably undercharging on rent by the time my folks relocated in 2016. Not everyone will get a bargain basement price on a home that suits their family's needs. The standard should be an achievable life for all the people who make communities in the West work: retirees, families with kids, computer programmers, ski instructors. Living in a place like Bend shouldn't have to rely on luck, an out-of-town paycheck, or generational wealth.

I set out to write this book because I wanted to follow a few people over a long period of time, to get a deep, personal sense of how the housing crisis affected them. I couldn't control the outcomes; I recorded the events. I sought to examine the commonly proposed solutions. I investigated the benefits and drawbacks of increasing density via missing middle housing, of subsidizing affordable housing production with taxpayer money, of utilizing land trusts as a model for low-cost homeownership. I wanted to pool the ideas in one place for policymakers, academics, homebuilders, renters, and homeowners to think about. My other hope for this book is that it not only gets more people talking about the toll of the housing crunch, but also draws attention to the resilience of Bend residents and those of any town across the United States, however transformed their circumstances.

▲ ▲ ▲

To get to the house where Greg Delgado rented a spare upstairs bedroom from a homeowner nicknamed Jay for $600 a month in July 2023, two years after we first came in contact, I turned into a development called Providence in the Mountain View neighborhood just within Bend's easternmost limits. Delgado must have seen my car pull close to the house and guessed it was me. Before I emerged from the car, a text message appeared on my iPhone: "Hola." I walked to the home at the end of the cul-de-sac.

Delgado opened the door in a lime-green muscle shirt, appropriate to the sweltering summer. Threads of gray in his hair evidenced that Delgado had celebrated his fifty-ninth birthday a few days prior. I went inside, and he told me about the party. It was the first time he had guests over since moving in. Celebrations started at 5:00 p.m., and about twenty people showed up. They crafted miniature Day of the Dead altars. Delgado made ceviche, carne asada, smoked salmon dip, and chunky salsa. There was a piñata and cake. One guest brought a few bottles of rosé, another friend a bottle of tequila. "I felt at home again," Delgado said. His demeanor was mellow as we caught up, seated in the living room. He relaxed in a chair. "The last three years have been like, 'Where is home?' and 'What does that feel like?' and feeling very transitory. I still feel somewhat transitory, but at least here, I feel a little grounded, and I feel comfortable." There were signs of his settling in. In the garage was a bike he had just bought. There were planters in the backyard, where he'd planted squash and corn. He tended to pass time either in his bedroom or on his laptop at the downstairs kitchen table, which was pushed up against a wall with a windowed view of the backyard.

In the living room, I asked Delgado how secure he felt. "At this point," he said, "I'm just blessed to be back in Bend." He'd prefer to live downtown again, because he loves to walk, and being on the edge of town is too far out for him. "But I'm blessed to be back in Bend," he repeated, "and I have to make sacrifices. So I accept that. But also, this is Jay's house." He said, "It's not a permanent housing situation for me. So that's still up in the air. It's like, where am I going to go next?" He still had the Ford shuttle bus on his father's property in Arizona to convert into something habitable. So far the old flooring was ripped out. He said, "Right now, I don't envision myself being able to afford a home ever." Eventually, he allowed, he might find somewhere to rent. "I don't know. I don't have the luxury of thinking ten years ahead. I'm just thinking of what I can do now. Like I said, I'm going to build that shuttle bus and go from there and see what I can do with that."

We walked to the second floor. Delgado showed me his room on the left side of the staircase. He typically watched television downstairs, but when he wanted to be by himself, his room had a small set with bunny-ear antennae by a wall. This was his "nest," a place to be alone, a place to clear his head, a place to turn off the lights and sleep. He'd doze off comfortably to the news. The room was decorated to his taste. A tapestry on the wall by the bed was strong with Día de Muertos imagery. A rose bloomed on the forehead of a broad-smiling skull and other skeletons danced all along the tapestry's border. He likes the holiday so much because it celebrates life. From the closet, he proudly withdrew one of his Nike Cortez Day of the Dead sneakers, the edition that was gray with a black Nike emblem. "Ain't that badass?" Delgado showed off the shoe. "Look, they even have skulls on the inside." He understood his life might continue on the move. Who knew how long he'd stay upstairs with his stuff?

The answer came the following January. Delgado texted me a video of an apartment he was renting for $1,720 a month—nearly double the $900 from Northwest Greeley Avenue and right in line with his prediction after the eviction, an eviction that thankfully didn't give him any trouble. He got into the single-bedroom place near Pilot Butte, and his phone camera showed a bunny-eared TV playing and a big comfy armchair and couch as he panned around the living room.

Delgado said: "My new home."

Notes

PREFACE

1   Kelli Rush Bach, Facebook post, November 6, 2016, https://www.facebook.
    com/1231611588/posts/pfbidoq83vqYskwt6BVNMNs6zX5jmPN4DZq17GBviB-
    VEu1aKjbUobU45hBccPf5zrRaCYel/?app=fbl.
2   Bach, Facebook post.
3   Dana Anderson, "Millennials Still Want Single-Family Homes,
    Even If It Means A Long Commute," Redfin News, November 21,
    2019 (updated October 6, 2020), https://www.redfin.com/news/
    millennial-homebuyers-prefer-single-family-homes/.
4   Redfin, "Redfin Survey: Millennials Still Want Single-Family Homes, Even if it
    Means a Long Commute," Cision PR Newswire, November 21, 2019, https://www.
    prnewswire.com/news-releases/redfin-survey-millennials-still-want-single-family-
    homes-even-if-it-means-a-long-commute-300962745.html.
5   Redfin, "Redfin Survey: Millennials Still Want Single-Family Homes, Even if it
    Means a Long Commute."
6   Sam Khater, Len Kiefer, and Venkataramana Yanamandra, "Housing Supply:
    A Growing Deficit," Freddie Mac, May 7, 2021, https://www.freddiemac.com/
    research/insight/20210507-housing-supply.
7   Adewale A. Maye and Kyle K. Moore, "The growing housing sup-
    ply shortage has created a housing affordability crisis," Economic
    Policy Institute, July 14, 2022, https://www.epi.org/blog/
    the-growing-housing-supply-shortage-has-created-a-housing-affordability-crisis/.
8   Lorelei Juntunen, "Landscape Report: Bend 2030," ECONorthwest,
    February 2017, 10, https://www.bendoregon.gov/home/
    showpublisheddocument/33009/636475427024930000.
9   Senator Ron Wyden's responses to my questions for this book came in an email
    from his spokesperson. Linea Gagliano, email to author, December 18, 2023.

CHAPTER 1

1   fortheloveofoldhouses, "304 NW Hunter Place, Bend, Oregon 97703," Instagram,
    October 19, 2023, https://www.instagram.com/p/CylUtRvr9y8/?img_index=1.
2   Liz Goodrich, "Know Home: Historic Homes of Bend," Deschutes Public Library,
    May 7, 2014, accessed October 8, 2023, https://www.deschuteslibrary.org/about/
    news/news?newsid=5581.
3   fortheloveofoldhouses, "304 NW Hunter Place, Bend, Oregon 97703."
4   See Josh Lehner, "Bend and Central Oregon, 2015 Update," Oregon Office
    of Economic Analysis, July 24, 2015, https://oregoneconomicanalysis.
    com/2015/07/24/bend-and-central-oregon-2015-update/. Lehner's commen-
    tary, discussed further in this chapter, arrived in 2015. The evidence as of 2023

showed that homebuilding did not accelerate quickly enough to stop prices from skyrocketing.

5   "304 NW Hunter Pl, Bend, OR 97703," Zillow, accessed November 6, 2023 and January 28, 2024, https://www.zillow.com/homedetails/304-NW-Hunter-Pl-Bend-OR-97703/60596196_zpid/.

6   Marli B. Miller, *Roadside Geology of Oregon*, 2nd ed. (Missoula: Mountain Press Publishing Company, 2014), 111.

7   Raymond R. Hatton, *High Country of Central Oregon*, 2nd ed. (Portland: Binford & Mort Publishing, 1987), 1.

8   Miller, *Roadside Geology of Oregon*, 111.

9   William G. Robbins, "Willamette Valley," Oregon Encyclopedia, updated July 31, 2023, https://www.oregonencyclopedia.org/articles/willamette_valley/.

10   Raymond R. Hatton, *Bend in Central Oregon*, 2nd ed. (Portland: Binford & Mort Publishing, 1986), 1.

11   Confederated Tribes of Warm Springs, "Bend Land Acknowledgement," City of Bend, accessed April 30, 2023, https://www.bendoregon.gov/government/city-council/land-acknowledgement.

12   "History," Confederated Tribes of Warm Springs, accessed April 30, 2023, https://warmsprings-nsn.gov/history/.

13   Hatton, *Bend in Central Oregon*, 11.

14   "Pilot Butte State Scenic Viewpoint," Oregon State Parks, accessed April 8, 2023, https://stateparks.oregon.gov/index.cfm?do=park.profile&parkId=33; "Pilot Butte State Scenic Viewpoint," Oregon State Parks, park brochure and map, 1–2, accessed June 18, 2023, https://stateparks.oregon.gov/index.cfm?do=main.loadFile&load=_siteFiles%2Fpublications%2FPilot_Butte_trail_and_interpretive_guide_Web_LOW_RES125826.pdf.

15   "Bend Early History," City of Bend, accessed April 30, 2023, 1, https://www.bendoregon.gov/Home/ShowDocument?id=29353.

16   Jason Stone, "Bend Bulletin," Historic Oregon Newspapers at the University of Oregon Libraries, accessed October 16, 2023, https://oregonnews.uoregon.edu/history/bendbulletin.

17   "Salutatory," *Bend Bulletin* (hereafter *Bulletin*), March 27, 1903, https://oregonnews.uoregon.edu/lccn/sn96088235/1903-03-27/ed-1/seq-2/.

18   Hatton, *Bend in Central Oregon*, 25–27.

19   City of Bend, "Bend Early History," 1.

20   Jonathan Bach, "High Desert, Higher Costs: The Dark Side of Bend's Runaway Housing Market," *Portland Business Journal*, May 13, 2021, https://www.bizjournals.com/portland/news/2021/05/13/bend-oregon-home-prices-poverty-with-a-view.html.

21   "No Drake Park Wasn't Named after the Ducks," *Bulletin*, May 29, 1981, 5, https://news.google.com/newspapers?id=JLVYAAAAIBAJ&sjid=Q_cDAAAAIBAJ&pg=6443%2C4495988; "Bend's Founder Left an Indelible Mark during His Stay," *Bend Magazine*, accessed October 7, 2023, https://bendmagazine.com/bends-founder-left-an-indelible-mark-during-his-stay/.

22   "Bend's Founder Left an Indelible Mark during His Stay."

23   "No Drake Park Wasn't Named after the Ducks."

24   "Bend's Founder Left an Indelible Mark during His Stay"; Deschutes County Historical Society, *Bend* (Charleston, SC: Arcadia Publishing, 2009), 18.

25   See Deschutes County Historical Society, *Bend*, 18, for a historical photo of Alexander Drake.

26 "No Drake Park Wasn't Named after the Ducks."

27 Deschutes County Historical Society, *Bend*, 18.

28 Quoted in Hatton, *Bend in Central Oregon*, 29.

29 Kenneth T. Jackson, *Crabgrass Frontier: The Suburbanization of the United States* (New York: Oxford University Press, Inc., 1985), 54–55.

30 Roderick Frazier Nash, *Wilderness and the American Mind*, 5th ed. (New Haven: Yale University Press, 2014), 44, 67; The Editors of Encyclopedia Britannica, "Romanticism," *Encyclopedia Britannica*, December 26, 2023, https://www.britannica.com/art/Romanticism.

31 Thomas R. Cox, *The Other Oregon: People, Environment, and History East of the Cascades* (Corvallis: Oregon State University Press, 2019), 103.

32 "Bend's Founder Left an Indelible Mark during His Stay."

33 Bach, "High Desert, Higher Costs."

34 *1911 Blue Book*, commemorative edition, compiled and issued by Secretaries of State Frank W. Benson and Ben W. Olcott (Salem, OR: Willis S. Duniway, State Printer, 1911; 2011), 13.

35 *Bulletin*, December 4, 1912, quoted in Hatton, *Bend in Central Oregon*, 54.

36 Benson and Olcott, *1911 Blue Book*, 9–11.

37 "History of Bend's Old Mill District – Our Story," Old Mill District, accessed April 7, 2023, https://www.oldmilldistrict.com/about/history/; Hatton, *Bend in Central Oregon*, 58.

38 *Bulletin*, January 19, 1916, quoted in Hatton, *Bend in Central Oregon*, 58.

39 Hatton, *Bend in Central Oregon*, 58.

40 Old Mill District, "History of Bend's Old Mill District – Our Story."

41 Cox, *The Other Oregon*, xii, 103–104.

42 For styles and proliferation of historic housing types, see Deschutes Historical Museum manager Vanessa Ivey, email to author, October 10, 2023. Ivey cited research by Michael Houser, a former local historic preservation planner, in her email.

43 Joshua Binus, "Shevlin-Hixon and Brooks-Scanlon Mills, Bend," Oregon History Project, a project of the Oregon Historical Society, accessed April 7, 2023, https://www.oregonhistoryproject.org/articles/historical-records/shevlin-hixon-and-brooks-scanlon-mills-bend/#.ZDCw3-zMLFp.

44 Hatton, *Bend in Central Oregon*, 43.

45 *Bulletin*, January 12, 1910, quoted in Hatton, *Bend in Central Oregon*, 43.

46 Hatton, *High Country of Central Oregon*, xi.

47 Hatton, *High Country of Central Oregon*, back cover.

48 Scott Hammers, "COCC professor, Masters Runner Hatton Dead at 83," *Bulletin*, March 11, 2015 (updated January 31, 2020), https://www.bendbulletin.com/local-state/cocc-professor-masters-runner-hatton-dead-at-83/article_5dcdf4bd-d85a-5511-8dac-add2507383d9.html.

49 Cox, *The Other Oregon*, 244.

50 Hatton, *Bend in Central Oregon*, vii.

51 Cox, *The Other Oregon*, 244–245.

52 Cox, *The Other Oregon*, 245; Ryanne Pilgeram, *Pushed Out: Contested Development and Rural Gentrification in the US West* (Seattle: University of Washington Press, 2021), 124–127.

53 Nash, *Wilderness and the American Mind*, 143.

54 Hatton, *Bend in Central Oregon*, 65.

55   "William H. Staats, Bend Pioneer, Dies in 1931," *Bulletin*, May 28, 2006, https://www.bendbulletin.com/lifestyle/william-h-staats-bend-pioneer-dies-in-1931/article_9f498500-2c49-52c9-a393-c910efa43059.html.

56   Hatton, *Bend in Central Oregon*, 65–66.

57   "Theodore Roosevelt and Conservation," National Park Service, updated November 16, 2017, https://www.nps.gov/thro/learn/historyculture/theodore-roosevelt-and-conservation.htm.

58   *Bulletin*, August 4, 1919, quoted in Hatton, *Bend in Central Oregon*, 66.

59   "Outplay Culture," Mount Bachelor, accessed July 24, 2023, https://www.mtbachelor.com/culture/outplay-culture/origins.

60   Tiah Edmunson-Morton, "Brewing Industry in Oregon," Oregon Encyclopedia, accessed June 18, 2023 (updated December 27, 2022), , https://www.oregonencyclopedia.org/articles/brewing-industry-in-oregon/.

61   Suzanne Roig, "Bill Smith, Architect of Bend's Old Mill District, Dies, Leaves Lasting Legacy," *Bulletin*, November 19, 2022, https://www.bendbulletin.com/localstate/bill-smith-architect-of-bends-old-mill-district-dies-leaves-lasting-legacy/article_077b5cb4-6856-11ed-a7cb-5bbaccf4498d.html#tncms-source=login; "Bill Smith Devoted Life's Work to Bend and Central Oregon," *Bend Magazine*, accessed October 17, 2023, https://bendmagazine.com/old-mill-district-developer-bend-bill-smith/.

62   Cox, *The Other Oregon*, xii, 244–248.

63   "Bend Housing Needs Analysis," City of Bend, August 31, 2016, 1–2, https://www.bendoregon.gov/home/showpublisheddocument/41161/636905768242400000.

64   "Comprehensive Housing Market Analysis Bend-Redmond, Oregon," US Department of Housing and Urban Development, September 1, 2021, 18, https://www.huduser.gov/portal/publications/pdf/BendRedmondOR-CHMA-21.pdf.

65   The Investopedia Team, "2008 Recession: What It Was and What Caused It," Investopedia, April 30, 2023, https://www.investopedia.com/terms/g/great-recession.asp.

66   Lehner, "Bend and Central Oregon, 2015 Update."

67   Associated Press, "Oregon's Recession is 'Poverty with a View,'" OregonLive, July 20, 2009, https://www.oregonlive.com/news/2009/07/oregons_recession_is_poverty_w.html.

68   Bach, "High Desert, Higher Costs."

69   Adam Hadi, "Construction Employment Peaks before the Recession and Falls Sharply throughout It," US Bureau of Labor Statistics, *Monthly Labor Review*, April 2011, 24, https://www.bls.gov/opub/mlr/2011/04/art4full.pdf.

70   "Comprehensive Housing Market Analysis Bend-Redmond, Oregon," US Department of Housing and Urban Development, August 1, 2018, 7, https://www.huduser.gov/portal/publications/pdf/Bend-RedmondOR-CHMA-18.pdf.

71   Adam Brookes, "Economic Crash in Oregon Boomtown," BBC News, updated September 4, 2009, http://news.bbc.co.uk/1/hi/8239227.stm.

72   "Comprehensive Housing Market Analysis Bend-Redmond, Oregon," US Department of Housing and Urban Development, September 1, 2021, 8–9, https://www.huduser.gov/portal/publications/pdf/BendRedmondOR-CHMA-21.pdf.

73   City of Bend, "Bend Housing Needs Analysis," 1, 15.

74   City of Bend, "Bend Housing Needs Analysis," 24–25.

75   Lehner, "Bend and Central Oregon, 2015 Update."

76   City of Bend, "Bend Housing Needs Analysis," 1–2.

77 Sean Meyers, "Women of Influence 2021: Lorelei Juntunen, ECONorthwest," *Portland Business Journal*, April 7, 2021, https://www.bizjournals.com/portland/news/2021/04/07/women-of-influence-2021-lorelei-juntunen.html.

78 Lorelei Juntunen, "Landscape Report: Bend 2030," ECONorthwest, February 2017, 4–6, https://www.bendoregon.gov/home/showpublisheddocument/33009/636475427024930000.

79 Juntunen, "Landscape Report: Bend 2030," 7–8.

80 Juntunen, "Landscape Report: Bend 2030," 9–10.

81 Juntunen, "Landscape Report: Bend 2030," 10–11; Lehner, "Bend and Central Oregon, 2015 Update."

82 Juntunen, "Landscape Report: Bend 2030," 15.

83 Brenna Visser, "City of Bend Creeps Closer to Housing Goal," *Bulletin*, December 24, 2019 (updated January 28, 2021), https://www.bendbulletin.com/localstate/city-of-bend-creeps-closer-to-housing-goal/article_7641b7e2-268c-11ea-a73e-b35ed24b2f54.html.

84 Emily Cureton Cook, "Bend Bulletin Owners Plan To Sell Everything and Dissolve the Company," Oregon Public Broadcasting, May 23, 2019, https://www.opb.org/news/article/bend-bulletin-owners-plans-dissolve-company-sell-newspapers/.

85 Phil Wright, "EO Media Group buys Bend Bulletin," *East Oregonian*, July 29, 2019, https://www.eastoregonian.com/news/local/eo-media-group-buys-bend-bulletin/article_e7907dfa-b20d-11e9-a9b2-4be6e2beadab.html.

86 Hatton, *Bend in Central Oregon*, 58.

87 Bach, "High Desert, Higher Costs."

CHAPTER 2

1   Colleen Sinsky, "The Rookie," JOIN PDX, October 15, 2010, https://joinpdx.org/the-rookie/.

2   Colleen Sinsky, "Interrupting Isolation," *Street Roots*, August 16, 2014, https://www.streetroots.org/news/2014/08/16/interrupting-isolation.

3   Colleen Sinsky, "Two Years of Vagabonding," *I'd Rather Be Here Now* (blog), October 1, 2016, https://colleensinsky.com/2016/10/01/two-years-of-vagabonding/.

4   Colleen Sinsky, "16 Things I Learned in 2016," *I'd Rather Be Here Now* (blog), January 5, 2017, https://colleensinsky.com/2017/01/05/16-things-i-learned-in-2016/.

5   Colleen Sinsky, "Guest Column: Bend's Housing Market is Forcing Me to Leave," *Bulletin*, November 13, 2020, https://www.bendbulletin.com/opinion/guest-column-bends-housing-market-is-forcing-me-to-leave/article_ba6155c8-2509-11eb-bff7-1fc114071f96.html.

6   Jonathan Bach, "High Desert, Higher Costs: The Dark Side of Bend's Runaway Housing Market," *Portland Business Journal*, May 13, 2021, https://www.bizjournals.com/portland/news/2021/05/13/bend-oregon-home-prices-poverty-with-a-view.html.

7   Bach, "High Desert, Higher Costs."

8   "2021 Impact Report," Central Oregon FUSE, accessed May 21, 2023, 2, 10, https://static1.squarespace.com/static/62d59a924c9c8000b94ea704/t/62e0336b2aecf74ea58dd2f2/1658860413379/FUSE+Impact+Report+2021.pdf.

9   "2021 Impact Report," 8.

10 "Permanent Supportive Housing," Oregon Housing and Community Services, accessed February 15, 2024, https://www.oregon.gov/ohcs/development/pages/

permanent-supportive-housing.aspx#:~:text=The%20objective%20of%20the%20
PSH,serve%20households%20experiencing%20chronic%20homelessness..

11   "2021 Impact Report," 8.

12   "Deschutes County Invests More Than $4.9 Million in Relief Funds,"
      Deschutes County, September 1, 2021, https://www.deschutes.org/bcc/page/
      deschutes-county-invests-more-49-million-relief-funds.

13   US Department of Housing and Urban Development, "Homeless Emergency
      Assistance and Rapid Transition to Housing: Defining 'Chronically Homeless,'"
      Federal Register 80, no. 233 (December 4, 2015): 7579175806, https://www.govinfo.
      gov/content/pkg/FR-2015-12-04/pdf/2015-30473.pdf.

14   "Definition of Chronic Homelessness," US Department of Housing and
      Urban Development, accessed May 21, 2023, https://www.hudexchange.info/
      homelessness-assistance/coc-esg-virtual-binders/coc-esg-homeless-eligibility/
      definition-of-chronic-homelessness/.

15   "Definition of Chronic Homelessness."

16   Conor Dougherty, Golden Gates: The Housing Crisis and a Reckoning
      for the American Dream (New York: Penguin Press, 2020; 2021),
      xxviii; Jenny Schuetz, "Oregon's New Rent Control Law is Only
      a Band-Aid on the State's Housing Woes," Brookings, March 1,
      2019, https://www.brookings.edu/blog/the-avenue/2019/03/01/
      oregons-new-rent-control-law-is-only-a-band-aid-on-the-states-housing-woes/.

17   David Madden and Peter Marcuse, In Defense of Housing (London: Verso, 2016), 17.

18   "Report of the Special Rapporteur on Adequate Housing as a Component
      of the Right to an Adequate Standard of Living, and on the Right to
      Non-Discrimination in This Context," United Nations, January 18,
      2017, 21, https://www.ohchr.org/en/documents/thematic-reports/
      ahrc3451-report-special-rapporteur-adequate-housing-component-right.

19   Adewale A. Maye and Kyle K. Moore, "The Growing Housing
      Supply Shortage Has Created a Housing Affordability Crisis,"
      Economic Policy Institute, July 14, 2022, https://www.epi.org/blog/
      the-growing-housing-supply-shortage-has-created-a-housing-affordability-crisis/.

20   Madden and Marcuse, In Defense of Housing, 82.

21   See also Matthew Desmond, Evicted: Poverty and Profit in the American City (New
      York: Crown Publishers, 2016), 299. As Desmond writes, "Poor families are living
      above their means, in apartments they cannot afford. The thing is, those apartments
      are already at the bottom of the market. Our cities have become unaffordable to
      our poorest families, and this problem is leaving a deep and jagged scar on the next
      generation."

22   Annie Nova, "How to Move on after an Eviction," CNBC, February 28, 2022,
      https://www.cnbc.com/2022/02/28/how-to-move-on-after-an-eviction-.html.
      Nova quoted a National Consumer Law Center staff attorney as saying, "Some
      landlords automatically deny applications based on eviction records regardless of
      outcome or context."

23   Desmond, Evicted, 296–299.

24   For a brief summary of the federal and state COVID-19 eviction moratoria around
      this time, see Jonathan Bach, "Federal Residential Eviction Moratorium Gets
      Another Extension, Likely the Last," Portland Business Journal, June 24, 2021,
      https://www.bizjournals.com/portland/news/2021/06/24/federal-eviction-
      moratorium-extension.html.

25 "Team," 350Deschutes, accessed February 16, 2024, https://350deschutes.org/about/team/.

26 US Census Bureau, "Oregon - Congressional District 2, Representative Greg Walden," accessed July 7, 2024, https://www2.census.gov/geo/maps/cong_dist/cd113/cd_based/ST41/CD113_OR02.pdf.

27 KTVZ News Team, "Rep. Walden Makes Swing through C. Oregon," KTVZ, January 20, 2014, https://ktvz.com/news/2014/01/20/rep-walden-makes-swing-through-c-oregon/.

28 City of Bend Police Department, *Case Report*, Scot Eliott, Case # 2014-00150112, Bend, Oregon: 2014, obtained by author under public records request in March 2023; Greg Delgado, email to author, March 20, 2023.

29 *State of Oregon vs. Gregorio Delgado (Case No. MI141498)*, disposition, August 6, 2014.

30 Greg Delgado for Senate, "About Greg Delgado for Senate," Facebook page, accessed May 20, 2023, https://www.facebook.com/degladoforsenate/about/?ref=page_internal.

31 US Census Bureau, "Bend city, Oregon," *Quick Facts*, accessed May 20, 2023, https://www.census.gov/quickfacts/bendcityoregon.

32 Jerry Garcia, "Latinos in Oregon," Oregon Encyclopedia, accessed October 17, 2023, https://www.oregonencyclopedia.org/articles/hispanics_in_oregon/; "Cape Blanco State Park," Oregon State Parks, accessed October 17, 2023, https://stateparks.oregon.gov/index.cfm?do=park.profile&parkId=44.

33 "Latinos in Central Oregon: A Community Profile in Statistics & Stories," Latino Community Association, October 2020, 5, 7, 10–11, https://latinocommunityas-sociation.org/wp-content/uploads/Latinos-in-Central-Oregon-10-11-20.pdf.

34 "Endorsements: State Senate District 27 & Measure 99," *Source Weekly*, October 12, 2016, https://www.bendsource.com/bend/endorsements-state-senate-district-27-and-measure-99/Content?oid=2765208.

35 "Editorial: Tim Knopp for State Senate," *Bulletin*, October 18, 2016 (updated Jan 31, 2020), https://www.bendbulletin.com/opinion/editorial-tim-knopp-for-state-senate/article_0f20918e-6e91-58ce-bb78-1af019c1b5e7.html.

36 Joshua Langlais, podcast interview with Greg Delgado, *A Community Thread*, accessed April 30, 2023, https://acommunitythread.com/greg-delgado.

37 Greg Delgado, "Re: Support for SB 608, Tenant Protections," Public Testimony, January 19, 2019, https://olis.oregonlegislature.gov/liz/2019R1/Downloads/CommitteeMeetingDocument/156280; Cait Boyce, in discussion with the author, October 2023; Greg Delgado, in discussion with the author, July 2021.

38 "Sales for account # 104483," Deschutes County Property Information, sale date September 15, 2021, https://dial.deschutes.org/Real/Sales/104483; Amended Annual Report for Second Half Enterprises, LLC, Oregon Secretary of State, e-filed December 3, 2021, 2, http://records.sos.state.or.us/ORSOSWebDrawer/Recordhtml/8434672; David McDonald, in discussion with the author, July 2024.

39 *Partners Property Management & Sales vs. Greg Delgado, et al. (Case No. 21LT01791)*, Plaintiff's Response to Defendant's ORCP 21A(8) Motion to Dismiss, 2.

40 *Partners Property Management & Sales vs. Greg Delgado, et al. (Case No. 21LT01791)*, Complaint, 1–3.

41 "Our Mission," Oregon Law Center, accessed February 25, 2024, https://oregon-lawcenter.org/about-olc/our-mission/.

42 *Partners Property Management & Sales vs. Greg Delgado, et al. (Case No. 21LT01791)*, audio recording of trial, June 3, 2021, obtained by author under public records request.

43 *Partners Property Management & Sales vs. Greg Delgado, et al. (Case No. 21LT01791)*, Motion for a Stay of Execution Pending Appeal and Setting Supersedeas Execution of Judgment Undertaking at Amount of Monthly Rent, June 8, 2021, 1–4.

44 *Partners Property Management & Sales vs. Greg Delgado, et al. (Case No. 21LT01791)*, Defendant Gregory Delgado's Declaration in Support of Defendant's Motion for a Stay of Execution Pending Appeal and Setting Supersedeas Execution of Judgment Undertaking at Amount of Monthly Rent, June 8, 2021.

45 "Settlement Agreement and Release of Claims" between Greg Delgado and Partners Property Management & Sales, June 11, 2021, copy obtained by author.

46 David McDonald, in discussion with the author, July 2024; "Sales for account # 104483," Deschutes County Property Information, sale date September 15, 2021, https://dial.deschutes.org/Real/Sales/104483.

47 See "How Does Eviction Affect Credit Scores?," Equifax, accessed January 15, 2024, https://www.equifax.com/personal/education/credit/score/articles/-/learn/how-does-eviction-affect-credit-score/.

48 Bryan Denson, "Christopher Boyce, Whose Spy Work Inspired 'The Falcon and the Snowman,' Finds Happiness in Oregon," OregonLive, March 6, 2014, https://www.oregonlive.com/politics/2014/03/christopher_boyce_who_inspired.html; Cait Boyce, in discussion with the author, October 2023.

49 MIG and ECOnorthwest, "City of Bend Housing Capacity Analysis 2025 to 2045 (DRAFT)," City of Bend, June 22, 2023, 25, https://www.bendoregon.gov/home/showpublisheddocument/56418/638252019592070000.

CHAPTER 3

1 D'Vera Cohn, "About a Fifth of U.S. Adults Moved Due to COVID-19 or Know Someone Who Did," Pew Research Center, July 6, 2020, https://www.pewresearch.org/fact-tank/2020/07/06/about-a-fifth-of-u-s-adults-moved-due-to-covid-19-or-know-someone-who-did/.

2 Conor Sen, "Booming 'Zoom Towns' Should Ease City Housing Costs," Bloomberg, August 5, 2020, https://www.bloomberg.com/opinion/articles/2020-08-05/remote-work-from-resort-towns-eases-housing-costs-in-big-cities.

3 Lilly Smith, "'Zoom Towns' are Exploding in the West," Fast Company, October 17, 2020, https://www.fastcompany.com/90564796/zoom-towns-are-exploding-in-the-west.

4 Greg Rosalsky, "Zoom Towns and the New Housing Market For the 2 Americas," NPR, September 8, 2020, https://www.npr.org/sections/money/2020/09/08/909680016/zoom-towns-and-the-new-housing-market-for-the-2-americas.

5 Lance Eliot, "Self-Driving Cars to Be Especially Welcomed in 'Zoom Towns,'" Forbes, March 12, 2021, https://www.forbes.com/sites/lanceeliot/2021/03/12/self-driving-cars-to-be-especially-welcomed-in-zoom-towns/?sh=430b35b37b29.

6 Ryanne Pilgeram, *Pushed Out: Contested Development and Rural Gentrification in the US West* (Seattle: University of Washington Press, 2021), 133–135.

7   "The Changing Needs of the West," Committee on Natural Resources House of
    Representatives, April 7, 1994, 69, https://www.govinfo.gov/content/pkg/CHRG-
    103hhrg79996/pdf/CHRG-103hhrg79996.pdf.

8   Colorado Office of Economic Development and International Trade,
    "VF Corporation Chooses Colorado as its New Global Headquarters,"
    Colorado Office of Economic Development and International Trade
    news release, August 13, 2018, https://oedit.colorado.gov/press-release/
    vf-corporation-chooses-colorado-as-its-new-global-headquarters.

9   Billy Duss, LinkedIn post, accessed May 18, 2023, https://www.linkedin.
    com/posts/billyduss_some-news-after-11-years-in-seattle-i-will-activity-
    6772588570483027968-wgNa?utm_source=share&utm_medium=member_desk-
    top.

10 Jonathan Bach, "High Desert, Higher Costs: The Dark Side of Bend's Runaway
    Housing Market," *Portland Business Journal*, May 13, 2021, https://www.bizjournals.
    com/portland/news/2021/05/13/bend-oregon-home-prices-poverty-with-a-view.
    html.

11 Damon Runberg, "Central Oregon Migration Patterns Before the Onset of the
    Pandemic," Oregon Employment Department, February 2022, originally accessed
    at https://www.qualityinfo.org/-/central-oregon-migration-patterns-before-the-
    onset-of-the-pandemic, copy obtained by public records request after hyperlink
    failed.

12 Brenna Visser, "State of the City: From Boom Town to 'Zoom Town,'" *Bulletin*,
    October 29, 2021 (updated December 4, 2021), https://www.bendbulletin.com/
    localstate/state-of-the-city-from-boom-town-to-zoom-town/article_0b781176-
    1a3e-11eb-ae88-cf8866bebd93.html; Bach, "High Desert, Higher Costs."

13 Kathleen McLaughlin, "Bend-Redmond Area Has Numerous Home-Based
    Workers," *Bulletin*, April 6, 2018 (updated January 31, 2020), https://www.bendbul-
    letin.com/business/bend-redmond-area-has-numerous-home-based-workers/
    article_8b35b576-595a-530f-bfc5-c2758dab4900.html.

14 See also, "Zoom Towns Appear to Be Real and Pandemic-Related Migration Looks
    to be Doubling Down on Existing Patterns of Growth," from Josh Lehner, "Zoom
    Towns are Real (Graph of the Week)," Oregon Office of Economic Analysis,
    October 27, 2020, https://oregoneconomicanalysis.com/2020/10/27/zoom-
    towns-are-real-graph-of-the-week/; see chapter 1 for extensive discussion of Bend's
    housing history and Lorelei Juntunen's ECOnorthwest report on low- and middle-
    income housing shortages.

CHAPTER 4

1   Hops_n_Boost, "STR" on r/Bend, Reddit, July 5, 2023, https://www.reddit.com/r/
    Bend/comments/14rrd47/str/.

2   Suzanne Moore, "30 Day Rental Transformation," Central Oregon Investor
    Network, accessed May 8, 2023, https://www.centraloregoninvestornetwork.com/
    learn/30-day-rental-transformation.

3   "Home," Central Oregon Investor Network, accessed May 8, 2023, https://www.
    centraloregoninvestornetwork.com/.

4   Sadie DiNatale, Rebecca Lewis, and Robert Parker, "Short-Term Rentals in Small
    Cities in Oregon: Impacts and Regulations," *Land Use Policy* 79 (December 2018):
    414, https://doi.org/10.1016/j.landusepol.2018.08.023.

5   Kromm Real Estate Team, "How to Manage a Bend OR Vacation Rental
      – Yourself," YouTube video, 13:01, July 7, 2022, https://www.youtube.com/
      watch?v=hfcJ8Gjbeoo.

6   "2022 Short Term Rental (STR) Code Amendments," City of
      Bend, accessed May 8, 2023, https://www.bendoregon.gov/home/
      showpublisheddocument/53834/638043485538400000.

7   City of Bend, "City Council Meeting," Video, 2:04:06, March 2, 2022, https://bend.
      granicus.com/player/clip/687?view_id=9&meta_id=56654&redirect=true&h=dbc
      920664bf1631c111d8bc6b559ac10.

8   Kromm Real Estate Team, "Newest STR Regulations Coming to BEND
      OR," YouTube video, 9:03, August 25, 2022, https://www.youtube.com/
      watch?v=Rx4p-Kv4-VA.

9   City of Bend, "City Council Meeting."

10   Kromm Real Estate Team, "Newest STR regulations coming to BEND OR."

11   City of Bend, "Bend City Council Approves Changes to Short Term Rental Rules,"
      October 5, 2022, https://www.bendoregon.gov/Home/Components/News/
      News/5463/29.

12   City of Bend, "Bend City Council Approves Changes to Short Term Rental Rules."

13   DiNatale, Lewis, and Parker, "Short-Term Rentals in Small Cities in Oregon,"
      407–408, 413.

14   City of Bend, "Bend City Council Approves Changes to Short Term Rental Rules."

15   DiNatale, Lewis, and Parker, "Short-Term Rentals in Small Cities in Oregon," 414.

16   City of Bend, "City Council Meeting."

17   HUDchannel, "PD&R Quarterly Update - Institutional Investors in Housing,"
      YouTube video, 1:39:58, December 8, 2022, https://www.youtube.com/
      watch?v=HWkNTTr_X8c&t=342s.

18   Jerusalem Demsas, "Meet the Latest Housing-Crisis Scapegoat," *Atlantic*,
      January 26, 2023, https://www.theatlantic.com/ideas/archive/2023/01/
      housing-crisis-hedge-funds-private-equity-scapegoat/672839/.

19   Lorelei Juntunen, "Landscape Report: Bend 2030," ECOnorthwest,
      February 2017, 8–10, https://www.bendoregon.gov/home/
      showpublisheddocument/33009/636475427024930000.

20   Josh Lehner, Twitter post, October 16, 2022, 8:13 p.m., https://x.com/lehnerjw/
      status/1581845758869143552; Josh Lehner, Twitter post, October 16, 2022, 8:22 p.m.,
      https://x.com/lehnerjw/status/1581848088494628864.

CHAPTER 5

1   "Stevens Road Tract Concept Plan," City of Bend, June 2022, accessed
      October 23, 2023, 2–4, 17–18, 42–44, https://www.bendoregon.gov/home/
      showpublisheddocument/52944/637890019140370000.

2   Brent Walth, *Fire at Eden's Gate: Tom McCall and the Oregon Story* (Portland:
      Oregon Historical Society Press, 1998), 243.

3   Sy Adler, *Oregon Plans: The Making of an Unquiet Land Use Revolution* (Corvallis:
      Oregon State University Press, 2012), 27.

4   Adler, *Oregon Plans*, 28–37.

5   Walth, *Fire at Eden's Gate*, 243.

6   Richard Rothstein, *The Color of Law: A Forgotten History of How Our Government Segregated America* (New York: Liveright Publishing Corporation, 2017), 48–49.

7   Adler, *Oregon Plans*, 50.

8   Walth, *Fire at Eden's Gate*, 39, 242–243.

9   Tom McCall, 1973 speech to the 57th Oregon Legislative Assembly, audio, 7:07, accessed May 19, 2023, available from Oregon Department of Land Conservation and Development at https://www.oregon.gov/lcd/OP/Pages/History.aspx.

10 Adler, *Oregon Plans*, 39.

11 Adler, *Oregon Plans*, 53.

12 Walth, *Fire at Eden's Gate*, 353–356; Adler, *Oregon Plans*, 52–58.

13 Adler, *Oregon Plans*, 55–58.

14 Adler, *Oregon Plans*, 79–82.

15 "History of Land Use Planning," Oregon Department of Land Conservation and Development, accessed April 26, 2023, https://www.oregon.gov/lcd/OP/Pages/History.aspx.

16 "Oregon's Statewide Land Use Planning Goals," Oregon Department of Land Conservation and Development, accessed April 26, 2023, https://www.oregon.gov/lcd/op/pages/goals.aspx.

17 "Comprehensive Plan: Preface Background," City of Bend, accessed March 1, 2024, https://bend.municipal.codes/CompPlan/Development_of_the_Plan.

18 "LCDC Order #1," Oregon Land Conservation and Development Commission, accessed April 26, 2023, https://www.oregon.gov/lcd/OP/Documents/original_goals_012575.pdf.

19 McCall, 1973 speech to the 57th Oregon Legislative Assembly.

20 Oregon Land Conservation and Development Commission, "LCDC Order #1," 29.

21 "Oregon Housing Needs Analysis Recommendations Report: Leading with Production," Oregon Department of Land Conservation and Development Oregon Housing and Community Services, December 2022, 6, https://www.oregon.gov/lcd/UP/Documents/20221231_OHNA_Legislative_Recommendations_Report.pdf.

22 "Oregon Housing Needs Analysis Recommendations Report," 6–7.

23 "Oregon Housing Needs Analysis Recommendations Report," 7.

24 Walth, *Fire at Eden's Gate*, 361.

25 "Former Oregon Gov. Tom McCall Dies at 69," *Washington Post*, accessed April 26, 2023, https://www.washingtonpost.com/archive/local/1983/01/09/former-oregon-gov-tom-mccall-dies-at-69/95e20e3a-d4c7-470c-8c56-6c7bdff764b0/.

26 University of Oregon land-use expert Rebecca Lewis made a similar point in an interview with the author. Rebecca Lewis, in discussion with the author, August 2021.

27 "The Changing Needs of the West," Committee on Natural Resources House of Representatives, April 7, 1994, 68–69, https://www.govinfo.gov/content/pkg/CHRG-103hhrg79996/pdf/CHRG-103hhrg79996.pdf.

28 Jonathan Bach, "Colleagues Remember ECOnorthwest Founder as Economist Grounded in Humanity," *Portland Business Journal*, May 5, 2021, https://www.bizjournals.com/portland/news/2021/05/05/ed-whitelaw-econorthwest-founder-dies-80.html.

29 Committee on Natural Resources House of Representatives, "The Changing Needs of the West," 68–69.

30   "Average annual pay by state and industry, 1994," US Bureau of Labor Statistics, news release, September 19, 1995, https://www.bls.gov/news.release/history/annpay_091995.txt.

31   Timothy Egan, "Economic Pulse: The Pacific Northwest - A Special Seport; Northwest's Fortunes, Once Grim, Thrive Despite National Recession," *New York Times*, March 14, 1991, https://www.nytimes.com/1991/03/14/us/economic-pulse-pacific-northwest-special-report-northwest-s-fortunes-once-grim.html.

32   Walth, *Fire at Eden's Gate*, 246. Walth distinguishes that, "McCall was prepared to take on the challenge of statewide land-use planning. . . . However, on this issue, McCall was not an environmentalist by definition, but a conservationist."

33   Egan, "Economic Pulse."

34   Bach, "Colleagues Remember ECOnorthwest Founder as Economist Grounded in Humanity."

35   "About Us," Thrive Hood River, accessed May 19, 2023, https://www.thrivehoodriver.org/about/.

36   Nigel Jaquiss, "First Lady, Inc.," *Willamette Week*, October 7, 2014, https://www.wweek.com/portland/article-23203-first-lady-inc.html; Aaron Mesh, "Former Oregon Gov. John Kitzhaber Agrees to Pay Hefty Penalty for Ethics Violations," *Willamette Week*, March 28, 2018, https://www.wweek.com/news/state/2018/03/28/former-oregon-gov-john-kitzhaber-agrees-to-pay-hefty-penalty-for-ethics-violations/.

37   Thrive Hood River, "Thrive's Land Use For 21st Century: Governor Kitzhaber's Remarks," YouTube video, 13:22, September 12, 2022, https://www.youtube.com/watch?app=desktop&v=vnVh7ygkBCE.

38   Rebecca Lewis, Robert Parker, Mary DeFollo, Eva Bailey, and Ben Noon, "Barriers to Housing Production in Oregon: Summary Report," prepared for Oregon Department of Land Conservation and Development by Institute for Policy Research and Engagement at the University of Oregon, October 2022, 18-19, 23, 38–39, https://bpb-us-e1.wpmucdn.com/blogs.uoregon.edu/dist/3/17202/files/2022/11/UO-IPRE-Barriers-to-Housing-Production-Summary-Report_Oct-2022.pdf.

39   Lewis, Parker, DeFollo, Bailey, and Noon, "Barriers to Housing Production in Oregon: Summary Report," 39–40.

40   Lewis, Parker, DeFollo, Bailey, and Noon, "Barriers to Housing Production in Oregon: Summary Report," 11, 38–39.

41   Jonathan Bach, "Infrastructure Costs May Derail Oregon Homebuilding Goals," *Portland Business Journal*, February 15, 2024 (updated February 16, 2024), https://www.bizjournals.com/portland/news/2024/02/15/oregon-housing-package-kotek-sb-1537-1530.html.

42   Lewis, Parker, DeFollo, Bailey, and Noon, "Barriers to Housing Production in Oregon: Summary Report," 43–44.

43   "House Bill 3318," Oregon State Legislature, accessed October 23, 2023, 1, https://www.bendoregon.gov/home/showpublisheddocument/51338/637714430350000000.

44   "Chapter 197 Comprehensive Land Use Planning I," OregonLaws, accessed March 3, 2024, https://oregon.public.law/statutes/ors_chapter_197.

45   Mary Kyle McCurdy, testimony on House Bill 3318, Oregon Legislative Information, June 22, 2021, 1, https://olis.oregonlegislature.gov/liz/2021R1/Downloads/PublicTestimonyDocument/32115

46 "Ordinance No. 2271," City of Bend, September 2016, accessed October
    24, 2023, https://www.bendoregon.gov/home/showpublisheddocu-
    ment/28477/636355345421470000; "Urban Growth Boundary Remand," City of
    Bend, accessed March 3, 2024, https://www.bendoregon.gov/government/depart-
    ments/growth-management/urban-growth-boundary-remand; "Bend Housing
    Needs Analysis," City of Bend, August 31, 2016, https://www.bendoregon.gov/
    home/showpublisheddocument/41161/636905768242400000.

47 McCurdy, testimony on House Bill 3318, 1.

48 Rory Isbell, testimony on House Bill 3318, Oregon Legislative Information,
    June 16, 2021, 1, 4, https://olis.oregonlegislature.gov/liz/2021R1/Downloads/
    PublicTestimonyDocument/32111.

49 Oregon State Legislature, "House Bill 3318," 5.

50 Isbell, testimony on House Bill 3318, 1.

51 Bruce Abernethy and Monica Desmond, testimony on House Bill 3318, Oregon
    Legislative Information, June 17, 2021, https://olis.oregonlegislature.gov/
    liz/2021R1/Downloads/PublicTestimonyDocument/32104.

52 Amy Warren, testimony on House Bill 3318, Oregon Legislative Information,
    June 22, 2021, https://olis.oregonlegislature.gov/liz/2021R1/Downloads/
    PublicTestimonyDocument/32109.

53 "Time for Workforce Housing in Bend," Central Oregon LandWatch, December
    13, 2021, https://www.centraloregonlandwatch.org/update/2021/12/13/
    building-a-better-bend.

54 "NorthWest Crossing: A Community Development Partnership," NorthWest
    Crossing, accessed January 1, 2024, https://northwestcrossing.com/about/.

55 Bend Magazine Staff, "Bend's NorthWest Crossing Neighborhood Offers
    Neighborhood Living with Amenities," *Bend Magazine*, April 2021, accessed March
    3, 2024, https://bendmagazine.com/bends-northwest-crossing-neighborhood-
    offers-neighborhood-living-with-amenities/.

56 MIG and ECOnorthwest, "City of Bend Housing Capacity Analysis 2025 to 2045
    (DRAFT)," City of Bend, June 22, 2023, 10–11, https://www.bendoregon.gov/
    home/showpublisheddocument/56418/638252019592070000.

57 City of Bend, "Stevens Road Tract Concept Plan," 64–67.

58 See also Bach, "Infrastructure Costs May Derail Oregon Homebuilding Goals."

CHAPTER 6

1   "Missing Middle Housing is a Transformative Concept that Highlights the Need
    for Diverse, Affordable Housing Choices in Sustainable, Walkable Places," Opticos
    Design, accessed February 25, 2024, https://opticosdesign.com/missing-middle-
    housing/; "About Daniel Parolek, Founding Principal," Opticos Design, accessed
    April 18, 2023, https://opticosdesign.com/about/staff/daniel-parolek/.

2   Chicago Humanities Festival, "Daniel Parolek: Thinking Big, Building
    Small," YouTube video, 59:21, November 13, 2019, https://www.youtube.com/
    watch?v=lHzTltos8gY&t=1s; Opticos Design, "Missing Middle Housing Forum -
    Portland, Oregon," YouTube video, 51:39, December 20, 2016, https://www.youtube.
    com/watch?v=Kaq2MYcfY8U; Opticos Design, "Dan Parolek explores Missing
    Middle Housing with ULI Idaho in Boise, March 9, 2016," YouTube video, 38:15, July
    21, 2016, https://www.youtube.com/watch?v=W2dRb9toUxY&feature=emb_title.

3   Opticos Design, "Missing Middle Housing Forum - Portland, Oregon."

4   Richard Rothstein, *The Color of Law: A Forgotten History of How Our Government Segregated America* (New York: Liveright Publishing Corporation, 2017), 44–48.

5   Jenna Davis, "The Double-Edged Sword of Upzoning," Brookings, July 15, 2021, https://www.brookings.edu/blog/how-we-rise/2021/07/15/the-double-edged-sword-of-upzoning/.

6   Nigel Jaquiss, "Tina Kotek Is Accomplished—and Struggles to Gain Traction With Some Democrats. Why?," Willamette Week, March 30, 2022, https://www.wweek.com/news/state/2022/03/30/tina-kotek-is-accomplishedand-struggles-to-gain-traction-with-some-democrats-why/.

7   "House Speaker Tina Kotek," Oregon State Legislature via WayBack Machine, accessed April 18, 2023, https://web.archive.org/web/20211030011154/https://www.oregonlegislature.gov/kotek/Pages/biography.aspx.

8   Oregon State Legislature, House, House Bill 2001 (Introduced), 2019 Regular Session, accessed May 17, 2023, 1, 3, https://olis.oregonlegislature.gov/liz/2019R1/Downloads/MeasureDocument/HB2001/Introduced.

9   Oregon State Legislature, "House Committee On Human Services and Housing 2019-02-11 1:00 PM," Video, 2:35:02, February 11, 2019, https://olis.oregonlegislature.gov/liz/mediaplayer/?clientID=4879615486&eventID=2019021333.

10   For a brief overview of YIMBYism, see Dougherty, *Golden Gates*, 35.

11   Scott Hammers, "Zone Change for Apartments on Bend's West Side Rejected," *Bulletin*, August 24, 2016, https://www.bendbulletin.com/localstate/zone-change-for-apartments-on-bend-s-west-side-rejected/article_5167869c-eb18-502b-b0b3-328306fdcd69.html.

12   Bulletin staff report, "Rental Vacancy Rate Hits 1.04 Percent in Region," *Bulletin*, June 4, 2016, https://www.bendbulletin.com/business/rental-vacancy-rate-hits-1-04-percent-in-region/article_931f8494-6889-58af-839e-48fe90b82c38.html; David Welton, "Fixing Bend's Housing Crisis," Bend YIMBY, September 21, 2016, https://bendyimby.com/2016/09/21/welcome/.

13   Welton, "Fixing Bend's Housing Crisis."

14   David Welton, "YIMBY Reading," Bend YIMBY, June 12, 2017, https://bendyimby.com/2017/06/12/yimby-reading/.

15   David Welton, testimony on House Bill 2001, Oregon Legislative Information, accessed May 2, 2023, https://olis.oregonlegislature.gov/liz/2019R1/Downloads/CommitteeMeetingDocument/157733.

16   Inge Fryklund, testimony on House Bill 2001, Oregon Legislative Information, accessed May 2, 2023, https://olis.oregonlegislature.gov/liz/2019R1/Downloads/CommitteeMeetingDocument/157735.

17   Katie Wilson, testimony on House Bill 2001, Oregon Legislative Information, February 13, 2019, https://olis.oregonlegislature.gov/liz/2019R1/Downloads/CommitteeMeetingDocument/159175.

18   "Bend Housing Needs Analysis," City of Bend, August 31, 2016, 1, https://www.bendoregon.gov/home/showpublisheddocument/41161/636905768242400000.

19   Deborah Imse, "Re: Please Support House Bill 2001," Oregon Legislative Information, February 11, 2019, https://olis.oregonlegislature.gov/liz/2019R1/Downloads/CommitteeMeetingDocument/158110.

20   Bend housing director Lynne McConnell makes a similar point later in this chapter.

21   Heather Richards, email to Taylor Smiley Wolfe, February 25, 2019, obtained via author's public records request.

22 Heather Richards, "RE: HB 2001," attachment to email to Taylor Smiley Wolfe, 2–3, February 24, 2019, obtained via author's public records request.

23 Taylor Smiley Wolfe, email to Heather Richards, February 25, 2019, obtained via author's public records request.

24 Oregon State Legislature, House, House Amendments to House Bill 2001, 2019 Regular Session, April 12, 2019, accessed May 17, 2023, 1, https://olis.oregonlegislature.gov/liz/2019R1/Downloads/MeasureDocument/HB2001/House%20Amendments%20to%20Introduced.

25 Oregon State Legislature, "House Committee On Human Services and Housing 2019-04-03 1:00 PM," Video, 1:26:47, April 3, 2019, https://olis.oregonlegislature.gov/liz/mediaplayer/?clientID=4879615486&eventID=2019041304.

26 "Oregon HB 2001 Middle Housing and Affordability Q&A," Sightline Institute, March 11, 2019, 1, https://olis.oregonlegislature.gov/liz/2019R1/Downloads/CommitteeMeetingDocument/186469.

27 Sightline Institute, "Oregon HB 2001 Middle Housing and Affordability Q&A," 2–3.

28 Sightline Institute, "Political Leadership for Abundant Housing," YouTube video, 1:15:20, April 15, 2022, https://www.youtube.com/watch?v=xw1c7Jo2BUk. A tip of the hat to journalist Conor Dougherty for conducting onstage interviews during this event.

29 "HB 2001 Enrolled," Oregon State Legislature/Oregon Legislative Information, accessed May 2, 2023, https://olis.oregonlegislature.gov/liz/2019R1/Measures/Overview/HB2001.

30 Will Parker, "Does Oregon Have the Answer to High Housing Costs?," *Wall Street Journal*, updated October 23, 2019, accessed July 8, 2024, https://www.wsj.com/articles/does-oregon-have-the-answer-to-high-housing-costs-11571823001.

31 govtinakotek, Threads post, March 4, 2024, 9:18 a.m., https://www.threads.net/@govtinakotek/post/C4GbTaJpxn7.

32 Brenna Visser, "Bend City Council Approves Code Changes Aimed at Increasing Housing," *Bulletin*, September 17, 2021 (updated October 23, 2022), https://www.bendbulletin.com/localstate/bend-city-council-approves-code-changes-aimed-at-increasing-housing/article_13ed214a-17f2-11ec-a878-ab97c9c2841d.html.

33 "House Bill (HB) 2001 Code Amendments Take Effect in November," City of Bend, October 7, 2021, https://www.bendoregon.gov/Home/Components/News/News/4819/29.

34 Rebecca Lewis, Robert Parker, Mary DeFollo, Eva Bailey, and Ben Noon, "Barriers to Housing Production in Oregon: Summary Report," prepared for Department of Land Conservation and Development by Institute for Policy Research and Engagement at the University of Oregon, October 2022, 38–39, https://bpb-us-e1.wpmucdn.com/blogs.uoregon.edu/dist/3/17202/files/2022/11/UO-IPRE-Barriers-to-Housing-Production-Summary-Report_Oct-2022.pdf.

35 "Accessory Dwelling Units," American Planning Association, accessed July 5, 2024, https://www.planning.org/knowledgebase/accessorydwellings/.

36 "Penn," Hiatus Homes, accessed March 16, 2024, https://www.hiatushomes.com/penn.

37 Jeff Mapes, "Oregon's Unique Growth Rules Have Preserved Open Space but also Led to New Fights," Oregon Public Broadcasting, August 19, 2022, https://www.opb.org/article/2022/08/19/oregon-land-use-laws-urban-growth-management-system-portland-conservation/.

38 "Housing Production Strategy Program - List of Tools, Actions, and Policies,"
    Oregon Department of Land Conservation and Development, revised February
    2022, https://www.oregon.gov/lcd/UP/Documents/Full%20Cover%20Letter%20
    and%20HPS%20List_with%20links.pdf.
39 "Housing Production Strategy Program - List of Tools, Actions, and Policies," 1, 3, 7.
40 Erin Kayata, "Take a Look Inside the Most Expensive Single-Family Home Ever
    Sold in Boston," *Boston*, March 22, 2023, https://www.bostonmagazine.com/
    property/2023/03/22/beacon-hill-record-breaker/#:~:text=Crosswords-,Take%20
    a%20Look%20Inside%20the%20Most%20Expensive%20Single%2DFamily%20
    Home,%2F2023%2C%204%3A10%20p.m.

CHAPTER 7
1   "Local Innovation and Fast Track (LIFT) Housing Program Annual Report to
    Interim Committees of the Legislative Assembly Related to Housing (HB 1582,
    2016)," Oregon Housing and Community Services, February 1, 2018.
2   Reagan Library, "President Reagan's Remarks at a Signing of the Tax Reform Act of
    1986, October 22, 1986," YouTube video, 13:46, June 15, 2016, https://www.youtube.
    com/watch?v=rloRibKfN8g.
3   Susan J. Popkin, "Proposed Cuts to Public Housing Threaten a Repeat of the 1980s'
    Housing Crisis," Urban Institute, June 1, 2017, https://www.urban.org/urban-wire/
    proposed-cuts-public-housing-threaten-repeat-1980s-housing-crisis.
4   Abt Associates Inc., "Development and Analysis of the National Low-Income
    Housing Tax Credit Database," prepared by Abt Associates Inc. for US Department
    of Housing and Urban Development Office of Policy Development and Research,
    July 1996, foreword by Michael A. Stegman, https://www.huduser.gov/portal//
    Datasets/LIHTC/report.pdf.
5   Mark P. Keightley, "An Introduction to the Low-Income Housing Tax Credit,"
    Congressional Research Service, January 6, 2023, 1, https://sgp.fas.org/crs/misc/
    RS22389.pdf.
6   Abt Associates Inc., "Development and Analysis of the National Low-Income
    Housing Tax Credit Database," 1-1; Keightley, "An Introduction to the Low-Income
    Housing Tax Credit," summary page.
7   "The Report on Tax Reform Options: Simplification, Compliance, and Corporate
    Taxation," The President's Economic Recovery Advisory Board, August 2010,
    79–80, https://obamawhitehouse.archives.gov/sites/default/files/microsites/
    PERAB_Tax_Reform_Report.pdf.
8   Chris Edwards and Vanessa Brown Calder, "Low-Income Housing
    Tax Credit: Costly, Complex, and Corruption-Prone," Cato Institute,
    November 13, 2017, https://www.cato.org/tax-budget-bulletin/
    low-income-housing-tax-credit-costly-complex-corruption-prone.
9   John Kitzhaber, email to author, February 22, 2023.
10 "President Biden Announces Key Regional Appointments for
    USDA and HUD," White House, January 13, 2022, https://www.
    whitehouse.gov/briefing-room/statements-releases/2022/01/13/
    president-biden-announces-key-regional-appointments-for-usda-and-hud/.
11 Margaret Salazar, LinkedIn resume, accessed February 28, 2024, https://www.
    linkedin.com/in/margaret-salazar-42ab6827/details/experience/.
12 Kevin A. Park, "The Federal Housing Administration: Bringing the Housing
    Finance System Out of a Chaotic Situation," Office of Policy Development and

Research, Summer-Fall 2020, https://www.huduser.gov/portal/periodicals/em/
SummerFall20/highlight2.html.

13   Margaret Van Vliet, Letter publicizing resignation from Portland Housing Bureau
director, Portland Housing Bureau, August 11, 2011, https://www.portlandoregon.
gov/fish/article/360555.

14   Governor's Office, "Governor Brown Appoints Claire Seguin as Interim Director
of the Oregon Housing and Community Services Department," State of Oregon
Newsroom, May 10, 2016, https://www.oregon.gov/newsroom/pages/NewsDetail.
aspx?newsid=208349.

15   Governor's Office, "Governor Brown Appoints Margaret Salazar as Director
of Oregon Housing and Community Services," State of Oregon Newsroom,
September 26, 2016, https://www.oregon.gov/newsroom/pages/NewsDetail.
aspx?newsid=208959.

16   Jeff Mapes, "Kate Brown Appoints Veteran Government Aide Jeanne Atkins to
Be Secretary of State," OregonLive, March 6, 2015, https://www.oregonlive.com/
mapes/2015/03/kate_brown_appoints_veteran_go.html.

17   "Oregon Housing and Community Services: Critical Improvements Needed to
Help Ensure Preservation of Affordable Housing for Low-Income Oregonians,"
Oregon Secretary of State's Office, December 2016, 1–2, http://records.sos.state.
or.us/ORSOSWebDrawer/Recordhtml/5080965.

18   "Oregon Housing and Community Services," 2.

19   "Oregon Housing and Community Services," 12.

20   "Oregon Housing and Community Services," 31.

21   Margaret Solle Salazar, Letter to Mary Wegner, Oregon Housing and Community
Services, November 29, 2016, 1, attached to "Oregon Housing and Community
Services."

22   Margaret Salazar, "Letter from the Director" in "Breaking New Ground: Oregon's
Statewide Housing Plan," Oregon Housing and Community Services, accessed
March 27, 2023, ii, https://www.oregon.gov/ohcs/Documents/swhp/swhp-full-
plan.pdf.

23   Oregon Housing and Community Services, "Statewide Housing Plan," YouTube
video, 16:49, November 21, 2018, https://www.youtube.com/watch?v=nL-it7B27ew.

24   Oregon Housing and Community Services, "Statewide Housing Plan," YouTube
video.

25   "Breaking New Ground," 3.

26   "Breaking New Ground," 29.

27   Oregon Housing and Community Services spokesperson, email to author,
December 20, 2022.

28   Jonathan Bach, "Cornerstone Apartments in North Salem Bring
Hope to Low-Income Families," Statesman Journal, August 17, 2018,
https://www.statesmanjournal.com/story/news/2018/08/18/
cornerstone-apartments-salem-low-income-housing-families/987617002/.

29   Author review of images to refresh memory from "Cornerstone Apartments,"
Neighborly Ventures, accessed May 1, 2023, https://www.cornerstoneoregon.com/;
Oregon Housing and Community Services, "Cornerstone Apartments, Salem - First
LIFT Project," YouTube video, 4:19, November 20, 2018, https://www.youtube.
com/watch?v=iHFg1NOmKjM.

30   Bach, "Cornerstone Apartments in North Salem Bring Hope to Low-Income
Families."

31 Oregon Housing and Community Services, "Cornerstone Apartments, Salem - First LIFT Project," YouTube video, 4:19, November 20, 2018, https://www.youtube.com/watch?v=iHFg1NOmKjM.

32 "Oregon Housing and Community Services," 7–8.

33 James Chen, "Private Activity Bonds (PAB) Explanation and Tax Treatment," Investopedia, updated April 22, 2022, accessed March 10, 2024, https://www.investopedia.com/terms/p/privateactivitybond.asp.

34 "2019 Annual Awards for Program Excellence Entry," Oregon Housing and Community Services, accessed May 1, 2023, https://www.ncsha.org/wp-content/uploads/Oregon-Rental-Housing-Encouraging-New-Production-2019.pdf.

35 "2019 Annual Awards for Program Excellence Entry."

36 Oregon Housing and Community Services spokesperson, email to author, December 20, 2022.

37 "OHCS Statewide Housing Plan Milestone 1 Update," Oregon Housing and Community Services, September 2019, 2, https://www.oregon.gov/ohcs/Documents/swhp/2019-09-SWHP-Quarterly-Summary.pdf.

38 Julie Cody, "Technical Advisory," Oregon Housing and Community Services, October 28, 2021, https://www.oregon.gov/ohcs/development/Documents/TAs/10-28-2021-TA-Bond-Conduit-LIHTC-Pause.pdf; Jonathan Bach, "Exclusive: Oregon Plans to Pit Affordable Housing Developers against Each Other over Incentives," *Portland Business Journal*, April 18, 2022, https://www.bizjournals.com/portland/news/2022/04/18/oregon-developers-may-have-to-compete.html.

39 Bach, "Exclusive: Oregon Plans to Pit Affordable Housing Developers against Each Other over Incentives."

40 "Affordable housing bond program," Metro, accessed May 1, 2023, https://www.oregonmetro.gov/public-projects/affordable-housing-bond-program.

41 Oregon Housing and Community Services, "4% Low Income Housing Tax Credits (LIHTC) & Private Activity Bond (PAB) Program Update & Process Overview."

42 Andrea Bell, "Federal Tax Bill: What It Could Mean for Affordable Housing," *Route Fifty*, January 31, 2024, https://www.route-fifty.com/management/2024/01/federal-tax-bill-what-it-could-mean-affordable-housing/393793/.

43 Jonathan Bach, "3 Takeaways from Landmark Report on Oregon's Housing Crisis," *Portland Business Journal*, November 15, 2022, https://www.bizjournals.com/portland/news/2022/11/15/oregon-housing-shortage-ohcs-dlcd-report-2022.html; "Oregon Housing Needs Analysis Recommendations Report: Leading with Production," Oregon Department of Land Conservation and Development Oregon Housing and Community Services, December 2022, 10, https://www.oregon.gov/lcd/UP/Documents/20221231_OHNA_Legislative_Recommendations_Report.pdf.

44 Oregon Housing and Community Services spokesperson Delia Hernández, email to author, March 17, 2023.

45 Bulletin Editorial Board, "Editorial: Affordable Housing Should Get a Needed Boost in Bend," *Bulletin*, July 6, 2023, https://www.bendbulletin.com/opinion/editorial-affordable-housing-should-get-a-needed-boost-in-bend/article_c504032e-1b54-11ee-8139-1f05059ec332.html.

46 Oregon Housing and Community Services, "$103.5 Million Awarded to 10 Affordable Housing Developments across the State," press release, July 11, 2023, https://t.e2ma.net/message/ysmp7ze/mfsr23wc.

47   ECOnorthwest, "The Impacts of the Lack of Housing Affordability on Economic Growth," prepared for the Bend Chamber of Commerce, November 7, 2022, 1, https://bendchamber.org/wp-content/uploads/2022/09/Final-Memo_110722.pdf.

48   ECOnorthwest, "The Impacts of the Lack of Housing Affordability on Economic Growth," 2.

49   ECOnorthwest, "The Impacts of the Lack of Housing Affordability on Economic Growth," 7. For median home sale prices, ECONorthwest cites *Median Price of Home Sold*, Central Oregon Association of Realtors, 2022.

50   ECOnorthwest, "The Impacts of the Lack of Housing Affordability on Economic Growth," 10.

51   ECOnorthwest, "The Impacts of the Lack of Housing Affordability on Economic Growth," 10.

52   Property information from "Rooted at Poplar," RootedHomes, accessed March 9, 2024, https://rootedhomes.org/communities/poplar; LIFT Homeownership funding information from Jackie Keogh, in discussion with the author, March 2024.

53   Katy Brooks, "Bend, Oregon: Housing Unaffordability Jeopardizes Economic Vitality," in Up For Growth, *Housing Underproduction in the U.S. 2023*, accessed October 31, 2023, 46–49, https://upforgrowth.org/apply-the-vision/2023-housing-underproduction/.

54   Property information from RootedHomes, "Rooted at Poplar"; mortgage cost estimate from Jackie Keogh, in discussion with the author, March 2024.

CHAPTER 8

1   Megan Lawson, senior economist with Headwaters Economics, made a similar comparison of "the four Bs: Bozeman, Bellingham, Washington . . . Boulder, Colorado" and Bend, according to a November 4, 2023, email newsletter from the *Bulletin* Editor Gerry O'Brien. I saw Lawson's comparison after I'd largely finished writing this chapter, but I make note of it as further evidence that such communities suffer from what Lawson called an "amenity trap." According to O'Brien's summary of Lawson's presentation during the local Chamber of Commerce Economic Impact Conference, "Basically, these areas are being loved to death, Lawson said." See Gerry O'Brien, "From the Editor's Desk: A Growing Concern," *Bulletin*, November 4, 2023, email newsletter.

2   Nicole Friedman, "Boise's Housing Market Boomed Early in the Pandemic. Now It Is Cooling Fast," *Wall Street Journal*, July 27, 2022, https://www.wsj.com/articles/boise-housing-market-cooling-down-zoomtowns-11658931254; Patrick Sisson, "Remote Workers Spur an Affordable Housing Crunch in Montana," Bloomberg, February 11, 2021, https://www.bloomberg.com/news/articles/2021-02-11/the-zoom-town-boom-in-bozeman-montana.

3   US Census Bureau, "Bend City, Oregon; Boulder City, Colorado," *Quick Facts*, accessed May 13, 2023, https://www.census.gov/quickfacts/fact/table/bendcityoregon,bouldercitycolorado/PST045222.

4   US Census Bureau, "Bend City, Oregon; Boulder City, Colorado."

5   "Housing Market Analysis & Needs Assessment Supplement," Root Policy Research, accessed May 13, 2023, 2–3, https://bouldercolorado.gov/media/5701/download?inline=.

6   Root Policy Research, "Housing Market Analysis & Needs Assessment Supplement," 12.

7   "Affordable Housing in Boulder," City of Boulder, accessed May 13, 2023, https://bouldercolorado.gov/guide/affordable-housing-boulder.

8   Editors of Encyclopaedia Britannica, "Boulder," Encyclopedia Britannica, November 8, 2021. https://www.britannica.com/place/Boulder-Colorado; "Who We Are," National Center for Atmospheric Research, accessed May 13, 2023, https://ncar.ucar.edu/who-we-are.

9   Burt Helm, "How Boulder Became America's Startup Capital," *Inc.,* from December 2013-January 2014 issue, accessed online May 13, 2023, https://www.inc.com/magazine/201312/boulder-colorado-fast-growing-business.html.

10   Laura Snider, "Boulder's Blue Line Turns 50," *Colorado Daily,* July 31, 2009, https://www.coloradodaily.com/2009/07/31/boulders-blue-line-turns-50/.

11   Albert A. Bartlett, "Recollections of the Origin of Boulder's Blue Line City Charter Amendment," Basin, September 26, 2000, http://bcn.boulder.co.us/basin/news/blueline.html.

12   Snider, "Boulder's Blue Line Turns 50."

13   "Open Space & Mountain Parks," City of Boulder, accessed May 13, 2023, https://bouldercolorado.gov/government/departments/open-space-mountain-parks/about.

14   "Affordable Housing in Boulder."

15   "30Pearl," City of Boulder, accessed May 24, 2023, https://bouldercolorado.gov/projects/30pearl.

16   Kriston Capps, "Boulder Will Host the First National 'YIMBY' Conference," Bloomberg, May 5, 2016, https://www.bloomberg.com/news/articles/2016-05-05/boulder-will-host-the-first-national-yimby-conference; Josh Stephens, "'YIMBY' Movement Heats Up in Boulder," Next City, June 21, 2016, https://nextcity.org/urbanist-news/who-are-yimby-first-meeting-boulder.

17   Agnew::Beck, "City of Boise Housing Needs Analysis 2021 Report," City of Boise, December 2021, 3–4, https://www.cityofboise.org/media/14362/boisehousinganalysis-2021-report.pdf.

18   Agnew::Beck, "City of Boise Housing Needs Analysis 2021 Report," 11.

19   Agnew::Beck, "City of Boise Housing Needs Analysis 2021 Report," 8.

20   "OLLI at MSU Friday Forum: Crisis! How Low Rental Inventory and High Rents Impact Us All, Part 2" on MSU Calendar, Montana State University, accessed May 24, 2023, https://www.montana.edu/calendar/events/43437.

21   Osher Lifelong Learning Institute at Montana State University Friday Forum, "OLLI at MSU Friday Forum: Crisis! How Low Rental Inventory and High Rents Impact Us All (Part 2)," Montana State University video, 1:19:33, October 14, 2022, https://montana.hosted.panopto.com/Panopto/Pages/Viewer.aspx?id=e0b3252b-b4d4-4261-8121-af310101b964.

22   Christopher Rugaber, "US Inflation at New 40-Year High as Price Increases Spread," Associated Press, June 10, 2022, https://apnews.com/article/key-inflation-report-highest-level-in-four-decades-c0248c5b5705cd1523d3dab377198 3b4.

23   "At a glance . . . ," NeighborImpact, accessed May 24, 2023, https://www.neighborimpact.org/wp-content/uploads/PDF/About-Us/At-A-Glance-2020-ENGLISH-1.pdf.

24   Osher Lifelong Learning Institute at Montana State University Friday Forum, "OLLI at MSU Friday Forum: Crisis! How Low Rental Inventory and High Rents Impact Us All (Part 2)."

25   Kathleen McLaughlin, "Who Can Afford to Live in the American West when Locals Can't?," *Guardian*, August 26, 2021, https://www.theguardian.com/society/2021/aug/26/american-west-income-inequality.

26   Ryanne Pilgeram, *Pushed Out: Contested Development and Rural Gentrification in the US West* (Seattle: University of Washington Press, 2021), 6–10, 18-19.

27   Pilgeram, *Pushed Out*, 19–20.

28   Pilgeram, *Pushed Out*, 31–33.

29   McLaughlin, "Who Can Afford to Live in the American West when Locals Can't?"

30   "The Community Land Trust Model," Kaniksu Land Trust, accessed April 10, 2023, https://www.kaniksu.org/housing.

CHAPTER 9

1   Information from Heritage Walk plaque outside Tower Theatre, donated by Tower Theatre Foundation, viewed October 2022.

2   Michelle Neiss, *City of Bend Community Perceptions Survey*, DHM Research, December 13, 2022, 7, https://www.bendoregon.gov/home/showpublisheddocument/54830/638096508472400000.

3   Gwynn Guilford and Nick Timiraos, "October Inflation Report Shows Consumer Prices Rose 7.7% From Year Earlier," *Wall Street Journal*, updated November 10, 2022, accessed January 22, 2024, https://www.wsj.com/articles/us-inflation-october-2022-consumer-price-index-11668050497.

4   "Mortgage Rates," Freddie Mac, accessed January 22, 2024, https://www.freddiemac.com/pmms.

5   Statista Research Department, "U.S. Single Family Homes - Statistics & Facts," Statista, February 20, 2023, https://www.statista.com/topics/5144/single-family-homes-in-the-us/#editorsPicks.

6   "Mortgage Rates," Freddie Mac, accessed January 1, 2024, https://www.freddiemac.com/pmms.

7   Taylor Orth, "One-Third of First-Time American Homebuyers Got Financial Help from Their Parents," YouGov, May 25, 2022, https://today.yougov.com/topics/economy/articles-reports/2022/05/25/american-homebuyers-finanancial-help-parents?utm_source=twitter&utm_medium=website_article&utm_campaign=housing_market.

8   Connor Ibbetson, "How Many People Had Help from Their Parents to Buy Their First Home?," YouGov, May 9, 2022, https://yougov.co.uk/topics/economy/articles-reports/2022/05/09/how-many-people-parents-help-first-home-deposit?_gl=1*0a07gd*_ga*NjcoOTk5Nzc3LjE2Nzc5ODk4NDQ.*_ga_DCHBLK4BVD*MTY3Nzk4OTgoMy4xLjEuMTY3Nzk5MDgyNi4wLjAuMA.

9   "Bend Housing Needs Analysis," City of Bend, August 31, 2016, 1–2, https://www.bendoregon.gov/home/showpublisheddocument/41161/636905768242400000.

10   Brenna Visser, "Homeless Population Grows by 17% in Central Oregon," *Bulletin*, May 6, 2022, https://www.bendbulletin.com/localstate/homeless-population-grows-by-17-in-central-oregon/article_d14d8d98-cd72-11ec-8b20-7be6e5def91f.html.

11   Brenna Visser, "Bend Homeless Man Is without a House, Not a Home," *Bulletin*, May 22, 2022 (updated July 16, 2022), https://www.bendbulletin.com/localstate/bend-homeless-man-is-without-a-house-not-a-home/article_1d6850e8-d0aa-11ec-b14f-47e6bff604f6.html.

12   BendChamber, "State of the City," YouTube video, 1:01:30, October 29, 2020, https://www.youtube.com/watch?v=SdrdAH177r0; Brenna Visser, "State of the City: From Boom Town to 'Zoom Town,'" *Bulletin*, October 29, 2020 (updated December 4, 2021), https://www.bendbulletin.com/localstate/state-of-the-city-from-boom-town-to-zoom-town/article_0b781176-1a3e-11eb-ae88-cf8866bebd93.html.

13   Brenna Visser, Twitter post, June 30, 2022, 8:55 a.m., https://twitter.com/brennavisser/status/1542537333202767872; Brenna Visser, Twitter post, June 30, 2022, 8:55 a.m., https://twitter.com/brennavisser/status/1542537334272405505; Brenna Visser, Twitter post, June 30, 2022, 8:55 a.m., https://twitter.com/brennavisser/status/1542537335337693184; Brenna Visser, Twitter post, June 30, 2022, 8:55 a.m., https://twitter.com/brennavisser/status/1542537336394698752.

14   David N. Welton, Twitter post, June 2022, 9:03 a.m., https://twitter.com/davidnwelton/status/1542539206702075905.

15   Mike Rogoway, "Oregon newspaper chain EO Media sells itself to Mississippi company," OregonLive, October 23, 2024, https://www.oregonlive.com/business/2024/10/oregon-newspaper-chain-eo-media-sells-itself-to-mississippi-company.html.

16   Suzanne Roig, "Workers Announce Intention to Unionize at the Bulletin, Redmond Spokesman," *Bulletin*, October 20, 2023, https://www.bendbulletin.com/business/workers-announce-intention-to-unionize-at-the-bulletin-redmond-spokesman/article_c25b4996-6f66-11ee-aa7e-0fc54a6553b2.html.

17   Energy Trust of Oregon spokesperson Julianne Thacher, email to author, March 9, 2023.

18   TRC Companies spokesperson Stephanie Berkland, email to author, March 9, 2023.

19   "An Overview of Waterless Composting Toilets," HomeBiogas, accessed November 9, 2023, https://www.homebiogas.com/blog/waterless-composting-toilet/.

20   Delgado Consulting LLC, "Articles of Organization," Oregon Secretary of State, February 7, 2022, accessed November 9, 2022, http://records.sos.state.or.us/ORSOSWebDrawer/Recordhtml/8554053.

21   Data courtesy of the Eviction Lab at Princeton University, Eviction Lab at Princeton University, accessed March 19, 2023, https://evictionlab.org/eviction-tracking/.

22   "City Council Meeting - Council Vacancy Interviews," City of Bend, January 11, 2023, https://bend.granicus.com/player/clip/730?view_id=9&redirect=true&h=9ec7723ae1ff80e8032f8a2c00228305.

CHAPTER 10

1   "Bend YIMBY News - 3/25/2024," Bend YIMBY, email newsletter, March 25, 2024.

2   Cassidy Mantor, "Modern Living with Sunrise Construction of Oregon," *Western Home Journal*, Spring and Summer 2023, 24–32.

3   Lorelei Juntunen of ECOnorthwest addresses the market dynamics at play in her comments later in this chapter.

4   Jillian Fortner and Barney Lerten, "Mt. Bachelor Offers its Seasonal Workers a New Housing Option, at Bend's Campfire Hotel," KTVZ, November 1, 2023, https://ktvz.com/news/business/2023/11/01/mt-bachelor-announces-seasonal-worker-housing-partnership-with-bends-campfire-hotel-52-beds-made-available/#:~:text=%E2%80%9CAt%20Mt.,contribute%20to%20this%20vibrant%20community; Morgan Owen, "Mt. Bachelor Announces Housing

Partnership with Campfire Hotel," *Bulletin*, November 4, 2023, https://www.bendbulletin.com/localstate/mt-bachelor-announces-housing-partnership-with-campfire-hotel/article_b4ed929c-7a78-11ee-b82d-53ae33e48001.html.

5   "OHCS Director Andrea Bell Joined Groundbreaking Ceremonies for More than 70 Affordable Homes in Bend," Oregon Housing and Community Services, October 16, 2023, https://t.e2ma.net/message/a6wnjoe/yw5y2pdd.

6   Jonathan Bach, "Gov. Tina Kotek Orders State to Nearly Double Per-Year Homebuilding," *Portland Business Journal*, January 11, 2023, https://www.bizjournals.com/portland/news/2023/01/11/gov-tina-kotek-orders-state-to-double.html.

7   Jay Lee and Michael Andersen, "Yes, Oregon, There is a Way to Build Enough Homes," Sightline Institute, February 7, 2023, https://www.sightline.org/2023/02/07/yes-oregon-there-is-a-way-to-build-enough-homes/.

8   Philip Kiefer, "3. Build It Better," *Outside*, March-April 2023, 56–57.

9   Jonathan Thompson, "On the Housing Supply-Side Theory," Land Desk, September 19, 2023, https://www.landdesk.org/p/on-the-housing-supply-side-theory?utm_source=profile&utm_medium=reader2.

10   Ryanne Pilgeram, *Pushed Out: Contested Development and Rural Gentrification in the US West* (Seattle: University of Washington Press, 2021), 124–127.

11   Jonathan Thompson, "Addenda to On the Supply-Side Housing Theory," Land Desk, September 22, 2023, https://www.landdesk.org/p/addenda-to-on-the-supply-side-housing?utm_source=%2Fsearch%2Fyimby&utm_medium=reader2.

12   Malia Spencer and Jonathan Bach, "A Bold Vision for Albina," *Portland Business Journal*, March 17, 2021, https://www.bizjournals.com/portland/news/2021/03/17/albina-vision-trust-portland-oregon.html.

13   See also the analysis from ECOnorthwest President and CEO Lorelei Juntunen later in this chapter.

14   "Wyden Proposes New Middle-Income Housing Tax Credit," United States Senate Committee on Finance, September 22, 2016, https://www.finance.senate.gov/ranking-members-news/wyden-proposes-new-middle-income-housing-tax-credit.

15   Senator Ron Wyden's responses to my questions for this book came in an email from his spokesperson. Linea Gagliano, email to author, December 18, 2023.

16   Alexander Hermann, Whitney Airgood-Obrycki, Nora Cahill, Peyton Whitney, "Middle-Income Housing Programs Emerge as Affordability Challenges Climb the Income Ladder," Joint Center for Housing Studies of Harvard University, July 1, 2024, accessed July 8, 2024, https://www.jchs.harvard.edu/blog/middle-income-housing-programs-emerge-affordability-challenges-climb-income-ladder.

17   For Katy Brooks's and Carly Colgan's online remarks, see Carly Colgan, LinkedIn post, July 8, 2024, accessed July 8, 2024, https://www.linkedin.com/feed/update/urn:li:activity:7216146232082059264/. I commented on the same LinkedIn post about "how vast and varied the income definitions for eligible middle-income renters are."

18   Danya Rumore and Philip Stoker, *Rural Gentrification and the Spillover Effect: Integrated Transportation, Housing, and Land Use Challenges and Strategies in Gateway Communities*, (Portland: Transportation Research and Education Center, 2023), 46.

19   US Census Bureau, "Moab City, Utah," *Quick Facts*, accessed November 21, 2023, https://www.census.gov/quickfacts/fact/table/moabcityutah/PST045222.

20   "Moab City Council approves active employment household ordinance," City of Moab, news release, August 3, 2022, https://moabcity.org/CivicAlerts.aspx?AID=395.

21   Jonathan Bach, "Portland Releases Long-Awaited Inclusionary Housing Study Findings," *Portland Business Journal*, July 13, 2023, https://www.bizjournals.com/portland/news/2023/07/13/portland-inclusionary-housing-zoning-study.html.
22   "Bend Housing Needs Analysis," City of Bend, August 31, 2016, 1–2, https://www.bendoregon.gov/home/showpublisheddocument/41161/636905768242400000. My argument is not novel. It harkens back to the very ideas presented in Bend's 2016 housing needs analysis.
23   "About Jake's," Jake's Diner, accessed November 19, 2023, http://jakesdinerbend.com/about-jakes/.

Index